Regulating S[
From Crime
to Neo-libe

C000156467

Edited by

Jane Scoular and Teela Sanders

⨂WILEY-BLACKWELL

This edition first published 2010
Editorial organization © 2010 Cardiff University Law School
Chapters © 2010 by the chapter author

Blackwell Publishing was acquired by John Wiley & Sons in February 2007. Blackwell's publishing programme has been merged with Wiley's global Scientific, Technical, and Medical business to form Wiley-Blackwell.

Editorial Offices
350 Main Street, Malden, MA 02148-5020, USA
9600 Garsington Road, Oxford OX4 2DQ, UK

For details of our global editorial offices, for customer services, and for information about how to apply for permission to reuse the copyright material in this book please see our website at www.blackwellpublishing.com

Registered Office
John Wiley & Sons Ltd, The Atrium, Southern Gate, Chichester, West Sussex PO19 8SQ.

Library of Congress Cataloging-in-Publication Data
Regulating sex/work : from crime control to neo-liberalism / edited by Jane Scoular and Teela Sanders.
    p. cm.
  ISBN 978-1-4443-3362-6
1. Prostitution. I. Scoular, Jane. II. Sanders, Teela. III. Title.

  K5295.R44   2010
344.05′44–dc22   201002329

A catalogue record for this title is available from the British Library.

Set in the United Kingdom by Godiva Publishing Services Ltd
Printed in Singapore by Fabulous Printers Pte Ltd

Contents

JOURNAL OF LAW AND SOCIETY
VOLUME 37, NUMBER 1, MARCH 2010
ISSN: 0263-323X, pp. 1–11

Introduction: The Changing Social and Legal Context of Sexual Commerce: Why Regulation Matters

JANE SCOULAR* AND TEELA SANDERS**

This volume seeks to respond to a particular moment in the study of commercial sex and its governance, pinpointed by an unprecedented rise in, and increased visibility of, sexual commerce and consumption and a corresponding growth in associated forms of regulation. Whilst common themes of controlling sexuality and changes in regulatory frameworks knit these papers into a coherent collection, the diversity of sex markets covered (male sex work, men who buy sex, pornography, bar dancing, legalized brothels, and sex shops) echoes the nuances of the 'sex industry' and challenges traditional academic concentration on narrow forms of prostitution. We discuss these dynamics in the context of post-industrial transformations of culture and sexuality in which what has been described as an 'unbridled ethic of sexual consumption' and 'soaring demand' for a variety of forms of commercial sex, are symptomatic of the way in which sexual commerce is increasingly 'specialised and diversified along technological, spatial and social lines'.[1] This leads to more visible availability in, and demand for, pornography, lapdancing, escorts, telephone sex, and sexual tourism, especially in developing countries'.[2]

In response, emerging sociological scholarship has sought to expand understandings of commercial sex beyond narrow studies of the traditional prostitution concept into the varied cultural forms which it takes. We can see this focus in, for instance, Agustín's 2007 special edition of *Sexualities* which considers, among other things, the discursive division between

* The Law School, University of Strathclyde, 141 St James' Road, Glasgow G4 OLT, Scotland
jane.scoular@strath.ac.uk
** School of Sociology and Social Policy, University of Leeds, Leeds LS2 9JT, England
T.L.M.Sanders@leeds.ac.uk

1 E. Bernstein, *Temporarily Yours: Intimacy, Authenticity, and the Commerce of Sex* (2007) 115.
2 E. Bernstein, 'The Meaning of the Purchase: Desire, Demand, and the Commerce of Sex' (2001) 2 *Ethnography* 375–406, at 389.

commercial and non-commercial sex and proposes the integration of cultural studies methodologies to the field. This approach opens up the analytical frame beyond endless moral debate and the over-emphasized and 'perpetually stigmatised' category of women selling sex, and ponder the much wider social and discursive field encompassed by the intersection of 'a range of activities that take place in both commerce and sex'. As Agustín explains:

> With the academic, media and 'helping' gaze fixed almost exclusively on women who sell sex, the great majority of phenomena that make up the sex industry are ignored, and this in itself contributes to the intransigent stigmatisation of these women ... commercial sex is usually disqualified and treated only as a moral issue. This means that a wide range of ways of study are excluded. A cultural-studies approach, on the contrary, would look at commercial sex in its widest sense, examining its intersections ... the everyday practices involved and try to reveal how our societies distinguish between activities considered normatively 'social' and activities denounced as morally wrong.[3]

In examining commercial sex, what this in turn requests is that we move beyond classic boundaries of 'prostitution' juxtaposed with other types of sex. There is a need to examine how sex which involves some form of commercial exchange fits into the broader cultural and social landscape. This fresh look at commercial sex examines the increasing mainstreaming and normalization of the sex industry. From their empirical work in the legal brothels of Nevada and examining the wider sex industries in the United States of America, Brents and Hausbeck remark:

> It is no longer useful to posit the sex industries as an 'other' to late capitalist industry. Research on the sex industries can tell us much about the effects of the economic infrastructure of mass consumption and the values and attitudes of consumer culture. Employing a framework grounded in economic and cultural shifts promises to add much to analyses of sex work. It historicises our understandings, situates changes in the economic contexts and the cultural meaning of sex in which sex work occurs, and invites examination of the social construction and material conditions of gender, sex and sexuality.[4]

Thus the increased mainstreaming of the sex industry has forced a welcomed adoption of a wider cultural analysis in terms of understanding commercial sex. Despite this, the regulation that has paralleled the industries' expansion remains hitherto under-theorized. This is what we seek to address in this volume.

The apparent 'unbridled ethic' of sex consumption has met with efforts to control the sale and organization of commercial sex via attempts both to stymie its supply and demand through the criminal law[5] and moves to

---

3 L. Agustín, 'New Research Directions: The Cultural Study of Commercial Sex' (2005) 8 *Sexualities* 618.

4 B.G. Brents and K. Hausbeck, 'Marketing Sex: US Legal Brothels and Late Capitalist Consumption' (2007) 10 *Sexualities* 425, at 436.

5 For an analysis of recent incursions into the demand/supply nexus, see V. Munro and M. Della Giusta (eds.), *Demanding Sex: Critical Reflections on the Regulation of Prostitution* (2008).

2

recognize the activity and seek to influence it by implementing systems of positive regulation. Phoenix and Oerton note the paradox:

> ... when sex appears to have become ever more subject to 'free' choice, greater openness and pluralism, there is a simultaneous proliferation of laws, policies and guidelines which seek to define the complex, vast and ever-changing 'rules of engagement' surrounding sex.[6]

Thus, the last decade has witnessed a flurry of regulatory controls across the globe. There have been significant changes in many countries' legislative frameworks for the control of commercial sex. In many cases this has involved an expansion in the punitive dimension, mirroring a wider culture of control which has resulted in behaviours that were not criminal becoming criminalized. Sweden, for example, has pioneered the outlawing of the purchase of sex and the United Kingdom (including Scotland) has sought to criminalize and responsibilize both sex workers and men who buy sex. This has been done through rehabilitation orders, 're-education' programmes, and increased policing – all of which is aimed at disrupting sex markets (see Scoular and Brooks-Gordon in this issue). This punitivism has been strengthened internationally, by a strong 'trafficking' discourse and over-simplified links between migrancy and the demand for commercial sex (see Weitzer in this issue). In punitive regimes, the collapsing into each other of discussions about voluntary commercial sex and forced sexual exploitation has left little distinction between very different types of sex markets and lived experiences. Even where some liberalization exists, it is rarely complete, often accompanied by punitive elements. For example, Sullivan (in this issue) shows that only some forms of prostitution are permitted in Australian states where sex work has been legalized, whilst the Netherlands has closed down several 'toleration zones' and reduced rights for migrant women working in the sex industry. Even the much heralded decriminal-ization of prostitution in New Zealand has failed to bring street sex work fully within its ambit.

The regulation of sex work in these contexts is, we argue, more complex than simply a case of sexual commerce being either legal or illegal. Just as the forms and analysis of commercial sex have become more complex, so too have its associated modes of regulation. In contrast to the more nuanced work that is developing in the wider field of commercial sex in other disciplines, studies on regulation and law frequently continue to assume not only a static regulatory target, but also home in on narrow modes of regulation – that of the powers at the disposal of the crime control professionals, particularly to control street prostitution. Just as the focus of academic commentary has been forced to move beyond the easy target of the vulnerable street worker to question the commercial sexual relations that are

---

6 J. Phoenix and S. Oerton, *Illicit and Illegal: Sex, Regulation and Social Control* (2005) 13.

3

less easy to govern, identify, and understand, so too must analyses of their regulation.

Law is typically characterized according to a legal/illegal dichotomy. Much campaigning follows this pattern, with one group (abolitionists) seeking to harness governmental power to protect those exploited by commercial sex. This 'protection' comes in the form of enticements to exit sex work, in addition to criminalizing purchasers, with the overall goal being the elimination of the sale of sex. Other campaigners seek governmental recognition of 'sex work' as a form of legitimate labour in order to gain the protection and rights that workers should enjoy. Phoenix and Oerton demonstrate how both of these causes are pursued in a context where there are increasing restrictions on sexual freedom as social control extends to the sexual.[7]

In this volume, we hope to move beyond uni-dimensional understandings of commercial sex, characterized by, for example, the overwhelming focus on the relatively insignificant phenomenon of street prostitution and the similarly blinkered approach to regulation apparent in the preoccupation with legal/illegal binaries and narrow sovereign-centered understanding of law (see Scoular's article). This will enable us to more fully appreciate the law's more complex relationship to society, and explore the way law and regulatory norms operate to support or to challenge the structures and conditions of the contemporary sex industry. In essence, we hope to match the increased sophistication in the sociological study of sex with a similarly complex study of the dynamics of contemporary regulation and to highlight that the law has a role in maintaining the current sex industries: for example, some forms of commercial sex have been made relatively mainstream and accessible as a result of economic and legal facilitation. Brents and Sanders argue that this generates a paradoxical need to retain hints of transgression and 'deviance' attached to commercial sex in order to maintain its appeal. The very fact that many aspects of the sex industry are tainted with illegality is its very attraction for many.

Thus, this collection seeks to explore an increasingly complex regulatory scene; one which, we suggest, takes the form of inter-related dynamics that broaden the levels of social control as well as intensifying the ways in which individuals are 'punished', 'rehabilitated', and 'rescued'. There has been a proliferation in modes of regulation – from the amplification of a crime-control model that seeks to criminalize even more participants in commercial sex and the use of new powers (for example, hybrid anti-social behaviour orders, rehabilitation orders) through to the expansion of administrative control via civil licensing and inspection. Much of this control and surveillance is executed by a range of third-party policing agents. Welfare agencies and professionals form a core part of this emerging regulatory machine: neighbourhood officers, outreach support workers, crime reduction

7 id.

4

officers, therapists, and drug treatment workers are all poised to watch, count, report on, and eventually criminalize those who are considered a nuisance to an imaginary ordered and civil society.

A MORE COMPLEX UNDERSTANDING OF LAW IN THE REGULATION OF SEX WORK

Thus, in the opening essay, Scoular sets the scene for a more complex reading of law's relationship to society. Arguing against claims that law is merely symbolic, Scoular explains, by drawing upon theories of governmentality, the continued relevance of law in processes which structure subjects, spaces, and forms of power in contemporary sex markets. It is the alignment of these processes with wider forms of neo-liberal governance that helps ensure a continuity across an apparently diverse legal system, which in many late-capitalist systems appears to follow a familiar trend of the denigration of street sex (as urban centres are gentrified) and the selective mainstreaming of other more profitable forms.

This framework allows us to offer a more accurate route map for future studies of the regulation of sex work. Its attraction is that it can accommodate the many contingencies under which sex work materializes and its regulation takes place. Examining the sex industry through a framework of governmentality can also operate according to differing modalities of power, recognizing the variations that emerge across time, space, and culture. Such a framework can allow for local variation as well as examining the sex trade through a global lens. Neo-liberalism is but one of the contexts in which regulation operates, and even then its impact may be varied in different settings. It may, as Kotiswaran notes, be less significant in different cultures where different customs and organization of sexual relations are present. Her paper, 'Labours in Vice or Virtue? Neo-liberalism, Sexual Commerce, and the Case of Indian Bar Dancing', argues that neo-liberalism is a peripheral issue in the context of the increased 'tolerance' shown towards bar-dancing in a recent Mumbai High Court ruling. This judgment, she argues:

> has less to do with the totalizing logic of neo-liberalism than a range of disparate factors including the distinct political economies of abolitionism pertaining to both bar dancing and sex work and the modes of resistance that female workers have offered in response.

As this contribution (and indeed others) show, we do not seek or claim some underlying unity between each of the contributions nor are we trying to reveal the traces of a vicious neo-liberal ideology hiding behind every form of regulation that is proposed, considered or implemented. The approach we advance is for a more complex understanding of regulation beyond legal/ illegal, appreciating regulation within a wider framework of governmentality, which can then be tied to contingent situations.

5

This framework can be used across a number of contexts. Hubbard and Coulmont demonstrate in their account of the changing regulation of sex shops in Britain and France over the last forty years how diverse forms of control have combined to restrict the location of sex shops, simultaneously shaping their design, management, and marketing. Describing the emergence of gentrified and 'designer' stores, their paper demonstrates that regulation in two quite different contexts has been complicit in a process of neo-liberalization that has favoured more corporate sex shops – without this having ever been an explicit aim of those who have argued for the regulation of sex retailing.

The governmentality framework can also allow for local variation and careful empirical testing as Sullivan demonstrates in her nimble examination of the partial legalized systems in two Australian states. Sullivan considers, in meticulous detail, the operation of complex regulatory agents and norms in New South Wales and Queensland, both of which have legalized some spaces of sex work. Paying close attention to the impact of similar yet different regimes on the safety, rights, and capacities of sex workers, Sullivan shows how a legalized regime can still create difficult working conditions but that, via legalization of brothels, some opportunities can be created to provide safe spaces for women.

The governmentality framework can help us understand what may appear to be the absence of regulation. What liberalism presents as freedom from law may be as significant as overt criminalization as it does not mean an absence of regulatory norms. As Rose and Miller note, constituting the realms of market and family as outwith direct sovereign governmental control does not free the private sphere from the operation of power.[8] Regulation, as Scoular says, must not be viewed solely in terms of political and state actions, or the imposition of law or police control. Rather, as Rose and Miller note, the separation of public and private spheres denotes a process in which 'liberalism identifies a domain outside "politics", and seeks to manage it without destroying its existence and autonomy'.[9] This 'management' involves the informal regulation by a range of forces and agents: for example, the market, the economy, experts, and individuals themselves. Thus, in the context of the unregulated forms of commercial sex that have proliferated in the United Kingdom following Wolfenden (which proposed to regulate only some public forms of commercial sex, notably indoor work and same-sex commercial work), the market, organized crime, and powerful business owners are key players in regulation, while sex workers, who occupy a position of political non-recognition, lack legal status and protection. This is demonstrated by the combined empirical studies of Sanders and Campbell, who show that the indoor premises are still open to

8 N. Rose and P. Miller, 'Political Power beyond the State: Problematics of Government' (1992) 43 *Brit. J. of Sociology* 173–205, at 180.
9 id.

6

violence, robbery, and unacceptable behaviour in a system that affords neither the workplace nor workers legitimacy or recognition.[10]

Male sex work is generally omitted from overt legislation, but Whowell's empirical snapshot offers an insight into the patterned and ordered nature of this form of commercial sex. The importance of the local dynamics of place and space are demonstrated by this study as Whowell argues:

> ... history and locality matter in choreographies of sex work, as well as the presentation of bodies through dress and demeanour. The micro-politics of solicitation, in this case, allow for the notion of self-regulation to be employed; and that rather than top-down mechanisms shaping the beat, locally deployed networks are important in the regulation of prostitution in this context. Rarely does policy consider how sex work is operationalized and practised on the ground, and the notion that spaces of commercial sex operating in different locales are shaped by different factors and networks.

Whowell documents thoroughly from her qualitative work how regulation is patterned by many different agents beyond the sex worker: by police, residents, outreach projects, and those who have vested economic interest in the street 'beat'. Therefore, what she terms the 'sexual choreography' of the street markets is regulated by those who are involved in the street beat from a multiple range of positions. Hence, the framework of governmentality goes well beyond official law, policy, and those involved in making it.

NEO-LIBERALISM AND THE PUNITIVE PARADOX

We have found this framework useful because it allows us to consider the paradox which emerges in many examples of legislative change that we have used as a stimulus to provoke the discussion in these papers. It is therefore our purpose in this collection, by documenting changes in the regulation of a range of sex markets from the United Kingdom, France, the United States, and Australia, to theorize the following paradox. The increase in oppressive and punitive approaches to regulating the sex industry, designed to deter participants and dislocate markets, comes at a time when the evidence suggests that both the supply and demand that fuels the sex markets, the diversification of those markets, and their embedded nature in social and economic infrastructures is more intense than ever. This paradox constitutes the most significant contemporary issue in relation to the study of sexual commerce and its regulation, yet it has not, so far, been explored in a sustained and coherent manner. Thus, we offer a novel departure in the area through our consideration of the production and commercialization of 'new' and shifting sex markets and the associated multifaceted and complex modes

---

10 T. Sanders and R. Campbell, 'Designing Out Violence, Building in Respect: Violence, Safety and Sex Work Policy' (2007) 58 *Brit. J. of Sociology* 1–18.

of regulation which operate within, and so often advance, neo-liberal power structures. The neo-liberalism in the title is not intended to be prescriptive (its influence is, of course, uneven, see Kotiswaran). However, when posed as a question, it allows us to consider the apparent paradox between the creeping neo-liberalism in many Western states, and the punitive sanctions that frequently accompany the increased mainstreaming of part of the sex industry.

Indeed it is ironic that, in the United States, where the proliferation of the sex industry is acutely visible in certain states, perhaps the most virulent moral campaigns and governmental embargos have taken place in response to the growth of the sex industry and to fears of its normalization in American society. Thus in the context of North America, as Weitzer notes, recent years have witnessed a considerable growth in the organized campaign committed to expanding criminalization of all forms of commercial sex. A powerful moral crusade has been successful in reshaping American government policy toward sex work, enhancing penalties for existing offences and creating new crimes. Weitzer explains how crusade organizations have advocated a strict abolitionist orientation toward all forms of commercialized sex, which are increasingly conflated with sex trafficking. Despite the many problems with this conflation, this movement has had significant impact on legal norms and government policies pertaining to sex work, trafficking or movement in persons and pornography as a species of commercial sexual exploitation.

Another theme in this volume is that of how 'demand' for commercial sex has been translated into a one-dimensional dynamics of male power and privilege. The paper by Attwood and Smith and that by Brooks-Gordon critically explore the assumptions that where there has been an increase in the 'demand' for commercial sex or different forms of pornography, this has become synonymous with patriarchy, violence, and the overall degradation of all women. Beyond moral debates regarding buying sex or accessing pornography, these papers identify the changes in post-industrial social spaces and, in particular, technological advances, which have altered how commercial sex is accessed. Technological advances which have facilitated sexual consumption as part of the 'unbridled ethic of consumption' have been targeted by regulators. In their paper, 'Extreme Concern: Regulating "Dangerous Pictures" in the United Kingdom', Attwood and Smith explain how increasing punitive legislation has been created in light of the increased accessibility of pornography. These authors critically assess the way in which the changing definitions of 'extreme' pornography has led to further policing of 'dangerous' sexualities and this additional control has also extended to other forms of sex commerce in the United Kingdom and in other jurisdictions, as outlined by Hubbard and Coulmont. Attwood and Smith argue against the legislation not only because it limits personal freedom but because the reasons for the outlawing are suspect, as it serves to mask a range of fears associated with apparent dangers of sex and

8

technology and the increased blurring of boundaries between public and private.

The limitation of personal freedom based on strict notions of what is sexually acceptable and in response to a wider campaign for gender equality, is well accounted for in the paper by Brooks-Gordon. Here, the recent attempts in Europe (namely, in Sweden and the United Kingdom) to criminalize the purchase of sex is critiqued. We learn how, through attempts to criminalize the 'punter', not only is the complex etiology of 'purchase' lost in the binary of legal or illegal, but the nuances of the relationship between seller and buyer are skirted over. Attempts to criminalize men who buy sex in the United Kingdom are broad-brush strokes to 'do something' about what is assumed to be 'the demand' for sex by predatory males. Yet the sex industry is diverse, catering for multiple sexualities which require different and nuanced working practices. In this collection, Brooks-Gordon and Whowell identify how gay, trans- or bi-sexual workers sell sex to a diverse range of lesbian, gay, trans-sexual, and straight clients who may be able-bodied or disabled. This raises interesting counter-rights claims, making sex work an interesting site for future human rights struggles.

BEYOND BINARIES

The framework also allows us to approach regulation while resisting its binaries. We argue there are similarities between the positions of criminalization and legalization as they operate alongside other modes of governance that are complicit with a neo-liberalism agenda that encourages forms of self-regulation as the mode of governance. Thus, for example, calls for increased protection often fail to recognize links between protection and control, so that abolitionism, by centring its campaigns on criminal justice control rather than wider social and economic justice, often become complicit in the wider politics of neo-liberalism. Recent activism to criminalize purchasers, while intended to advance equality, may in fact collude with a strong 'culture of control'. This does little to tackle structural issues, such as the feminization of poverty, that creates some of the precarious positions that are an issue not only in sex work but in many sectors of the economy. As Scoular notes, one of the perverse consequences of intervening in prostitution through the mechanism of criminal justice is that it often increases, rather than decreases, the levels of riskiness, vulnerability, and poverty of women in prostitution, especially those women who tend to get targeted most – street-based sex workers.

The apparent decriminalization of female soliciting that accompanies abolitionism is similarly more complex. The prevalent victim model, whereby inclusion depends on exiting from prostitution, takes place in a social context of punitive welfarism. This has potentially more far-reaching consequences than the previous explicit regime of criminalization, as the

9

discourses of responsibilization and self-help operate in more insidious ways, seeking to harness the self-governing and self-correcting capacities of individuals and, in so doing, co-opt more radical political objectives to a wider form of neo-liberal control.[11]

Those assuming decriminalization moves outside this labyrinth into some laissez-faire utopia, ignore at their peril the myriad of regulatory apparatuses and personnel accompanying this regulatory model. As Scoular notes, and Sullivan's careful empirical work attests, decriminalization or legalization do not result in or require an absence of law but rather deploy law in different ways. These modes can operate regardless of whether commercial sex is prohibited or permitted. Increasingly individualized forms of control are present, not only in exit strategies, but also in the licensing system of the Netherlands which, as Scoular says:

> encourage workers to self-regulate their behaviour in the interests of public health promotion, to conform to certain modes of working in order to meet the conditions of registration. Inclusion is offered to those who 'can perform the rituals of middle class society'[12] with all of the typical exclusions based on age, status, race, health and class that this entails.

In Sullivan's examination of the legalization of some forms of sex work in two Australian states, she notes the connection to wider forms of regulation. Whether this means or amounts to an improvement in conditions for women is a matter of empirical not ideological testing.

Thus, in order properly to evaluate the usefulness of legal approaches, we must be cognisant of contingent conditions and ancillary forms of regulation. This ensures the critical eye looks beyond the rhetoric of law to its regulatory processes and the nuances that impact on (mainly female) sex workers. The symbiotic relationship with street sex work continues to retain a distinction between good and bad sex workers – those who are invisible and 'civil' enjoy apparent freedom at the expense of even greater control of others who are anti-social. As Kotiswaran concludes, 'the prospects for redistributive law reform for all sexual workers are dim unless the arbitrary legal distinctions drawn between markets in sexual labour are overcome'. The rhetoric of rights and resources for some should not be peddled at the expense of marginalizing those who are very vulnerable – yet this seems to be the consistent result whatever the form regulation takes, although Sullivan offers some hope.

Therefore we need to work towards a form of politics that does not feed into modes of governance that have such poor outcomes for so many, especially the most vulnerable female sex workers. Thus, as Maggie O'Neill notes in our final chapter, politics needs to move away from regulatory

11 J. Scoular and M. O'Neill, 'Regulating prostitution. Social inclusion, responsibilization and the politics of prostitution reform' (2007) 47 *Brit. J. of Criminology* 764–78.
12 B. Sullivan, 'Prostitution Law Reform in Australia. A Preliminary Evaluation' (1999) 18 *Social Alternatives* 9–14.

10

categories of identity towards more radical forms of politics that disrupt simple divisive binaries and allow resistance in the context of dominant structures. She offers an alternative framework for a cultural materialist analysis of sex work. This is centred upon inclusion, facilitated by participatory methods. It seeks to develop a radical democratic imaginary by creating spaces for dialogue and fostering more integrated horizontal and vertical processes of inclusion around the principles of social justice and cultural citizenship[13] that include inclusion, rights, recognition, respect, and redistribution for sex workers. These are principles that can unite and foster collaboration between groups, including sex workers, and that are concerned with an enlarging space for social justice.

Alas, it is only if there is an understanding of the links between regulation and governance that we can move towards a more informed, inclusive, and transformative politics of prostitution reform. It is hoped that this collection of essays is the beginning of a more enlightened and critical approach that inspires more work which looks beyond the binary of illegal/legal to the complexities of commercial sex and its regulation.

---

13 J. Pakulski, 'Cultural Citizenship' (1997) 1 *Citizenship Studies* 73–86.

JOURNAL OF LAW AND SOCIETY
VOLUME 37, NUMBER 1, MARCH 2010
ISSN: 0263-323X, pp. 12–39

What's Law Got To Do With it?
How and Why Law Matters in the Regulation of Sex Work

JANE SCOULAR*

Drawing on recent empirical work that considers the relationship between different legal approaches to the 'problem' of prostitution, this article argues that the frequently drawn distinction between apparently diametrically opposed positions, such as prohibitionism and legalization, is certainly less significant than is often assumed and may, in fact, be illusory. This lack of distinction raises serious questions as to law's role in regulating sex work. In response to claims that law is 'merely' symbolic in its influence, I argue that these similarities arise precisely because law does matter (albeit in a different way from that assumed by a sovereign-centred understanding of the legal complex), and offer a complex and critical account of the role of modern law in regulating sex work. This approach not only more accurately elucidates the ways in which law supports dominant structures, in this case neo-liberalism, but offers some optimism for its (albeit limited) potential to transform.

INTRODUCTION

A discussion of the regulation of sex work typically begins by highlighting the distinctions between different regulatory approaches. Researchers, campaigners, and policy makers frequently review the apparent distinctions between prohibitionist (prohibits prostitution and penalizes prostitutes and pimps, but not necessarily clients), regulationist (seeks to regulate rather than prohibit or abolish prostitution, for example, through legalization), and abolitionist systems (seeks to abolish prostitution by penalizing clients and pimps but not prostitutes), before recommending or adopting an approach which best supports their own particular socio-political and ethical contexts

* *The Law School, University of Strathclyde, 141 St James' Road, Glasgow, G4 0LT, Scotland*
jane.scoular@strath.ac.uk

and projects.[1] Such neat classifications are, however, problematic, given that these terms describe general political and social aspirations regarding how best to regulate commercial sex and that considerable gaps inevitably exist between these objectives and the modes of intervention utilized to implement them.[2] Even more distant are the effects in the social realm of these various laws, policies, and techniques put in place by governments and other social actors. Thus, a 'top-down' approach relays a false impression of unity in policy settlements that are always provisional, often contradictory, and generally reflective of 'the varied and complex political influence of competing discourses and organized interests'.[3] Moreover 'state-centred' approaches fail to account for local conditions, which often appear incongruous with the terms of the formal law. Indeed, recent empirical research, including my own work with colleagues in three European countries, reveals that apparently contrasting legal approaches can produce similar results,[4] even in the apparently diametrically opposed systems of criminalization and legalization. Strikingly, Sweden and the Netherlands, despite being described as representing a 'two-way ideological mirror',[5] appear to display remarkably similar results on the ground in terms of the increased marginalization of more public forms of sex work (street sex work) and its participants, and a relative inattentiveness to many forms of indoor work.

These continuities between commercial sex markets, across cultural and legal differences has led one author, Laura Agustín, to question law's very relevance in the field of commercial sex.[6] Given the dominance of legal solutions in both state responses to the 'problem' of prostitution and its salience in campaigns by those who seek justice for those involved, such impotence would have important, and potentially damning, consequences. Yet, as I argue below, while this prognosis appears to be a logical conclusion from the findings, it fails to account for the ways in which modern forms of

---

1 See, for example, J. Kilvington, S. Day, H. Ward, 'Prostitution Policy in Europe: A Time of Change?' (2001) 67 *Feminist Rev.* 78–93; Council of Europe, Resolution 1579 (2007) 'Prostitution – Which stance to take?', at: <http://assembly.coe.int/Main.asp?link=/Documents/AdoptedText/ta07/ERES1579.htm>.

2 J. Phoenix, *Regulating Sex for Sale: Prostitution, Policy Reform and the UK* (2009) 14.

3 J. West, 'Prostitution: Collectives and the Politics of Regulation' (2000) 7 *Gender, Work and Organization* 106–18, at 106.

4 P.J. Hubbard et al., *Regulating the spaces of sex work: assessing the impact of prostitution law: Full Research Report.* ESRC no. RES-000-22-1001 (2007); See, also, E. Bernstein, *Temporarily Yours: Intimacy, Authenticity, and the Commerce of Sex* (2007) ch. 6.

5 B. Hobson, *Uneasy Virtue: The Politics of Prostitution in the American Reform Tradition* (1987) 30, cited in Bernstein, id., p. 145.

6 L. Agustín, 'Sex and the Limits of Enlightenment: The Irrationality of Legal Regimes to Control Prostitution' (2008) 5(4) *Sexuality Research & Social Policy* 73–86.

13

legal power operate to support hegemonic power relations 'despite a persistent gap between law in the books and law in action'.[7]

To be fair to Agustín, this dynamic has yet to be adequately theorized in what is now a vast literature on sex work, and one in which law occupies a significant position. By using insights derived from theories of governmentality, which reveal the productive and adaptive nature of power, I hope to begin the process of offering a more critical account of the role of modern law in regulating sex work in neo-liberal contexts. I will argue that the fact that contrasting regulatory approaches have the same empirical effects is precisely because law *does* matter (alongside other variables), albeit in a different way than that assumed by many positivist policy makers and academic commentators, including Agustín.

I begin, however, by outlining the empirical findings that reveal remarkable similarities in apparently contrasting regulatory approaches to prostitution. It is this paradox which has sparked this critical inquiry into the role of law in contemporary society.

EXPLORING THE PARALLELS IN ABOLITIONIST AND REGULATORY APROACHES TO SEX WORK IN THE CONTEXT OF NEO-LIBERALISM

The history of prostitution control shows that major reform is episodic and related to wider social transformations, to shifts in economy, culture, and 'nation states'.[8] Significant legislative change in the West has, for example, accompanied the period of transition from feudalism to industrialization and

---

7 S. Silbey, 'After Legal Consciousness' (2005) 1 *Annual Rev. of Law and Social Science* 323–68.

8 J.R. Walkowitz, *Prostitution and Victorian Society* (1980); C. Smart, *Feminism and the Power of Law* (1989). My aim in beginning with law is not to suggest it as the primary lens through which to understand the operations of commercial sex, as to do so would be assume it as a universal ethic which limits both the 'the social and discursive field' (Agustín, op. cit., n. 6, at p. 75). As Rose and Valverde note:

> The intellectual premises and analytic methods of legal studies tend to presuppose that objects and problems form within the workings of law itself. But in order to analyse the ways in which problems form at the intersection of legal and extra-legal discourses, practices and institutions, it is necessary to de-centre law from the outset.

(N. Rose and M. Valverde, 'Governed by law?' (1998) 7 *Social and Legal Studies* 541–53, at 545). Thus in explaining how prostitution becomes a target for regulation, law is shown to form only part of wider social processes (such as medicine, public health, health, religion, the nation state) involved in the problematization and regulation of sex work. Yet, to decentre law is not to expel it or render it insignificant as legal processes, institutions, and functionaries do play a vital role, alongside other factors, in creating targets for regulation and authoring other modes of regulatory power.

14

from that period to present-day late capitalism. Such rapid change resonates throughout the social body, appearing to threaten to disrupt the perceived social fabric and its associated norms. The threat and experience of this social rupture provokes considerable anxieties on the part of certain groups, who seek to control the social order in order to preserve hegemonic forms of power relations.[9] During such periods of flux, issues of problematic consumption (alcohol, gambling, and prostitution) and dangerous identities have been convenient and familiar 'targets' for programmes and campaigns of moral regulation.[10] Prostitution, which combines both of these elements, thus appears throughout history as 'a dense signifier around which a variety of social anxieties' can be expressed.[11]

Thus, during the intense social and economic transformation which characterized the Victorian era, moral panics around syphilis, venereal disease, and an imagined 'white slavery trade'[12] expressed wider cultural anxieties over the overlapping processes of urbanization, immigration, and women's shifting roles. Encouraged by a broad coalition of feminists and religious groups who had made saving fallen women their mission, the Contagious Diseases Acts of 1864, 1866, and 1869 constructed the prostitute as morally and physically dangerous and vulnerable, justifying the intensive moral, social, and legal regulation of many unmarried working-class women.[13] In so doing, the public's individual moral and social health

---

9 S. Cohen, *Folk Devils and Moral Panics: The Creation of the Mods and Rockers* (1972).

10 A. Hunt, *Governing Morals: A Social History of Moral Regulation* (1999). This target setting could be explained according to the dynamics of moral panics, which as Cohen famously noted, often centre upon 'folk devils'; figures for anxiety to be projected upon, and ultimately regulated, controlled or even expelled so that order (and authority) be restored. Thus a number of moral panics could be said to have been inscribed upon the prostitute body. This term, while apt in describing some aspects of prostitution campaigns, may not be useful as a term of general application. (It may be useful with regards aspects of trafficking campaigns: see Weitzer in this volume (pp. 61–84) and the brilliant piece by J. O'Connell Davidson, 'Will the real sex slave please stand up?' (2006) 83 *Feminist Rev.* 4–22, which does particularly well not to minimize the real concerns faced by migrants and those involved in sexual and domestic labour but queries the reduction of complex social factors into a unitary victimized model that so few women can occupy.) It may not, however, offer the best conceptualization of a more cyclical process that, while involving a great deal of moral entrepreneurialism, does not so much create 'folk devils' as call upon identities that are always and already 'spoiled' (I thank Jo Phoenix for this insight). Thus I use the term 'target setting' for processes of moral politics to capture this process more accurately.

11 Phoenix, op. cit., n. 2, p. 12.

12 Bernstein, op. cit., n. 4, p. 13; R. Clifford, *What Women Might Do with the Ballot: The Abolition of the White Slave Traffic* (1912) 132.

13 This included forcing them to wear distinguishing apparel, exclusion from parts of cities, and the sanctioning of compulsory medical treatment and confinement. See Walkowitz, op. cit., n. 8; L. Mahood, *The Magdalenes: Prostitution in the Nineteenth Century* (1990).

15

appeared to be secured, helping to consolidate a particular image of the nation state as healthy and enlightened, all of which facilitated its colonial expansion. As Burton notes, the spectre of sexual slavery employed in campaigns and reforms at this time operated to conceal their facilitation of a wider colonialist project.[14]

This parallels with the present late-modern period and the dynamics of globalization which provide much of the impetus behind the recent flurry of legislative activity in international prostitution laws. Here the major shifts and increased fluidity in the movement of people, capital, and commodities brought about by globalization and late-capitalist restructuring, alongside a burgeoning sex industry, have incited a similar broad coalition of the religious right, moral puritans, and radical feminists around an abolitionist mission.[15] This modern 'unholy' alliance has coalesced around a crusade to combat what it regards as 'modern sexual slavery', a term applied variously to the 'trafficking' of women and girls for purposes of prostitution and to commercial sex more generally. 'Saving fallen women' has returned to the policy frame, yet while there is continuity with the earlier nineteenth-century campaigns, its reappearance relates to a new global economic and political context and invokes new forms of governance.[16] Once again, the trafficked bodies of sex workers provide a useful metaphor for violated state boundaries and act as a trope for a more general politics of security:[17]

> the putative re-emergence of the 'white slave trade' triggered multiple initiatives intended to protect the sovereign spaces of the European Union as much as the sovereign bodies of women.[18]

The form these multiple initiatives have taken is contingent upon different political traditions and arrangements, meaning that the same forces (that is, globalization) have been the impetus behind what are often cast as opposing regulatory frameworks, the most notable being efforts to criminalize men in Sweden and to legalize voluntary sex work in the Netherlands.[19]

---

14 A. Burton, *Burdens of History: British Feminists, Indian Women and Imperial Culture 1865–1915* (1994).
15 Abolitionism is informed both by moral and religious views regarding the proper place of procreative sexual monogamy. Radical feminist doctrine plays an increasingly critical role in marking out prostitution as an area requiring special attention. Its theory of sexuality and the state casts prostitution not simply as an example of women's oppression but as a foundational idea that predetermines women's social, sexual, and economic subordination.
16 J. Scoular and M. O'Neill, 'Regulating prostitution. Social inclusion, responsibiliza-tion and the politics of prostitution reform' (2007) 47 *Brit. J. of Criminology* 764–78.
17 See Hubbard et al., op. cit., n. 4, p. 140; C. Aradau, *Rethinking Trafficking in Women: Politics Out of Security* (2008).
18 Hubbard et al., id.
19 Bernstein, op. cit., n. 4, p. 148.

In 1998 Sweden took the unprecedented step of prohibiting the purchase, but not the sale, of sexual services, specifically criminalizing those who 'obtain casual sexual relations in return for payment'.[20] Commentators describe this as an attempt to assert a coherent national identity in the face of perceived national anxiety over entry into the EU, growing migration, and increased permissiveness in Europe.[21] Thus, as Kulick notes, in light of the increasing availability and commodification of commercial sex (threatening to blur boundaries between 'public and private and licit and illicit sex') and the spectres of Europeanization and globalization (that threaten Sweden with immediate and literal blurring of its national boundaries), the referent prostitute comes to symbolize the order of things and attempts to protect her also represent attempts to reinforce both cultural and geopolitical boundaries.[22]

Alongside these dynamics, as I have previously highlighted,[23] an influential role was played by a particularly hegemonic form of state feminism' which infused Sweden's conservative social policy norms with radical feminist ideology to produce a law that cites gender equality as its key objective:[24]

> Gender equality will remain unattainable so long as men buy, sell and exploit women and children by prostituting them ... Prostituted persons are the weaker party, exploited by both the procurers and the buyers ... By adopting the legislation Sweden has given notice to the world that it regards prostitution

---

20 The Prohibition of the Purchase of Sexual Services Act 1998, 408 states: 'A person who obtains a casual sexual relation in return for payment will be sentenced – unless the act is punishable under the penal code – for the purchase of sexual services to a fine or a term of imprisonment not exceeding six months.' Norway and Iceland have since followed Sweden's lead, with both countries outlawing the purchasing of sex in 1999.

21 A. Gould, 'The Criminalisation of Buying Sex' (2001) 30 *J. of Social Policy* 437–56; D. Kulick, 'Sex in the New Europe: The Criminalisation of Clients and Swedish fear of Penetration' (2003) 3 *Anthropological Theory* 199–218.

22 Kulick, id., p. 207.

23 J. Scoular, 'Criminalising "Punters": Evaluating the Swedish position on Prostitution' (2004) 26 *J. of Social Welfare and Family Law* 195–210.

24 A belief that prostitution symbolizes women's oppression and is, therefore, incompatible with women's equality underlies the official discourse in Sweden. This connection was bolstered by the new law's positioning as part of a package of measures to counteract violence against women. Entitled *Kvinnofrid*, which roughly translates as women's peace, it includes legislation on rape, domestic violence, and sexual harassment. Yet there are a number of problems in defining prostitution straightforwardly as violence against women: see Scoular, id.; J. Scoular and M. O'Neill, 'Legal Incursion into Supply/Demand: Criminalising and Responsibilising the Buyers and Sellers of Sex in the UK' in *Demanding Sex: Critical Reflections on the Regulation of Prostitution*, eds. V.E. Munro and M. Della Giusta (2008) 13–35.

17

as a serious form of oppression of women and children and that efforts must be made to combat it.[25]

Thus, apparent equality is achieved in the Swedish model by moving from criminalizing women in prostitution to penalizing men's role as purchasers and diverting women as victims to social work services focused on 'encouraging' exiting from prostitution.

A similar socio-economic climate and fears surrounding immigration hidden within the spectre of trafficking, resulted in a very different legal response from the Dutch who, in the same year as the Swedish law came into force, voted to legalize commercial sex in brothels. Despite the Dutch system's frequent caricaturing as the archetypal liberalized system, a careful understanding of the reforms shows that what was intended to be a pragmatic response has been in effect a selective and uneven approach to the issue.

It is evident from political debates on the issue that one of the main purposes of the new law was to reduce gendered exploitation in this area. This was thought to be achieved by drawing a distinction between voluntary and forced prostitution, as Outshoorn explains:

> Prostitution is no longer a controversial moral issue, but is now defined as sex work, provided the work is done voluntarily. Prostitutes are entitled to social insurance and can unionise if employed; they also have to pay taxes. Sex employers have to observe labour law, health and safety regulations, and pay social insurance and taxes. Brothels are permitted within certain areas and have to comply with local regulations; pimping is no longer a criminal offence. Forced prostitution, often tied to the trafficking of women, is to be eliminated. Traffickers can be sentenced to an 8-year prison sentence.[26]

In Sweden, there have been a number of evaluations of the law since its inception, though none has provided a straightforward comparison of the situation before and after the legislation. In keeping with the ideological nature of the reform, many surveys and governmental claims focus on changes in public opinion which are of course not of themselves direct indicators of behaviour. Thus, despite claims of the law's widespread support, which varies according to reports, a much smaller proportion of the public feel that the law is working.

In terms of the practical effects of the new law, the consistent message across a number of evaluations and sources, including those conducted by governmental departments, is of a temporary reduction in street sex work, leading to the displacement of women and men into more hidden forms of sex work and the worsening of conditions for those who remain on the

---

25 Ministry of Industry, Employment and Communications, 'Prostitution and trafficking in women: Fact sheet' (2003) 1.
26 J. Outshoorn, 'Pragmatism in the Polder: Changing Prostitution Policy in The Netherlands' (2004) 12 *J. of Contemporary European Studies* 165–76, at 165.

streets.[27] Despite the fact that purchasing sex was criminalized irrespective of location, the law has been selectively enforced, with the main focus being on the highly visible spaces of street prostitution.[28] Although relatively small by international comparison,[29] street sex work became 'the' overwhelming target of media attention, public expenditure, and police efforts, with seven million kronor (over £500,000) being given to the police to enforce the law, leading to an initial but probably only temporary, reduction in its activity as a result of targeted enforcement.[30]

This led to a classic displacement with a concomitant rise in 'hidden' forms of prostitution evidenced by the increase in an already expanding, yet little regulated, market in sex accessed via the Internet, in pornographic magazines, and via informal networks, for example, taxi drivers and hotels.[31] Many Swedish social workers have reported that some of the women who had been selling sex from the streets have now been forced to move into illegal brothels or to work alone from indoor locations. Such a move leaves these women more isolated than before, which arguably exposes them to greater risks of violence, and leaves them open to the forms of harm that are more common in indoor settings, for example, economic exploitation.[32]

Conviction rates have been low, amounting to around five hundred in the ten years since the law was enacted.[33] Research by the police board and others noted that, of cases filed by the police, the majority of investigations were discontinued due to insufficient evidence[34] and few proceeded to court.[35]

---

27 Socialstyrelsen (SoS), *Kännedom om prostitution 1998–1999* (2000); SoS, *Prostitution in Sweden 2003 – Knowledge, Beliefs and Attitudes of Key Informants* (2004); SoS, *Kännedom om prostitution* (2007); Brottsförebyggande Rådet (BRÅ), *Förbud mot Köp av Sexuella Tjänster: Tillampningen av Lagen under Första Året* (2000); A. Nord and T. Rosenberg, *Rapport: Lag om Förbud mot Köp av Sexuella Tjänster. Metodutveckling Avseende Åtgärder mot Prostitution* (2001).

28 Hubbard et al., op. cit., n. 4.

29 It has always been low in comparison to other European countries, with street prostitutes never totalling more than 1000 nationally, Kulick, op. cit., n. 21, p. 220.

30 This was recently followed in July 2008 by a new Action Plan on prostitution (Ministry of Integration and Gender Equality, *Action Plan against Prostitution and Human Trafficking for Sexual Purposes* (2008)), with a further 200 million kroner for international action and further educational measures to 'help [the people] rethink their attitudes' ('Government gets tough on sex trade' *The Local*, 16 July 2008). The focus again is on the symbolic implementation of the law and not on improving the material condition of sex workers.

31 SoS, op. cit., n. 26.

32 M.A. Barnard, G. Hurt, C. Benson, and S. Church, 'Client violence against prostitutes working from street and off-street locations: A three-city comparison' (2002) ESRC Violence Research Programme.

33 'Swedish prostitution: gone or just hidden?' *The Local*, 10 January 2008.

34 BRÅ, op. cit., n. 26.

35 Nord and Rosenberg, op. cit., n. 26, p. 208.

19

There is even less information on numbers exiting, on what social support exists for this, and of its effectiveness.[36]

Thus, the law, despite governmental claims, has had little evidenced impact on supply or demand but, rather, has achieved a restructuring between 'visible' street working and 'invisible' off-street work.[37] Alongside this, a number of reports note the law's negative impact on the most socially marginalized individuals who remain working outdoors. This was due to greater policing, a drop in custom leading to lower prices, less choice of clients, quick transactions, and consequently, greater risk taking,[38] a finding echoed in Östergren's interviews with women, who reported experiencing greater stress and danger on the streets.[39] Thus, criminalizing the purchase of sex in order to provide greater protection for women in prostitution has had the paradoxical effect of generating higher levels of risk and danger to those most vulnerable to risk – street-based sex workers.

Evidence from the Dutch system reveals a similar pattern in operation. The new law allows for licensed forms of work and so does not condone all instances of prostitution. For those deemed to be voluntarily engaged in sex work in a brothel setting, the previous restrictions on prostitution were removed from the criminal code (these were in any event rarely enforced through the previous system of 'regulated tolerance').[40]

For those who could meet these conditions, there was some evidence of improved working conditions within regulated brothels.[41] Yet workers also experienced increased control. They were, for example, required to produce documents in order to identify their status (their age and residential or immigration status), and encouraged to self-regulate their behaviour in the interests of public health, with social workers and public health workers alike encouraging prostitutes to conform to certain modes of working according to licensing conditions and business norms.[42]

36 Numbers if they were available would in all likelihood be diminished given the recession's impact on the economy and job market and the increasingly retraction of the welfare state, factors that are noted to impact negatively on women's ability to exit sex work: see S.A. Månsson and U.C. Hedin, 'Breaking the Matthew Effect: On Women Leaving Prostitution' (1999) 8 *International J. of Social Welfare* 67–77. See, also, Scoular and O'Neill, op. cit., n. 16.
37 Hubbard et al., op. cit., n. 4; L. Johansson and K. Persson, *Perspektiv på prostitution* (2004).
38 Nord and Rosenberg, op. cit., n. 26.
39 P. Östergren, 'Sex Workers Critique of Swedish Prostitution Policy' (2004) available at: <http://www.petraostergren.com/pages.aspx?r_id=40716>.
40 C. Brants, 'The Fine Art of Regulated Tolerance: Prostitution in Amsterdam' (1998) 25 *J. of Law and Society* 621–35.
41 I. Vanwesenbeeck, M. Höing, and P. Vennix, *The social position of prostitutes in the regulated circuit a year after the change* (2002); A.L. Daalder, *Lifting the Ban on Brothels: Prostitution 2000–2001* (2004); A.L. Daalder, *Prostitution in the Netherlands since the lifting of the brothel ban* (2007), available at <www.wodc.nl/images/ob249a_fulltext_tcm44-83466.pdf>.
42 Vanswesenbeeck et al., id.

20

The costs of compliance and conditions imposed by this system prioritized certain businesses and locations, leading to the constriction of the legal market in sexual services and the promotion of more corporatized forms.[43] The majority of sex workers lack the financial resources to set up on their own and would in any case resist a formalized employer/employee relationship, preferring an independent contractor status. Alongside this, many workers by reason of age, nationality or health-status are excluded from a formalized system. Notably, street sex work does not feature in the system of positive regulation. Indeed, many authorities appeared to assume that by licensing some brothels they somehow dispensed with the need to provide space for outdoor workers; thus *tippelzones*[44] in Amsterdam, Rotterdam, and Herleen have all closed since the repeal of the brothel ban.[45]

The net effect of the new law was a constricted legal sector with better working conditions for a small minority who were also subject to increased regulation and a wider displacement to a larger unregulated illegal sector. This has significant implications as noted in Daalder:

> The various developments in the prostitution sector would appear to be resulting in a growing division in the prostitution world ... The combination of inspections in the regulated sector and ... limited enforcement efforts in the unregulated sector results in a situation where involuntary prostitutes, underage prostitutes or illegal prostitutes have relocated from the regulated sector to the unregulated sector. These forms of prostitution are characterised by a lack of supervision and by poor accessibility for support workers, leaving [them] even more vulnerable to exploitation and making their position worse rather than better.[46]

SAME DIFFERENCE?

Thus, despite legalization and abolitionism being frequently cast as oppositional in policy, media, and academic circles,[47] with political lines drawn accordingly, the aforementioned evaluations and recent empirical work reveals that the difference in policy effects between these two positions is not as marked as rhetoric would suggest.[48] For example, my own work

---

43 Hubbard et al., op. cit., n. 4; 'In Amsterdam the reported number of legal brothels halved with the introduction of the law, Amsterdam to Cut Brothels in Half' *BBC*, 6 December 2008.
44 These are areas where street prostitution is tolerated by the police and where certain services, for example medical and social, may also be provided.
45 City of Amsterdam, *Voortgangsrapportage sluiting Tippelzone (de ontwikkelingen sinds de sluiting van de Theemsweg* (2004).
46 Daalder, op. cit. (2004), n. 41, p. 50.
47 Kilvington et al., op. cit., n. 1.
48 This includes my own work with P.J. Hubbard et al., 'Re-regulating sex work in the EU: prostitute women and the new spaces of exception' (2008) 15 *Gender, Place and Culture* 137–52; Bernstein, op. cit., n. 4; Agustín, op. cit., n. 6.

21

with Hubbard, Matthews, and Agustín[49] contrasts these two European 'extremes' with the United Kingdom system, showing considerable common ground, notably in terms of the lack of attention paid to many forms of indoor work and the increasing marginalization of street sex work.

Bernstein made similar observations when comparing the Dutch and Swedish systems with previous fieldwork conducted in her native San Francisco:

> In San Francisco, Stockholm and Amsterdam, three quite disparate versions of policy reform in the late 1990s resulted in a common series of alterations to the social geography of sexual commerce: the removal of economically dis-enfranchised and racially marginalised street walkers and their customers from gentrifying city centres; the de facto tolerance of a smaller tier of pre-dominantly white and relatively privileged indoor clients and workers; and the driving of illegal migrant sex workers further underground.[50]

The congruence between these empirical findings is striking, raising important questions as to the significance of law. At one level, the similarities could be explained by a gap between formal law and its implementation. There are, as documented, practical forces and concerns that mean that what is intended in the different responses just does not play out on the ground in either system: thus those implementing the Swedish law focused almost exclusively on the most visible forms of sex work, leading to a displacement and an almost de facto tolerance of more private forms of commercial sex. At the same time, the Dutch promise of pragmatic regulation was not taken, or could not be taken up by many who continued to operate beyond the regulatory system, excluded from its protection. But do these practical issues offer sufficient explanation as to why systems that have selected diametrically opposed approaches continue to display such similar results?

One possible attempt to address this issue at a deeper, more analytical level is provided by Agustín who argues that this lack of distinction is evidence that law simply does not matter, with much of sexual commerce taking place despite its supposed legal status. In the sections that follow I take issue with this verdict as I explain why and how law *does* matter in shaping contemporary sex markets in similar ways, which fits within a broader content of neo-liberalism. It is the contention of this article that law does form part of the explanation, but only if it is properly theorized through the lens of governmentality. I argue that, regardless of substantive or even practice differences, there are important parallels in the way in which law is operationalized in the service of power that unites both regimes, and it is only if we adopt a more complex understanding of law in modern society that we can appreciate its continued relevance.

---

49 Hubbard et al., op. cit., n. 4.
50 Bernstein, op. cit., n. 4, p. 146.

22

Agustín's work in the area of commercial sex has offered important boundary-breaking insights. In proposing the integration of a cultural studies approach to the field she has joined others[51] in opening up the analytical frame beyond endless moral debate and the over-emphasized and 'perpetually stigmatized' category of women selling sex, to take in the much wider social and discursive field encompassed by the intersection of 'a range of activities that take place in both commerce and sex':

> With the academic, media and 'helping' gaze fixed almost exclusively on women who sell sex, the great majority of phenomena that make up the sex industry are ignored, and this in itself contributes to the intransigent stigmatization of these women ... commercial sex is usually disqualified and treated only as a moral issue. This means that a wide range of ways of study are excluded. A cultural-studies approach, on the contrary, would look at commercial sex in its widest sense, examining its intersections ... the everyday practices involved and try to reveal how our societies distinguish between activities considered normatively 'social' and activities denounced as morally wrong.[52]

Her work on migration and labour markets similarly rejects the stereotypes of passive trafficked victims and benign saviours, a reductionist caricature which obscures the processes of global capitalism (which depend upon marginalized migrant groups[53]) and the, at times, parasitic interests of what she terms 'rescue industries'.

In a recent special edition of *Sexuality Research and Social Policy*, Agustín attempts a similar shift in perceptions as regards the legal regulation of commercial sex. Following on from her previous work which is heavily influenced by Gray's anti-enlightenment project,[54] she argues against what she regards as a misplaced faith that progress and emancipation will emanate through more enlightened law reform. The belief in increased social harmony through better laws is, she argues, irrational and myopic as law has little bearing on the ways in which the sex industry functions:

> In the domain of commercial sex, the search for the most rational, most just, and least upsetting model goes on, but almost exclusively in debates on socio-legal regimes that aim to prohibit or permit, punish, or tolerate the provision of sex for money. Based on moral and ethical worldviews, these assume that

---

51 This follows important work such as M. O'Neill, *Prostitution and Feminism: Towards a Politics of Feeling* (2000); S. Bell, *Reading, Writing and Rewriting the Prostitute Body* (1994).

52 L. Agustín, 'New Research Directions: The Cultural Study of Commercial Sex' (2005) 8 *Sexualities* 618.

53 L. Agustín, *Sex at the Margins: Migration, Labour Markets and the Rescue Industry* (2007).

54 J. Gray, *Enlightenment's Wake: Politics and Culture at the Close of the Modern Age* (1995).

progress, in the hope of better societies with better social justice and harmony will result.[55]

On the contrary, the fact that legal systems are characterized by non-compliance, with seemingly contrasting systems producing similar results means that for Agustín, the law is largely irrelevant in regulating contemporary forms of sex work:

> [I] dispute the usual assumption that these laws make reality on-the-ground very very very different. On the contrary, if someone were to come to Earth from Mars, they would look at commercial sex in the USA, which mostly has meant criminalising laws, and look at it in New Zealand or the UK or Germany, and not see much difference at all. The endless debating about legal systems to control prostitution is bizarrely irrelevant, except for its symbolic value.[56]

While I would agree with much of Agustín's descriptive account with regards the empirical effects of many law reforms, her prescriptive account of law is less convincing. While it is certainly the case that the legal doctrine is over-privileged in much analysis of prostitution, and while I would agree that blind faith in the law is, of course, unsustainable as a political and intellectual position, it does not necessarily follow from this that law does not matter in any significant way in shaping the contours of contemporary sex work.

There are two related aspects of Agustín's expulsion of law that I highlight as particularly troubling. First, by taking law at face value, Agustín offers a limited understanding of modern legal power and thus underestimates its role in authorizing and shaping contemporary power relations. Secondly, and relatedly, by failing to appreciate the specificity of modern legal power, there is a concomitant failure to appreciate law's (albeit circumscribed) potential to transform. By contrast, utilizing insights from theories of governmentality, I offer a new approach to the study of the regulation of sex work. I use this to revisit the aforementioned empirical findings to show how law matters in neo-liberal settings, in constructing the space, subjects, and systems of governance, and conclude by arguing how law could matter in future struggles.

WHY LAW MATTERS: CRITIQUING THE EXPULSION OF LAW

Agustín, in setting out what she terms her anti-statist approach, rightly recognizes that to view commercial sex through the lens of legal doctrine frames the subject too narrowly. Yet her own analysis is similarly afflicted as

---

55 Agustín, op. cit, n. 6, p. 74.
56 See <http://www.nodo50.org/Laura_Agustin/bad-reporting-prostitution-law-and-the-bbc-> which featured on her incredibly informative web blog, 'Border Thinking on Migration, Trafficking and Commercial Sex'.

she relies on a limited and out-dated juridical understanding of law which reinscribes the monism she rejects in all other categorizations. Law, in Agustín's thesis, is reduced to its sovereign expression: that which is enacted[57] or judged by the legislature and judiciary and then enforced by the policing agencies of the executive.[58] Thus, when legal rules that seek to criminalize or legalize prostitution do not activate this juridical structure, they are rendered impotent. In Agustín's schema, when 'reality' does not relate directly to law's pronouncements, it is rendered irrelevant:

> Almost all of the effects of legal regimes refer to the large, sometimes very large numbers of people who operate outside or against the law (whatever is in place) and a main element of all of these regimes is toleration, areas outside of the system in which the whims of local police and municipal politicians decree whether those who sell sex can be prosecuted.[59]

Yet, can these people and their actions be accurately described as 'outside or against the law' or as 'areas outside the system'? The impression given here is of law as a free-floating entity, with society going on outside of it. The relationship between law and society cannot be easily separated nor cast as merely symbolic (without a much greater account of what symbols mean), as law is imbricated in the very power relationships that constitute society. This more complex relationship cannot be captured by the analytical tools Agustín uses in her critique: 'rational/irrational' is not a sufficiently nuanced analytical device to consider the relationship between modern law and power, and operates instead to stymie the potential of her analysis. The charge of irrationality against law tells us little about its relationship to contemporary power structures; rationality is simply part of law's rhetoric. As Valverde and Rose remind us:

> There is no such thing as 'The Law'. Law, as a unified phenomenon governed by certain general principles is a fiction. This fiction is the creation of the legal discipline, of legal textbooks, of jurisprudence itself, which is forever seeking for the differentia specifica that will unify and rationalize the empirical diversity of legal sites, legal concepts, legal criteria of judgement, legal personnel, legal discourses, legal objects and objectives.[60]

Rationality, then, is simply a device used by positivist projects in their attempts to unify law 'jurisprudentially or genealogically' in order to present an image of a law as a bounded rational system. By assuming that law is only expressed in this framework, Agustín shares the myopia of positivist jurisprudence which assumes 'an internally coherent legal system' which has 'a state monopoly on the classification of law'.[61] This fails to recognize the

---

57 Or posited (hence the term positivism).
58 K. Walby, 'Contributions to a post-sovereigntist understanding of law: M. Foucault, Law as Governance and Legal Pluralism' (2007) 16 *Social and Legal Studies* 551–71, at 552.
59 Agustín, op. cit., n. 6, p. 75.
60 Rose and Valverde, op. cit., n. 8, p. 545.
61 W. Twining, *Globalisation and Legal Theory* (2000) 232.

25

ways in which law adapts to changes in power more generally; how law matters in modern societies. Sovereign/juridical power may describe a particular operation of legal power but it is not the only, nor indeed the most significant way that power manifests itself in contemporary late-capitalist societies. While positive law may well still be in place, and indeed is frequently called upon to address the problem of prostitution, juridical structures are no longer adequate in themselves to describe the multiple ways in which modern legal power operates in this field.[62]

To be fair, critical legal work is not sufficiently developed in the field of prostitution,[63] with studies tending, like Agustín, to focus on legal rules and their shortcomings, yet failing to elucidate properly the ways in which law operates in modern societies. While there is increasing recognition that 'law shapes but does not determine the extent of sexual exchange',[64] there is little by way of analytical explanation, or connection to wider theory on the operation of law in late modernity. This article strives to begin such a process. Utilizing the insights derived from Foucault's genealogical method and theories of power, it develops a more complex understanding of law in society, one that can recognize its significance without overestimating its power. Insights derived from Foucault's theory of governmentality, which advances an understanding of power beyond the focus on its location in a specific site to an awareness of its changing techniques and rationalities of control, is vital in understanding the shifts in modern legal power which mirror the more diffuse forms of power in modernity.[65] Viewing law through the lens of governmentality allows us to appreciate that law has adapted from a juridical repressive model towards more productive forms, making it still pertinent to the regulation of contemporary forms of sex work.

Applying Foucault's theory to law has been controversial and this may have influenced Agustín's limited appreciation of law which does seem out of step with her previous work which is infused by post-structuralism yet strangely stops at law. There is some precedence to this. At various points in his early writings, Foucault appeared to eschew law from his account of the changing configurations of power:

> We must eschew the model of Leviathan in the study of power. We must escape from the limited field of juridical sovereignty and state institutions, and instead base our analysis of power on the study of the techniques and tactics of domination.[66]

---

62 V.E. Munro, 'Legal Feminism and Foucault – A critique of the Expulsion of Law' (2001) 28 *J. of Law and Society* 546–67, at 556.

63 For a fuller attempt to fill this void, see J. Scoular, *The Subject of Prostitution* (2010).

64 M. Neave, *Inquiry into Prostitution: Final Report* (1985).

65 M. Foucault, *The History of Sexuality, Vol. 1* (1979).

66 M. Foucault, *'Two Lectures' in Power/ Knowledge: Selected Interviews and Other Writings, 1972–1977*, ed. C. Gordon et al. (1980) 102.

The rise of disciplinary and bio-power appears to herald the demise of juridical forms and law would, therefore, appear to recede:[67]

> It is a question of orienting ourselves to a conception of power which replaces the privilege of the law with the viewpoint of the objective ... the privilege of sovereignty with the analysis of a multiple and mobile field of force relations.[68]

This has led some writers to conclude that law has little bearing on modern societies, a point Agustín seems to echo. Yet, the antagonism between juridical codes and disciplinary measures is hard to square with Foucault's wider theoretical insights, a point made by a number of academics who have sought to recover law from its expulsion from the Foucauldian project.[69] Ewald and Tadros, for example, make the semantic distinctions between the writer's use of the terms *juridical*, which describes legal structures of power, and *law*, which describes the legal processes through which power operates. They point out that Foucault tended to collapse these terms in his earlier work[70] giving the impression of law receding when in fact all he meant to imply was the declining significance of juridical structures of power, not law and legal processes which may remain an important mechanism through which new forms of power operate and as vital 'technique[s] and tactic[s] of domination'.[71]

This seems a more likely interpretation as it would be somewhat anomalous for Foucault not to extend his recognition of the creativity of power relations to the legal complex. Indeed, as Munro notes, it would only be if we were to assume that Foucault understands law according to an outdated Austinian model, as commands backed by threats, that it would make sense to regard him as consigning the power of law to a past epoch of sovereign rule.[72] However, as seems more likely, assuming that he took a wider view of legal power, accepting that it too has been transformed as it adapts to changes in power more generally, we can recognize the withering of juridical power without assuming as a corollary a lessening significance of law. As Foucault himself would appear to confirm:

> Another consequence of this development of bio-power was the growing importance assumed by the action of the norm at the expense of the juridical system of the law ... I do not mean to say that the law fades into the

---

67 A. Hunt and G. Wickham, *Foucault and Law: Towards a Sociology of Law as Governance* (1994) 40; Smart, op. cit., n. 8.

68 Foucault, op. cit., n. 66, p. 102.

69 A. Hunt, 'Foucault's expulsion of law: Toward a Retrieval' (1992) 17 *Law and Social Inquiry* 1–38.

70 F. Ewald, 'Norms, Discipline and Law' in *Law and the Order of Culture*, ed. R. Post (1991); V. Tadros, 'Between Governance and Discipline: The Law and Michael Foucault' (1998) 18 *Oxford J. of Legal Studies* 75–103; Rose and Valverde, op. cit., n. 8.

71 Foucault, op. cit., n. 66, p. 102.

72 Rose and Valverde, op. cit., n. 8, p. 542.

background or that the institutions of justice tend to disappear, but rather that the law operates more and more as a norm, and that the judicial institution is increasingly incorporated into a continuum of apparatuses (medical, administrative, and so on) whose functions are for the most part regulatory.[73]

Thus, as Foucault confirms, while law may no longer provide the model for power relations in society, it remains a vital process through which modern power relations operate; 'a medium rather than a principle of power'.[74] This suggests not the supplementation of sovereignty by discipline, or the displacement of law but rather its embedding within governmental strategies that increasingly centre on the routine administration of lives,[75] a point confirmed by the sheer profusion of social laws that have accompanied the development of modern normalizing societies. As Rose and Valverde so perceptively note:

> The legal complex had itself become welded to substantive, normalizing, disciplinary and bio-political objectives having to do with the re-shaping of individual and collective conduct in relation to particular substantive conceptions of desirable ends. The legal complex, that is to say, had been governmentalized.[76]

It is this governmentalization that explains law's continued relevance in shaping the contours of contemporary forms of sex work. As law adapts to the wider social and political culture of neo-liberalism, typified by a decentred economy and forms of governance that operate at a distance, it too increasingly reflects its 'economized model'[77] of power, operating through, not simply over, lives.

This model implies not less power but rather its more rationalized deployment as it is operates productively for the protection of lives, not simply by threatening to take them away (though this remains in the background).[78] While there may be less government there is more governance, as power operates through normative discourses (including law) to produce subjects as effects of power and to 'structure the[ir] possible field of action'[79] in ways that so often align with wider social structures. Thus in the

---

73 Foucault, op. cit., n. 66, p. 144.
74 S. Veitch, E. Christodoulidis, and L. Farmer, *Jurisprudence: Themes and Concepts* (2007) 242.
75 Foucault, op. cit., n. 66, p. 144
76 Rose and Valverde, op. cit., n. 8, p. 543
77 id.
78 Sullivan describes the schizophrenic nature of late-modern criminal justice processes in which 'socially inclusive neo-liberal techniques of regulation can co-exist with more overt forms of control and repression: R. Sullivan, 'The Schizophrenic State: Neo-Liberal Criminal Justice' in *Crime, Risk and Justice: The Politics of Crime Control in Liberal Democracies*, eds. K. Stenson and R. Sullivan (2001).
79 M. Foucault, 'The subject and power' in *Michel Foucault: beyond structuralism and hermeneutics*, eds. H.L. Dreyfus and P. Rabinow (1982) 212–21, at 221.

context of a retracted or dismantled welfare state, individuals are increasingly responsible for their own well-being which is all the time more aligned to market norms. For those who fail in this task of ethical self-discipline, exclusion is their fate. Thus, modern systems of governance may actually augment and allow the carceral system to function better – by identifying for criminalization those who cannot self-correct.[80]

By corollary, modern law operates as much through freedom, rights, and norms as it does through censure, to regulate the complete lives of individuals rather than simply to prevent certain actions. In this context it operates both through the 'empowering' systems of licensing and welfare-inspired interventions designed to liberate women from the oppressive 'reality' of commercial sex. In order to examine how law matters in this more complex way, we need to take a more expansive view beyond the legal/illegal, inside/outside binaries that Agustín employs, beyond law's positivist presentation (as a 'unified phenomenon carried out by specialist institutions'[81]), and, as Valverde and Rose advise, examine instead what 'law is doing'.[82] This allows us to move beyond the 'dreary debate between sovereignty and discipline',[83] as both are shown to be involved in contemporary forms of governmentality.

The insights of governmentality suggest a new focus for future regulatory studies: to examine the ways in which law regulates and legitimates the operations of discipline, as it is 'these operations, rather than juridically imposed interdictions that constitute the fabric of the modern subject'.[84] This signals a new, but important, direction for research in the area of prostitution policy.

The hypotheses it yields will, of course, require further empirical testing.[85] With that caveat in place, I return to consider what law is doing in each of the aforementioned jurisdictions. Using an adaptation of Valverde and Rose's four foci of normalizations, authorizations, subjectifications, and spatializations, which they offer as a useful guide to analyse the legal complex from the perspective of government, I suggest that it is precisely because law does matter, in shaping subjects, spaces, and forms of power in

---

80 A system which itself is increasingly tasked 'to transform and reconstruct self-reliance in the excluded': N. Rose, 'Government and Control' (2000) 40 *Brit. J. of Criminology* 321–39, at 335.
81 Rose and Valverde, op. cit., n. 8, p. 550.
82 Hunt and Wickham, op. cit., n. 67, p. 99; Rose and Valverde, id.
83 Rose and Valverde, id., p. 550.
84 Tadros, op. cit., n. 70, p. 103.
85 I make these claims tentatively as these studies did not set out with this specific methodology in place. This area requires much more detailed empirical work that can capture nuances in regulatory regimes; a fine example is Sullivan's work in this collection, where she carefully illustrates the impact of different modes of regulation for different groups of sex workers in two Australian states, both of which are often collapsed into one national scene and one homogeneous group.

line with wider forms of neo-liberal governance, that a continuity is ensured across these apparently diverse legal systems.

HOW LAW MATTERS

1. *Norms*

By examining what law is doing in both cases, it becomes apparent that despite the difference in rhetoric, legal strategies for the governance of sex work share a number of similarities in terms of their regulatory ambitions. Empirical evidence points to two parallel processes in which prostitution becomes a target for the state's wider efforts to responsibilize citizens, while simultaneously maintaining spaces for the operation of the capitalist economy.

Processes of licensing and exiting operate to normalize particular forms of citizenship and sexual activity which enhance a broader structure of consumption, rendering deviant those who cannot through poverty, race, immigration status or health meet these increasingly restricted norms of citizenship, and marginalizing unproductive spaces. As Bernstein notes:

> both the state policing of the street-level sex trade and the normalization of other forms of commercial sex business reveal a shared set of underlying economic and cultural interests; the excision of class and racial Others from gentrifying inner cities, the facilitation of the post-industrial service sector, and the creation of clean and shiny urban spaces in which middle-class men can safely indulge in recreational commercial sexual consumption.[86]

This normative order is established not through law as such but via a continuum of regulatory mechanisms of which it forms part. Law has no privilege in this system but it does play a vital role in authorizing other forms of knowledge, helping to shape content, and empowering a much wider group of regulatory agents in exercising more diffuse forms of power.

2. *Authorizations*

Examining the extended forms of governance operating in this area may enlighten us more about what law is doing than the statute book. Thus, in the context of Sweden and the Netherlands, despite differences at a sovereign level in prostitution policy, law authorizes and operates though a number of quasi-legal forums (john schools, exiting programmes, rehabilitation schemes, and licensing boards) and techniques (anti-social behaviour orders, fines, rehabilitation orders, licenses) in which an extended group of regulatory agents exercise normalizing power: 'all the little judges of

---

86 Bernstein, op. cit., n. 4, p. 141.

conduct [who] exercise their petty powers of adjudication and enforce-ment[87] in what Valverde and Rose call 'the bureaucratic workings of our over-governed existence'.[88]

These forums feature a hybridization of legal and non-legal authority. The state's role appears to recede but it may actually be augmented by a wider range of control mechanisms and forms of professional intervention that may be even more pervasive than the previous systems. Licensing decision making is devolved to a wider group, yet operates to reaffirm the dividing lines between legitimate and illegitimate forms of commercial sex. Indeed, it may be more useful than direct control as delegated authority refines law more minutely in response to shifting realities on the ground and employs a wider group of authorities in its realization. This ensures that the wider structures of governmentality fit with local conditions while appearing to comply with the liberal objection to state interference.

Thus, in the case of the Netherlands, while street sex work has not been outlawed it has been made more and more difficult, as a number of municipalities in closing their *tippelzones* have dispensed with their previous assumed duties to provide safe places for street sex work. Similarly the economic and racial segregation apparent in indoor settings appears distant and accidental as it is effected by powers exercised by diverse groups.

In Sweden decriminalization premised on exiting may actually signal a wider range of control mechanisms and forms of professional intervention which are even more pervasive than the previous system of fines. Thus, the apparent increased 'protection' promised by reforms results in the increased policing of many women's lives.[89]

3. Subjectifications

> There is a question which is essential in the Modern Tribunal, but which would have had a strange ring to it 150 years [ago]: 'Who are You?'[90]

Foucault's observation in *The Dangerous Individual* is that law in normalizing societies is increasingly concerned with lives rather than with acts. This is evident in the current preoccupation with particular subjects and spaces of sex work and the operationalizing of forms of governance to save, empower, responsibilize, and ethically reconstruct individuals – all testament to law's increasing normalizing ambitions as it acts alongside other discourses to construct 'the fabric of the modern subject'.[91] In doing so it

---

87 Rose and Valverde, op. cit., n. 8, p. 546.
88 id.
89 J. Phoenix, 'Youth Prostitution Policy Reform: New Discourses, Same Old Story' in *Women and Punishment: The Struggle for Justice*, ed. P. Carlen (2002) 82.
90 M. Foucault, 'The Dangerous Individual' in *Politics, Philosophy, Culture: Interviews and Other Writings 1977–1984*, ed. L.D. Kritzman (1988) 126.
91 Tadros, op. cit., n. 70, p. 103.

31

operates not ideologically, as there is always resistance, nor through the simple imputation of legal consciousness,[92] but through a process of subjectification, encouraging self-projects in ways that align with the diverse objectives of legislation.[93] Thus, if we examine the *continuities* in the projects of self-governance promoted in each jurisdiction, we begin to see that the commonly accepted opposition between victim and agent may not be as marked when viewed through a governmental lens. Thus, through parallel forms of subjectification, both licensing and exiting operate to encourage subjects to perform as 'self-governing, rational actors' required by the wider context of neo-liberalism and to identify those who cannot self-manage or who resist normalization in order that they be excluded.

Thus when we look to Sweden and ask what law is doing with regard to the types of subjectifications it encourages, we see that while it decriminal-izes selling sex (due to women's assumed victimhood), it replaces this with a

92 The term legal consciousness is not the most useful concept to apply in this context as it is often limited to understanding 'what particular individuals think and do'. Thus, as with Agustín, when individuals do not follow or self-identify with law, it risks being rendered insignificant. For example, in a study of street-based drug-using women by Levine and Mellema, law did not feature prominently, leading them to conclude that the literature on legal consciousness over-privileged law, which was in their findings less important than other structural factors (K. Levine and V. Mellema, 'Strategizing the Street: How Law Matters in the Lives of Women in the Street-Level Drug Economy' (2001) *Law and Social Inquiry* 169, 179). While not disputing these findings, I would again caution against their implications for a wider analysis of law in society. The problem with such analyses is that they take too literal an approach to law and tend to examine law only in its sovereign sense, as a singular power in a hierarchy of norms, ignoring the myriad of ways that modern law operates as part of a complex regulatory apparatus focused on lives. An analysis informed by governmentality would, as I argue above, avoid the simple imputation of subjects as 'against the law' or even 'outside the law' when the law and their quasi-legal status very much structures their daily activities. Silbey, in 'After Legal Consciousness', appears to make a similar argument, without linking directly to governmentality. She explains that legal consciousness as a theoretical concept has become too compromised,

> the relationships among consciousness and processes of ideology and hegemony often go unexplained, legal consciousness as an analytic concept is domesticated within what appear to be policy projects: making specific laws work better for particular groups or interests.

(Silbey, op. cit., n. 6, p. 323.) In order to retain a critical edge, understandings of legal consciousness must, according to Silbey, be able to explain how different experiences of law become synthesized into a set of circulating schemata and habits often seemingly connected to persistent 'forms of inequality and domination characteristic of industrial capitalism' (id., p. 325, citing L. Kalman, *The Strange Career of Legal Liberalism* (1996)). I would suggest these schemata are better explained via theories of governmentality and its foci of spatializations, subjectifications, norms, and authorizations which offer a much-needed specificity to a complex area. I suggest, then, a synthesis of legal consciousness literature and governmentality to provide an important corrective to this literature.

93 Rose and Valverde, op. cit., n. 8.

system of welfare and therapeutic interventions which operate to support wider systems of neo-liberal governance.

Despite being heralded as a 'renewed welfare approach', which in any event is not necessarily benign, as my previous work with Maggie O'Neill[94] points out, contemporary forms of governance operate through these techniques of responsibilization. Techniques of 'exiting' women from prostitution must be viewed in the wider context of neo-liberalism in which welfare states, including the much renowned Swedish system, are retracting and being replaced by systems of private insurance, thus leading to increasing conditionality in citizenship and penality for those who cannot meet their terms/manage risks. In this context social exclusion is not tackled by structural change but via individual re-education, re-training, and entry into legitimate economies and relationships. By prioritizing 'exiting' as a means of facilitating social inclusion rather than offering recognition, rights or redistribution to sex workers as a group, abolitionist systems promote forms of self-governance which require active citizens to self-regulate according to the norms of the family and the market. Those who act responsibly by adopting appropriate lifestyles via work and norms of sexuality are offered inclusion, those who do not or cannot and instead remain in sex work (which retains its criminal label) are further excluded, having failed to meet the increasingly normalized terms of citizenship in late-capitalist societies.

The increased focus on male clients involves the promotion of similar individuating modes of governance. Despite the rhetoric of gender equality, the increased punitiveness towards (some) purchasers represents no more than the shifting of the 'whore stigma' to a new deviant group. Responsibility becomes increasingly narrowed to client motives and individual sexual ethics, which are pathologized rather than explained in relation to their historical specificity and to the social and economic institutions that themselves structure the relations of gender domination.[95] When action is taken through criminalization, or via the quasi-legal forums of john schools and name-and-shame campaigns, it typically operates on 'a lower-tier of male heterosexual practices' or to 're-gender sexual stigma in certain middle class fractions',[96] leaving the more mainstream corporate and private market untouched.

The system of regulationism in the Netherlands encourages similar forms of self-governance and produces analogous exclusions. Research suggests that legalized systems create a two-tiered (if not more) industry, as the costs and norms of compliance are too onerous for most individuals and small brothel owners to bear. Thus, it overwhelmingly favours profitable sex

94 Scoular and O'Neill, op. cit., n. 16.
95 Scoular, op. cit., n. 23, p. 206.
96 Bernstein, op. cit., n. 4, p. 115.

33

businesses which, as Brents and Hausbeck note, can now hardly be described as 'other' to late-capitalist industries.[97]

Alongside this, the system of licensing encourages workers to self-regulate[98] their behaviour in the interests of public health promotion, to conform to certain modes of working in order to meet the conditions of registration. Inclusion is offered to those who 'can perform the rituals of middle class society'[99] with all of the typical exclusions based on age, status, race, health, and class that this entails. This point is well illustrated in an advert which followed the decriminalization of brothels in New South Wales:

> ... tall, blonde and stylish, she recently completed her tertiary marketing course and is looking for employment in the field ... She provides her own condoms ... and comes complete with a medical certificate.[100]

This 'ideal' typifies the rational subjects encouraged by these processes, as law operates alongside practices, such as public health, to create and maintain what Scott calls a 'responsible prostitution population'.[101] The low take-up rate in the Netherlands indicates that very few can conform to this responsibilized model, meaning that while licensing can offer some increased improvement in the working conditions for a small section of workers, it also operates to identify and exclude those who cannot meet the increasingly conditional nature of citizenship, for example, migrants, the underage, and drug-users, all of whom are not incorporated within the framework of regulatory protection.

Thus in both systems, the moral engineering of advanced liberal governance has co-opted feminist concerns into techniques of governance and control. Whether based on a recognition of sex workers' inherent agency or victimhood, social exclusion is being used as leverage for increased control rather than for increased social justice. Empowerment simply operates to sanction forms of self-governance that support neo-liberal interests. As Cruikshank notes, the recent proliferation of state-sponsored programmes of empowerment must be treated with critical caution, as even while they are utilizing the vocabulary of radical politics, their promise of emancipation may be merely rhetorical as they 'endeavour to operationalise the self-

---

97 B.G. Brents and K. Hausbeck, 'Marketing Sex: US Legal Brothels and Late Capitalist Consumption' (2007) 10 *Sexualities* 425–39.

98 Sex workers rather than clients are encouraged to self-regulate their behaviour in the interests of public health promotion, with social workers and public health workers alike encouraging prostitutes to conform to certain modes of working: see Hubbard et al., op. cit., n. 4, p. 142.

99 B. Sullivan, 'Prostitution Law Reform in Australia. A Preliminary Evaluation' (1999) 18 *Social Alternatives* 9–14.

100 'Happy Hooker's Rich Pickings: It's a Bed of Roses for $200-an Hour Beauty' *Sunday Telegraph*, 6 August 1995, cited in J.G. Scott, *How Modern Governments Made Prostitution a Social Problem* (2005) 264.

101 Scott, id., p. 252.

34

governing capacity of the governed in the pursuit of governmental objectives'.[102] Yet what both processes do well is to identify those who cannot perform, rendering them vulnerable to exclusion or banishment.

4. *Spatializations*

Valverde and Rose use the term 'spatializations' to describe the governable spaces demarcated not by law but by the 'everyday knowledges' of order and disorder produced by a whole range of regulatory agents, from local authorities, businesses, organized crime, security firms, and policing authorities. This results in a 'patchwork' of local norms, of which law forms just part, marking certain conduct as desirable/undesirable, legitimate/illegitimate, according to its place. Street sex work typically appears alongside other behaviours such as begging and soliciting, loitering, vagrancy and sleeping rough that are marginalized as space is increasingly structured according to 'a territorial division between the excluded and the included, between the spaces of consumption and civility and the savage spaces on the margins'.[103] This exclusionary demarcation of citizenship ties in with my earlier work with colleagues which paid particular attention to the way in which new laws were being used to shape the legal geography of sex work. In Sweden and the Netherlands (and indeed the United Kingdom) we noted similarities, with abolitionist-inspired law and regulatory devices both being used as tools for eradicating particular spaces of prostitution, noticeably street sex work, while less visible forms take place outwith the scrutiny of the authorities. Thus, in Sweden, enforcement has largely focused on the most visible forms of sex work, leading to almost de facto tolerance of indoor and more private forms of commercial sex. In the Netherlands the protection offered via regulationism does not extend to street sex work, which 'cannot be incorporated within legitimate, regulated and surveyed economic spaces'.[104] For example in Amsterdam, a combination of the normalization of certain indoor settings and the non-recognition of outdoor settings produced the following spatial divisions:

> Amsterdam's tippelzone finally closed in December 2003, meaning that there is now nowhere for sex workers to solicit legally in Amsterdam. Only around fifty street workers are thought to operate in the city, and only in areas where police surveillance is less stringent. Given there were between 8000 and 10,000 sex workers in Amsterdam before the repeal of the brothel laws, but

---

102 M. Dean, *Governmentality: Power and Rule in Modern Society* (1999) 67; B. Cruikshank, *The Will to Empower: Democratic Citizens and Other Subjects* (2004) 103; D. Garland, '"Governmentality" and the Problem of Crime: Foucault, criminology, sociology' (1997) 1 *Theoretical Criminology* 173–214.
103 Rose and Valverde, op. cit., n. 8. See, also, J. Hermer, 'Keeping Oshawa Beautiful: Policing the Loiterer in Public Nuisance By-Law' (1997) 12 *Canadian J. of Law and Society* 72–94.
104 Hubbard et al., op. cit., n. 48 p. 149.

35

only 1500 or so now work in licensed brothels and clubs, the suggestion is that there has been a major growth in offstreet work in unregulated bordels (brothels), flats and cellars, mainly well away from a city centre increasingly dedicated to organised, corporate forms of sex work.[105]

Thus despite the differences in formal law, more sophisticated forms of spatial governance operate to produce similar geographies of legitimate and illegitimate sex, with safe spaces for consumption and civility coded as indoor/private and the street increasingly denigrated and most heavily surveilled.[106] As noted in my earlier European work with colleagues:

> while it might be assumed that the Dutch model of legalisation, the UK abolitionist system and the Swedish prohibitionist approach would have very different consequences ... the weight of evidence points to similarities ... street prostitution is being increasingly repressed (and displaced) by the state on the grounds that it is benignly seeking to protect both prostitutes and communities. Through a contrary set of moves, prostitutes hence 'disappear' beyond the bounds of respectable visibility (and often the protection of the state and law): even in instances where prostitution has been brought within the ambit of state licensing systems (e.g. the Netherlands), critics allege a failure to address many of the issues of gendered inequality occurring in such off-street spaces.[107]

OUTSIDE LAW?

This more complex process of governance offers a more nuanced account of law's power over subjects. This contrasts with Agustín's account, where she describes the issue of compliance (or lack of) as involving rational subjects deciding to deviate from the law and its norms:

> many of those to be regulated avoid participating in regulatory projects (even if they know about them), rather prioritizing their personal convenience, goals and financial advantage (apparently preferring to be marginalized, pitied, vilified and criminalized).[108]

As the work on governmentality shows this is a reductive view of the relationship between law and subjectivity. Law operates through freedom as much as through censure; through both the 'empowering' systems of licensing and welfare inspired interventions designed to liberate women from the oppressive 'reality' of commercial sex. The insight that power is productive and not simply repressive makes the liberal notion of freedom from the law naïve. It also complicates the distinction between legal/illegal and questions the presence of those 'outside or against' law whom Agustín's claims to

---

105 id.
106 id.
107 id.
108 Agustín, op. cit., n. 6, p. 73.

undermine relevance of law in contemporary sex markets. These people may be outwith law's sovereign rule/terms but they cannot escape its normalizing influence;[109] as Tadros notes, 'liberation from the blunt technology of the juridical does not prevent the individual being subjected to the loving force of bio-power'.[110]

Bio-power thus explains the position and indeed fate for many of those who exist outside law's formal terms yet remain subject to its disciplining power. In previous work with Hubbard et al., we used Agamben's[111] term '*homo sacer*' to describe these marginalized figures excluded from the law's protection yet subject to its power,[112] existing on the threshold of the sovereign state, in a state of liminal drift:[113]

> Stripped of workers' rights, dignity and adequate protection, those prostitute women excluded from political life and state recognition appear vulnerable to exploitation and are inevitably reduced to a form of 'bare life'.[114]

Such exclusion, re-figured to match the contemporary situation, has always been the destiny of those deemed prostitutes, whose identity, reductive as it is, exists to maintain the citizenship of others, and to preserve the boundaries between the economy and sexuality, work and affective labour. Thus, the neo-liberal techniques of control outlined above operate to augment an on-going hegemonic moral and political regulation of sex workers.[115]

Yet, ironically, insights from governmentality may also offer some hope for law's limited potential to challenge these injustices. A further benefit of Foucault's work is his insights into resistance. As power is immanent in our social practices and conduct, so too is resistance, albeit circumscribed by the context within which it operates. As law does not operate ideologically (as there is always resistance) or directly via consciousness (as it is more than simply what people think and do) but through its increased governmentality in shaping the subjects, spaces, and forms of power, it is within these spaces that some leverage could be applied to loosen the legal complex from being welded to the power of the norm.

---

109 Agustín almost recognizes this as she quotes Saskia Sassen who describes the informal economy as a coherent and necessary 'outgrowth of advanced capitalism': S. Sassen, *Globalization and Its Discontents* (1998) 155. What she fails to explain is how this coherence is achieved; is it simply a matter of ideology? Or is the capitalist system maintained through a more complex system of governance, of which law forms a part, which encourages individuals to operate primarily as consumers (*homo economicus*) and structures spaces and forms of citizenship, inclusion and exclusion accordingly?
110 Tadros, op. cit., n. 70, p. 103.
111 G. Agamben, *Homo Sacer: Sovereign Power and Bare Life* (1998).
112 Hubbard et al., op. cit., n. 4; K. Mitchell, 'Geographies of identity: the new exceptionalism' (2006) 30 *Progress in Human Geography* 1–12.
113 Z. Bauman, *Wasted Lives: Modernity and Its Outcasts* (2004).
114 Hubbard et al., op. cit., n. 4, p. 149.
115 Scoular and O'Neill, op. cit., n. 16.

Given there is no outside of law to effect such challenge, we must work within its structures. Foucault's genealogical approach shows us that while law has become increasingly governmentalized, it has not been fully colonized; it still operates according to a sovereign model, albeit to a much more limited extent which could be utilized as part of a strategy of resistance. As Rose and Valverde note, 'Not all legal power is juridical and not all non-legal power is non-juridical, thus it can be deployed both to extend and to contest normalized political strategies.'[116] Thus, the radical democratic agenda outlined by O'Neill in this collection could feature a modest role for law. The recent renaissance in human rights ideals and their embedding in international and domestic systems may offer a useful vehicle for her calls for recognition, redistribution, and rights, yet they may also provide a foil for increased normalization. In the context of neo-liberalism, the legal complex tends to form a key part of wider processes that constitute social life (in normalized societies) rather than working to alter or change it, and sadly in many recent reform attempts, feminists have colluded with this wider normalizing agenda. The balance, as ever, depends on who utilizes law, how they do so, and in what context: whether, for example, the terms 'sex worker' or 'exploitation' are used to reify exclusionary forms of identity, and essentialist forms of citizenship while obscuring material conditions (thus supporting law's normalizing power) or whether these terms can transcend binaries and give way to wider politics of resistance.

CONCLUSION

In this article I have sought to argue against an uncritical dismissal of law's role in regulating and structuring the conditions of contemporary sex work. Despite findings that apparently contrary legal positions produce similar results on the ground, I wish to argue that this lack of distinction is, in part, due to law's involvement in wider forms of governmentality that operate to support a wider neo-liberal context. This means that while it makes sense to de-centre law from our analysis, we simply cannot ignore it.

Law's increasing hybridization with norms means that it is imbricated in the everyday world. This suggests a much more expansive, extensive role, meaning that while Agustín is right to de-centre law, we cannot expel its relevance. Law and society are mutually constitutive: law may occupy a more modest position and effect a less direct power than sovereign rule, yet it may take a more potent form as it increasingly operates alongside other normative ordering practices to shape subjects, identities, practices, and spaces. While law can no longer be regarded as the primary source of power, there is no place outside its control.

---

116 Rose and Valverde, op. cit., n. 8, p. 543.

Rather than expel law, we need a more complex analytical framework to understand its contemporary relevance. Such a framework can be developed by applying insights from theories of governmentality to the studies on the regulation of sex work. This offers a fuller appreciation of the wider legal complex, and its role in regulating and authorizing the spaces, norms, and subjects of contemporary sex work. It also explains law's role in maintaining the systems of governmentality, across legal systems, that exacerbate these injustices and forms of bare life that have become hallmarks of late-industrial capitalist societies.

In arguing for the continued relevance of law I do not intend to reinstate an imperialist, uncritical positivist position. I argue instead for its strategic use in order to 'pursue a deconstructivist agenda *within* legal arenas and discourses'.[117] This requires an acute understanding of law as a mode of regulation as well as an understanding of how it could be how harnessed as a tool of resistance. As Tadros notes:

> rather than the structure or fabric which constitutes our society, the law is a machine which oils the modern structures of domination, or which, at best achieves a tinkering on the side of justice.[118]

In order to tinker more on the side of justice rather than domination, one has to be critically aware of how modern forms of governance and control operate. This article, it is hoped, begins this process as it allow us to see that law *does* matter in the regulation of sex work and could matter, albeit in a different way than was thought before.

117 R. Sandland, 'Between Truth and Difference: Poststructuralism, Law and the Power of Feminism' (1995) 3 *Feminist Legal Studies* 14.
118 Tadros, op. cit., n. 70, p. 102.

JOURNAL OF LAW AND SOCIETY
VOLUME 37, NUMBER 1, MARCH 2010
ISSN: 0263-323X, pp. 40–60

Mainstreaming the Sex Industry:
Economic Inclusion and Social Ambivalence

BARBARA G. BRENTS* AND TEELA SANDERS**

*This paper seeks to analyse the expansion of commercial sex through
processes of mainstreaming in economic and social institutions. We
argue that cultural changes and neo-liberal policies and attitudes have
enabled economic mainstreaming, whilst social ambivalence continues
to provide the backdrop to a prolific and profitable global industry. We
chart the advancement of sexual consumption and sexual service
provision in late capitalism before defining the concept of 'mainstreaming' applied here. We use the case studies of Las Vegas and
Leeds to identify various social and economic dimensions to the
mainstreaming process and the ways these play out in law and
regulation. While social and economic processes have integrated
sexual services into night-time commerce, remaining social ambivalence fuels transgression and marginalization of the industry which in
fact assists the mainstreaming process. Finally, we project some
implications for gender relations, work, and inequalities as a result of
the integration of sexual services into the economy.*

INTRODUCTION

This paper seeks to analyse the expansion of commercial sex through
processes of mainstreaming in economic and, to a lesser extent, social
institutions. We argue that cultural changes and neo-liberal policies and
attitudes have enabled economic mainstreaming, whilst social ambivalence
continues to provide the backdrop to a prolific and profitable global industry.
We initially chart the advancement of sexual consumption and sexual service

* Department of Sociology, University of Nevada, Las Vegas, Las Vegas NV
89154-5033, United States of America
barb.brents@unlv.edu
** School of Sociology and Social Policy, University of Leeds, Leeds LS2
9JT, England
T.L.M.Sanders@leeds.ac.uk

provision in late capitalism before defining the concept of 'mainstreaming' applied in this paper. From our work, we use the case studies of Las Vegas, United States of America, and Leeds, United Kingdom to identify various social and economic dimensions to the mainstreaming process and the ways these play out in law and regulation.

While social and economic processes have integrated sexual services into night-time commerce, remaining social ambivalence fuels transgression and marginalization of the industry which in fact assists the mainstreaming process. Finally, we project some implications for gender relations, work, and inequalities as a result of the integration of sexual services into the economy.

ANALYSING THE RISE OF COMMERCIAL SEX

International travel, mobility, changes in consumption patterns, more leisure time, and neo-liberal state policies, have increased the visibility of sexual commerce in a global economy. The media has made much of the mainstreaming of sexual commerce.[1] Globalization has encouraged a dramatic growth in a worldwide sex industry that was worth 'at least $20 billion a year and probably many times that', the *Economist* estimated in 1998.[2] Moffat and Peters used Internet data to calculate that the indoor massage parlours business in the United Kingdom was worth approximately £534 million per annum in 1999.[3] Jones et al. cautiously estimate the annual turnover of lap-dancing bars in the United Kingdom to stand at £300 million in 2002.[4] In the United States, an industry report estimated adult entertainment to be worth more than $12 billion in 2005.[5] Two of the largest lap-dancing club chains reported earnings of around $60 million each in 2008.[6] Analysts say that these companies are proving to be fairly recession resistant, holding profits well compared to many companies, despite economic downturns. These economic 'facts' suggest prevalence and durability, contributing to what commentators such as McNair and Attwood

---

1 See S. Paasonen, K. Nikunen, and L. Saarenmaa, *Pornification: Sex and Sexuality in Media Culture* (2007).
2 'Giving the Customer What He Wants' *Economist*, 14 February 1998.
3 P.G. Moffatt and S.A. Peters, 'Pricing Personal Services: An Empirical Study of Earnings in the UK Prostitution Industry' (2004) 51 *Scottish J. of Political Economy* 675–90.
4 P. Jones, P. Shears, and D. Hillier, 'Retailing and the Regulatory State: A Case Study of Lap Dancing Clubs in the UK' (2003) 31 *International J. of Retail and Distribution Management* 214–19, at 215.
5 M.L. Freridge, *Adult Entertainment in America: A State of the Industry Report* (2006).
6 'More Women Working in Adult Entertainment' *MSNBC*, 30 March 2009, available at <http://www.msnbc.msn.com/id/29824663//>. The two companies are VCG Holding, owning more than twenty nightclubs, and also Rick's Cabaret.

describe as an increased respectability, both in how these businesses look and what people think of them.[7]

Despite this increased social presence, very little research has investigated the *processes* of mainstreaming and what this reveals about law, regulation and social change. Therefore, in this paper we ask two questions: how have sexual businesses accomplished the move towards acceptability in non-sex industry commercial networks and what has been the effect on the supply of and demand for sexual consumption and labour? In answering these questions, we hope to shed light on the economic and social mechanisms underlying the process of mainstreaming. Both the supply of and demand for sexual commerce has important implications for our understandings both of gender and sexuality in the workplace – given that sexual labour is a mainstream work option for a significant proportion of women in society – and for wider gender inequalities in society.[8]

This paper will rely on a comparative study of sexual commerce in two cities: Las Vegas, Nevada, a large tourist-based city in the western United States, and Leeds, a large metropolitan city in the north of England. Comparative qualitative research of informal economies is important as it offers insights into the establishment of wider global trends that span continents and contexts. These two cities were chosen due to the high levels of sexual commerce visible in their night-time economies. After a brief discussion of the concept of mainstreaming and the economic and social forces driving it, we will examine three facets of mainstreaming in these two cities: the economics of the industry, the regulation of the sex industry, and the effectiveness of their social integration. The study will then discuss the effects of these efforts on the supply of and demand for sexual consumption and labour, and what this reveals about the law and regulation of sexual commerce in today's societies.

DEFINING MAINSTREAMING

Just what does 'mainstreaming' mean? Both popular and academic accounts use the term in different ways. One of the most common uses has been to refer to the expansion in the size of the sex industry in the United Kingdom, the Unites States, and across the globe.[9] Mainstreaming also has been associated with the spread of the adult entertainment industry into businesses

---

7 B. McNair, *Striptease Culture: Sex, Media and the Democratization of Desire* (2002); F. Attwood, 'Sexed Up: Theorizing the Sexualization of Culture' (2006) 9 *Sexualities* 77–94.

8 Note that throughout the paper we are referring to the adult female heterosexual sex industry unless otherwise stated.

9 'The Business of Pornography' *U.S. News & World Report*, 10 February 1997; 'How Big Is Porn?' *Forbes*, 25 May 2001; McNair, op. cit., n. 7.

42

that do not directly supply sex, such as the growth of profits from adult videos via pay per view for large hotel chains, or the role of the sex industry in fuelling Internet commerce in general. The term mainstreaming has also described some sex workers, like adult film stars Jenna Jameson or Sasha Grey, who have crossed over into mainstream film and television.[10] Both media and academic research note a shift in the social classes typically associated with the sex industry. Media increasingly highlight the growth of both middle-class consumers and workers in adult markets, and with that a subtle shift in the perceived respectability of those involved in the industry.[11]

The concept of mainstreaming thus involves two interrelated factors, economic integration and social integration. Economic mainstreaming involves processes that push businesses toward smoother integration with mainstream economic institutions. Economic mainstreaming can involve changes in business forms, marketing, and distribution whereby sex businesses look and act like majority, conventional, ordinary, normal businesses. For example, mainstreaming sex-industry businesses can adopt traditional business forms such as corporate structures, vertical and horizontal integration, chains, franchises, marketing techniques, and traditional forms of financing. Mainstreaming can include horizontal integration, where a sexual business owns non-sexual businesses, such as a brothel that also owns a restaurant. Sex-industry businesses can be more integrated with other businesses by relying on non-sex industry businesses for marketing, advertising, distribution, manufacturing, or other business services. Mainstreaming also involves changes in marketing. Their look, feel, product and image embodies a conscious attempt to mimic aspects of non-sexual products and services (such as retail outlets that look like traditional storefronts or other night-time leisure venues, packaging that is non-sexual, labels for services that cast the service as a less transgressive one). Quite often these attempts to 'look' more mainstream are coded with class – upscaling in order to move away from traditional working-class sexual codes. Mainstreaming also includes a variety of techniques to bring in newer markets that may not otherwise have purchased sexual services or goods, including marketing to women and more diversity in age, ethnicity, and even sexual orientation.

Social mainstreaming shifts cultural attitudes toward the acceptability of sexuality as a legitimate form of commerce and pushes businesses toward

---

10 *MSNBC*, op. cit., n. 6. Jenna Jameson is an award-winning erotic film star, owns a multimedia adult entertainment company, and has also appeared on a number of mainstream American television sitcoms and other shows. Sasha Grey is an adult film star who appeared in a Spring 2009 mainstream film directed by Steven Soderbergh, *The Girlfriend Experience*.

11 Academic researcher Elizabeth Bernstein notes a specific trend of more middle-class women entering the sex industry to make a living, and selling sexual services to a mainly middle-class audience on the Internet. See E. Bernstein, *Temporarily Yours: Intimacy, Authenticity, and the Commerce of Sex* (2007).

smoother integration with mainstream social institutions. This is most visible in the arena of advertising where the sexualized female form (and to a lesser extent male bodies) sells a range of products from cars to clothing to deodorant. Bodies, physicality, and sexuality as modes of commercialization in all aspects of consumerism have allowed the direct and indirect purchase of sexual services to become more visible and accessible on the high street and in public spaces. There are some specific examples that support this point: research by Storr and Comella, for example, describes the increasing respectability as both sex toys (aimed at women through the Ann Summers high-street chain) and adult videos are increasingly marketing toward women.[12] It appears that other parts of the commercial sex industry are following this example, with Nevada's legal brothels similarly relying on business associations for lobbying, using corporate business structures, adding restaurants, and marketing to more upscale and female customers.[13] Thus, commercial sex has become mainstreamed as a direct consequence of broader social changes in the relative acceptability of bodies as commodities.

LATE CAPITALISM AND MAINSTREAMING

Academic researchers have pointed out changes in late-capitalist culture and economies that encourage and 'normalize' the growth of sexual commerce. Late-capitalist mass consumption has encouraged a pornographication of culture, a liberalization of sexual attitudes, and more egalitarian attitudes toward intimacy with an element of disposability about relationships if they are not providing full satisfaction.[14] Commentators such as media analyst Brian McNair label the persistence of a culture and media that encourage sexual revelation, voyeurism, and sexualized looking as 'striptease culture'.[15] This 'sexed-up' nature of contemporary society forms the backdrop to understanding the prevalence and visibility of sex venues in Western society.[16]

12 M. Storr, *Latex and Lingerie: Shopping for Pleasure at Ann Summers* (2003); L. Comella, 'It's Sexy. It's Big Business. And It's Not Just for Men' (2003) 7 *Contexts* 61–3.
13 K. Hausbeck and B.G. Brents, 'Inside Nevada's Brothel Industry' in *Sex for Sale*, ed. R. Weitzer (2000); B.G. Brents and K. Hausbeck, 'Marketing Sex: U.S. Legal Brothels and Late Capitalist Consumption' (2007) 10 *Sexualities* 425–39. B.G. Brents, C. Jackson, and K. Hausbeck, *The State of Sex* (2010).
14 A. Giddens, *The Transformation of Intimacy: Sexuality, Love, and Eroticism in Modern Societies* (1992); McNair, op. cit., n. 7; S. Jackson and S. Scott, 'Sexual Antinomies in Late Modernity' (2004) 7 *Sexualities* 233–48; U. Beck and E. Beck-Gernsheim, *The Normal Chaos of Love* (1995); G. Hawkes, *A Sociology of Sex and Sexuality* (1996); Z. Bauman, *Liquid Love: On the Frailty of Human Bonds* (2003); K. Plummer, *Intimate Citizenship: Private Decisions and Public Dialogues* (2003).
15 McNair, op. cit., n. 7; Attwood, op. cit., n. 7; R. Gill, *Gender and the Media* (2007).
16 McNair, id.; Attwood id.; Gill, id.

Other major social changes interplay with the dynamic changes of sexualized culture. As religion declines, it loses its power as a sexual regulator, as the promotion of traditional sexual values is increasingly questioned or rejected.[17] The market takes these opportunities apparent in social change and seeks to exploit any changes in sexual values. Studies are also demonstrating an increasing commercialization or commodification of intimacy and a heightened sexualization of gendered forms of work.[18] Thus, sexuality has become a central component of late-capitalist consumer culture.

Mainstreaming of the sex industry is invariably linked to wider patterns in leisure consumption, travel, and the hedonistic search for relaxation and pleasure. Global tourists increasingly consume services that sell escapism, themed adventure, spectacle, fantasy, voyeurism, and even transgression. Workers increasingly sell emotions, performances, and connections in an unequal context. The sexualization of work is particularly noticeable in empirical studies of the tourism, leisure, beauty, and restaurant industries.[19]

These transformations are affecting industries and work outside of the sex industry, and there is a large literature debating what this means for identity. Adkins notes that the material conditions of both sex workers and women who work in other industries are similar because 'sexual servicing of men may not be specific to the "sex industry" but rather is a common feature of women's waged work'.[20] In other words, sex work and mainstream service work are becoming increasingly similar.[21]

Yet also in this context a now globalized sex industry itself has grown tremendously, as legal and illegal services and a myriad of sexual products flood First World markets and connect rich consumers (male and female) with poor workers throughout the developed and developing world.[22] Thus,

---

17 J. Scott, 'Changing Attitudes to Sexual Morality: A Cross-National Comparison' (1998) 32 *Sociology* 815–45

18 A.R. Hochschild, *The Managed Heart : Commercialization of Human Feeling* (1983); L. Adkins and V. Merchant, *Sexualizing the Social: Power and the Organization of Sexuality* (1996); E. Illouz, *Consuming the Romantic Utopia: Love and the Cultural Contradictions of Capitalism* (1997); L. Adkins, *Revisions: Gender and Sexuality in Late Modernity* (2002); V.A.R. Zelizer, *The Purchase of Intimacy* (2005).

19 P. Crang, 'It's Showtime: On the Workplace Geographies of Display in a Restaurant in Southern England' (1994) 12 *Environment and Planning D: Society and Space* 675–704; L. Adkins, *Gendered Work: Sexuality, Family and the Labour Market* (1995); M. Tyler and P. Abbott, 'Chocs Away: Weight Watching in the Contemporary Airline Industry' (1998) 32 *Sociology* 433–50; P. Black, *The Beauty Industry: Gender, Culture, Pleasure* (2004).

20 L. Adkins, *Gendered Work: Sexuality, Family and the Labour Market* (1995) 158.

21 B.G. Brents and K. Hausbeck, 'Sex Work Now: What the Blurring Boundaries around the Sex Industry Means for Sex Work, Research and Activism' in *Beyond Divides: Exploring Money, Power and Intimacy in the Sex Industry*, eds. M. Ditmore, A. Levy, and A. Willman (2010).

22 For an account, see M. Padilla, *Caribbean Pleasure Industry: Tourism, Sexuality, and AIDS in the Dominican Republic* (2007).

45

even as the sex industry is normalized, it also feeds the transgressive attractions of the sex industry.[23] Even middle-class workers in First World countries find themselves turning to sex work for a liveable wage in a social structure conditioned by high-cost urban living and comparatively low wages for long hours.

NEO-LIBERAL REGULATION

Most certainly, the massive global economic and social changes of the last century have been a driving force in affecting the mainstreaming of the sex industry. This has been accelerated by neo-liberal policies of deregulation which have restructured local and national governances processes and supported the globalization of markets on a wider scale than previously possible. The growth of a neo-liberalism in the past forty years has meant, across the world, governments have increasingly designed policies to remove regulations seen as reducing market competition to allow business to flourish. Notions of individual liberty and responsibility have replaced protective regulations and social supports. This has allowed all sorts of enterprises to expand, including the sex industry.

This rhetoric of the free market and individual freedom has spread to the regulation of morality and sexuality. The obscenity, sodomy, and anti-pornography laws that once constrained sexual behavior and consumption are increasingly challenged by a more general legal ethic which reflects the morality of the market, the contract, and the principle of free choice. The new technologies, specifically the Internet, that drive the mainstreaming of sex industries have remained largely unregulated by official agencies and lie outside the remit of other advertising regulations.[24]

Consumption promotes a morality where personal choice is elevated to a moral right. Choice, be it choice of lifestyle or choice of product, is quickly becoming the new moral principle of our age. The service industry also allows for personal relations to be marketed as uncomplicated, free, contractual arrangements within the market. This new moral principle means that the content of the choice is irrelevant; it is the right to choose that matters. In other words, this free-market liberalism has also been injected into our personal morality.[25] This can be understood sociologically as a consequence of the transformations in individuals and society brought about

---

23 C. Seib et al., 'Commercial Sexual Practices Before and After Legalization in Australia' (2008) *Archives of Sexual Behavior*, published online 30 December 2008 at <http://www.springerlink.com/content/d432686008581243/>.

24 T. Sanders, M. O'Neill, and J. Pitcher, *Sex Work, Policy and Practice* (2009); P. Jenkins, *Beyond Tolerance: Child Pornography on the Internet* (2001).

25 G. Hawkes, *A Sociology of Sex and Sexuality* (1996); M. Prasad, 'The Morality of Market Exchange: Love, Money, and Contractual Justice' (1999) 42 *Sociological Perspectives* 181–214.

by consumerism. Bauman describes the present era as a 'liquid modernity' – a mass consumer culture in which a society of producers has become a society of consumers, where individuals become the commodities. It is these social, economic, and cultural changes that have promoted the growth of the sex industry as a consumer right and choice.[26]

While many of these changes promote economic and social integration of sexual commerce, there remains social ambivalences. In the United States, these changes have been at the centre of what some call culture wars.[27] There remains considerable anxiety about the specialness of sex and its 'rightful' place in socially proscribed conventional intimate relationship.[28] There is increasing polarization over moral issues such as abortion, same-sex marriage, and variable degrees of tolerance of permissive sexual relations between different social classes, racial and ethnic groups, urban and rural dwellers, especially in the United States. The United Kingdom is equally in some turmoil when it comes to establishing norms regarding what types of sex are acceptable. Recent years have seen a positive shift in the formal recognition of diverse sexualities. In the United Kingdom, same-sex unions were legalized through civil partnerships in 2004. The Gender Recognition Act in 2004 increased rights for those seeking gender reassignment. Yet, alongside this, there are very distinct areas targeted as morally and socially corrupt: sex in public, cottaging, sado-masochism, pornography, and prostitution have been subject to increased criminal controls.[29] So, even as we document a liberalization of sexual attitudes and gender scripts, there is also entrenchment around traditional roles, practices, and values. It is clear that gender, as well as sexual attitudes and practices, are in the midst of a major transformation that is best understood in conjunction with changes in other realms, such as the economy, labour, leisure, commodity, culture, and the self.

Thus, while massive global and social changes drive the mainstreaming of the sex industry, particularly in economic institutions, social ambivalences often find their way into the law and regulations affecting the sex industry. Certainly neo-liberal politics encourages many localities to pass regulations that encourage entrepreneurialism. In doing so, they often do not or cannot discriminate on type of business, making it easier to establish sex-work venues. Examples from Las Vegas and the Licensing Act 2005 in the United Kingdom (both detailed below) demonstrate the ways in which official

26 Z. Bauman, *Liquid Modernity* (2000).
27 L. Duggan and N.D. Hunter, *Sex Wars: Sexual Dissent and Political Culture* (1995); R. Weitzer, 'Deficiencies in the Sociology of Sex Work' (2000) 2 *Sociology of Crime, Law and Deviance* 2; R. Weitzer, 'The Politics of Prostitution in America' in *Sex for Sale*, ed. R. Weitzer (2000) 159–80.
28 Jackson and Scott, op. cit., n. 14.
29 P. Johnson, 'Ordinary Folk and Cottaging: Law, Morality, and Public Sex' (2007) 34 *J. of Law and Society* 520–43.

mechanisms have supported the growth of different sex markets. Even in areas that criminalize all (such as Las Vegas city itself) or some aspects of commercial sex (as in the United Kingdom where there is an official policy encouraging the 'eradication' of street-sex markets), commercial sex can still thrive. Yet governments rarely enthusiastically embrace mainstreaming sex businesses. From religious organizations to fundamentalist feminist organizations, there are powerful social movements that put considerable pressure on governments to keep remaining regulations on certain sex businesses. Thus, pressures toward economic integration are tempered by considerable social ambivalences.

We now turn to a comparison of sexual commerce and regulation in Leeds and Las Vegas, illustrating the way in which the informal sexual economies in these two cities are reflectant of these larger trends in economic and social mainstreaming.

THE TALE OF TWO CITIES

1. *Leeds*

The city of Leeds is a dominant economic and cultural metropolis in the north of England. It has a population of approximately 750,000 people with a further 100,000 people working in the city. Its history of being a predominately white, working-class Yorkshire location remains, with the more recent addition of smaller communities from Pakistan, India, Bangladesh, China, and the African Caribbean. The engineering and manufacturing base that made Leeds an important town during the nineteenth-century Industrial Revolution has become more of a service economy, with media, communications, teaching, and research becoming significant during the twentieth century. Amongst other educational institutions, Leeds now hosts two large universities with an average annual student population of 45,000, and is rated by students as one of the best university locations in the country. Over the past decade the city centre has become a hotbed of regeneration for businesses, urban dwellings (high rise apartment blocks), and high-end retail and entertainment.

The city has a reputation for a lively night-time economy. It has a large music scene with a nightlife tailored to a range of interests and age groups. Notably, the city is a mecca for 'hen and stag parties' (pre-marriage single-sex celebrations which revolve around alcohol), and has a visible commercial sex industry. It is this relative visibility, accessibility, and tolerance of commercial sex which enables the city to be compared relatively with Las Vegas. The city has recently seen a large growth in the number of lap-dancing clubs. As of the time of writing, there were twelve such bars throughout the city centre, considerably more than rival cities and arguably the highest number outside London. While direct sexual services are illegal,

48

there is still a thriving trade in street and off-street markets. A local sex work project, Genesis, has contact with approximately six hundred women in saunas, flats, and escorts and a further two hundred women working on the street in any one year.[30] These figures identify that there has been some level of official tolerance of the sex industry historically, particularly in the indoor sex markets. It is only with recent government pressure that the local authority has taken an eradication approach.

2. *Las Vegas*

Las Vegas, Nevada is a city of nearly two million people, located in the deserts of the western United States. Las Vegas has been one of the fastest growing cities in the United States for the past ten years, fuelled largely by a tourist economy that has grown up around legalized gambling.[31] Called a 'triumph of globalised postindustrial capitalism',[32] Las Vegas's resorts market glamour, spectacle, fantasy, and adventure through images of vice, gambling, sex, and sin. The city advertises, 'what happens in Las Vegas stays in Las Vegas'.[33] Las Vegas in 2008 ranked twelfth globally on the number of air passengers and is the forty-eighth most visited city in the world.[34] Las Vegas attracts 39 million visitors who spend more than $41 billion per year. Nearly 20 per cent of the population has immigrated from Mexico, Latin America, and other parts of the world to work in casino and construction jobs.

While the resorts thrive on selling sin and sexuality, the very powerful resort industry association distances itself from any association with the adult entertainment industry. The desire to keep gambling legitimate means corporate resort owners, who have lots to lose, must keep a visible profile cleansed of other vices. As a result, Las Vegas's thriving sex industry is not that much bigger than many resort and convention cities in the United States. As of 2007, there were thirty seven gentlemen's clubs with nearly 100,000 registered dancers in the Las Vegas area. There are many adult boutiques, bookstores, and fetish stores that cater mainly to tourists, as locals are fairly

---

30 Direct sexual services sell sexual intercourse and related contact, such as prostitution. Indirect sexual services sell sexual interactions or images not involving genital contact with customers, including bondage and discipline, lap dancing, massage, adult film or magazines.

31 P.I.O. US Census Bureau, 'U.S. Census Bureau News Press Release: Nevada in Focus: Census Bureau Pre-Caucus Snapshot' 16 January 2008.

32 M. Gottdiener, C.C. Collins, and D.R. Dickens, *Las Vegas: The Social Production of an All-American City* (1999). H. Rothman, *Neon Metropolis: How Las Vegas Started the Twenty-First Century* (2002).

33 Gottdiener et al., id.

34 C. Bremner, 'Top 150 City Destinations: London Leads the Way' (2007), available at: <http://www.euromonitor.com/Top_150_City_Destinations_London_Leads_the_Way>.

conservative when it comes to sexual entertainment. There is a thriving legal outcall dancing industry where dancers visit hotel rooms and homes. Most of these women then sell sex illegally for tips. Nevada is unique in the United States for having legal brothel prostitution in rural counties, although there are no brothels in the major resort cities.[35]

Las Vegas's expertise has been in using sexuality and vice as a marketing tool, something it has done well since the 1940s. Yet it does so in ways that make vice mainstream and palatable to middle-class consumers. In other words, it is able to market sexuality as both mainstream and transgressive, as we will discuss later.

MAINSTREAMING SEX INDUSTRIES AND THE LAW

While neo-liberal politics promotes laws that encourage economic integration of sexual commerce, social ambivalence often pushes contradictory regulations. In this section we examine the integration of sexual commerce with mainstream economic, legal, and social institutions in Leeds and Las Vegas.

1. The mainstreaming sex industry in Leeds

In many ways, the scale and history of the sex industry in Leeds is not comparable to the rich and infamous history of its counterpart in Las Vegas. Key economic and social differences, such as the relative lack of tourism in Leeds, the international profile, and even the desert location, mean that the two cities are very different in their abilities to soak up, facilitate, and therefore mainstream the sex industry. However, Leeds, like Las Vegas, is increasingly relying on a service and entertainment sector to bolster its economic base. Leeds has interesting dimensions which offers insights into how the mainstreaming process is taking place in the United Kingdom.

Like Las Vegas, officials in Leeds have regulated the sex industry in two distinct ways. First, the direct sex market, particularly street prostitution, has been heavily policed in recent years, following central government's agenda to eradicate prostitution as set out by the Home Office's *Coordinated Prostitution Strategy* in 2006.[36] The focus in Leeds also shifted beyond the visible street markets as police raided and closed indoor premises such as brothels and working flats to further 'disrupt the sex markets', in line with

---

35 K. Hausbeck, B.G. Brents, and C. Jackson, 'Sex Industry and Sex Workers in Nevada' (2006), available at <www.unlv.edu/centers/cdclv/healthnv/health_ contents.html>.

36 T. Sanders, *Sex Work: A Risky Business* (2005); T. Sanders, 'Controlling the Anti-Sexual City: Sexual Citizenship and the Disciplining of Female Sex Workers' (2009) 9 *Criminology and Criminal Justice* 507–25.

50

government objectives. These two activities have been fuelled by the rhetoric of street prostitution as public nuisance and the 'trafficking' moral panic that has exaggerated the extent of the problem, and drawn policy and resources away from prostitution in general, towards specific forms of sexual exploitation. Yet, despite years of police crackdowns, dedicated officers, and intolerance towards voluntary sexual services, there is a persistence of street and off-street direct sex markets (even if numbers and visibility fluctuate).

Second, indirect sexual services are tolerated. Recent changes in laws regulating non-sex-industry businesses have facilitated this tolerance. In a prime example of the modern state supporting free market economics, the 2005 Licensing Act reduced previous constraints placed upon premises selling alcohol.[37] The law allowed, for the first time, businesses to remain open for twenty-four hours after a minimal risk assessment. Lap-dancing bars were not given any specific licensing assessments but came under the same requirements as any other alcohol venue, including the same risk assessments regarding anti-social behaviour and violence. As these venues are rarely involved with these affrays, and the 'risks' are often assessed as minimal, essentially the licensing law gave a green light to entrepreneurs to open lap-dancing bars.

Since then, the number of strip clubs and other night-time entertainment has dramatically increased in Leeds. These legal venues sidle alongside 'ordinary' pubs and bars in the high street in the centre and on the periphery of the leisure zones. Lap-dancing clubs cater to all wallets, tastes, and social occasions. The hierarchy of lap-dancing bars goes from the 'cheap and cheerful' larger venues which host 'free' student nights where dances can be purchased 'two for the price of one'; middle-of-the-range clubs where there is a stricter entrance code and fee; and at the top of the hierarchy there are elite 'members-only' clubs which boast chic and sophisticated surroundings, charge higher prices for entrance, drinks, and dances and are more exclusive regarding clientele (aiming for spendthrift businessmen). This hierarchy is made up of national and multinational operators as well as independent owners. These venues are highly visible on the main streets of Leeds city centre, both physically through flashing neon signs, and public advertising via posters, flyers, and discount coupons. Where clubs are placed in the hierarchy is reflected in the types of advertising, branding, image, offers, and promotion tactics they utilize and even by the physical presence of door staff and attendants.

There also have been very public plans for a 'superclub' to be opened next to the city's main train station. The huge poster at the intended location advertising the new 'superclub' is next to the most expensive traditional hotel in town. It boasts a £1 million refurbishment of the building and promises a venue that will host a hundred dancers each night. Currently the new club is offering customers 'limited free memberships' and promises of

---

37 For a review of the consequences of the law, see P. Hadfield, *Bar Wars: Contesting the Night in Contemporary British Cities* (2006).

51

'VIP and champagne lounges.' Reminding the public that this is indeed a *supply* as well as a demand economy, the poster also recruits for dancers. The blatant advertising of this 'superclub' and the visibility of strip venues in general demonstrate the level of economic tolerance regarding commercial sex in the city.

While there is considerable integration with mainstream economic institutions, there remains social ambivalence. In 2008 politicians were pressured from a small number of communities to close down lap-dancing venues that were considered to be located in inappropriate places. In addition, the anti-sex industry lobby (Object) has campaigned against exotic dancing as an acceptable job for women, taking the line that such objectification is exploitative and oppressive. Hence, 2009 sees government proposals to reform lap-dancing regulations by reclassifying them as 'sex encounter establishments' giving local councils greater powers to take into account local concerns and community objections. This may see a reduction of lap-dancing bars in the future or indeed the closure of existing venues. But then there are most likely to be other regulatory loopholes that will allow businesses to operate, especially in an economic downturn. Even if legislative changes should tighten the freedom on lap-dancing bars that is currently being exploited, economic incentives remain for lap-dancing venues to thrive and become a serious slice of the night-time economy. Therefore, in Leeds, like other large cities in the United Kingdom, the visibility and accessibility of commercial sex as both a form of labour and consumption is on a relative spectrum to that found in Las Vegas.

2. *The mainstreaming sex industry in Las Vegas*

Despite its iconic status as the symbolic centre of the sex industry, Las Vegas has a contradictory approach to its sex industry. On the one hand, the direct sex market, particularly street prostitution, is heavily policed, on the other hand, indirect sexual services are fairly well accepted. Most of the motivation for regulatory approaches to the sex industry revolves around the adult industry's relationship with the tourism industry. First, officials seek to keep visible prostitution out of the resort areas. Prostitution is illegal in Las Vegas metropolitan area. Police institute occasional crackdowns on street prostitution, enforcing stiffer penalties on women working near resort areas. Authorities also attempt to police indoor direct sexual services. The legal outcall industry greatly irritates local officials, and the vice department run 'stings' to catch women illegally selling sex in hotels while on a legal outcall to dance. The local police department claims to have made 5,000 vice related arrests in 2008, although most workers are back at work the following day.[38] Because the outcall referral business is legal, business owners cannot be

---

38 'Vice Enforcement's Top Offenders: Police Are Taking Unprecedented Steps to Keep Prostitution Offenders Off the Streets' *Las Vegas Rev. J.*, 15 February 2009.

52

arrested. In fact, outcall businesses advertise on flyers distributed by individuals on public sidewalks outside the casinos, much to the dismay of the resort industry. These adverts are clearly promoting sexual services. The resort industry and local officials have tried hard to get rid of these hawkers, but free speech advocates have successfully defended their right to remain.

In addition to local government controls, some large casinos use their own private security to discourage visible soliciting in casino bars, although some casinos are more diligent than others. Some of the largest resorts are rumoured to have their own assembly of high-class sex workers readily available for VIP customers. Despite these efforts, illegal prostitution thrives in Las Vegas. There are some who estimate that there are more than 3,000 indoor sex workers at any one time, more on the weekends.[39]

The second approach by officials is limited tolerance toward other indirect sexual services. All adult businesses, clubs, bookstores, and novelty stores are subject to special zoning regulations preventing much mixing with mainstream retail outlets. For the most part, they are subject to the same business and alcohol licenses as other mainstream organizations. In some cases, businesses can deal in limited adult content and not be subject to regulations. Adult bookstores, for example, are only regulated as adult stores if more than 35 per cent of gross sales come from sexually explicit content.

Most strip clubs operate just outside the resort corridors. A few clubs are located in the major tourist areas because they were there before zoning was instituted. Strip clubs are subject to regulations on clothing and how near dancers may be to customers. There is a range of clubs from the downmarket to the ultra chic. But the majority of those in and around the resort areas are mega clubs that can employ as many as three hundred women a night. Some have very upscale décor and a few have on-site restaurants. Most are corporate owned, and almost all of the large national chains have clubs in Las Vegas. Strip clubs have been hoping to get inside casinos for years, but because the gambling industry does not want to be associated with prostitution, the chances of an actual club inside a casino seems remote. At the same time, sexy nightclubs, burlesque and topless dancing revues have long been a part of casino businesses with long-standing semi-nude shows available at ordinary theatres.

Though strip clubs are treated as mainstream businesses, they are often subject to much more surveillance than other businesses. The local police department continually patrols strip clubs for signs of prostitution. A very high-profile federal investigation caught several local officials who had received bribes from a local strip club owner in exchange for favourable regulations.[40] In spite of this, the industry seems to be thriving. Perhaps as a

39 Hausbeck et al., op. cit., n. 35.
40 A brief description of the investigation, 'Political Corruption: The Galardi Investigation', and an archive of all relevant news stories is at *Las Vegas Rev. J.* website: <http://www.reviewjournal.com/news/galardi/>.

sign of just how economically mainstream the sex industry is becoming, the Sin City Chamber of Commerce formed in 2004, and by 2008 had a membership of more than 500 businesses. Yet this story also belies the cultural ambivalence of the sex industry, even in Las Vegas. The Sin City Chamber of Commerce was formed when the two founders, who worked for the Las Vegas Chamber of Commerce at the time, began to see the Chamber discriminate against the growing numbers of adult businesses who sought to be members. The two pioneers told the authors in an interview that they decided to start their own chamber precisely because they believed there was a lot of money to be made by accepting these businesses. Among their 500 members, 80 per cent are mainstream, non-sexual businesses (such as accountants, plastic surgeons, and lawyers), 15 per cent are adult and 5 per cent are gay and lesbian businesses.

The organization promotes both economic and social mainstreaming. The founders say that their business is based on both economics and an identity of being open to all business. Their mission statement, which appears at the bottom of their web pages, states their desire to 'promote, with equality, respect and fairness, the businesses that provide the products and services that Sin City Las Vegas is noted for worldwide'.[41] Mainstream businesses join because they recognize there are profits in providing services to adult-related businesses, including advertising, printing, financial services, attorneys, apparel, and travel agencies. Dedicated, friendly and non-judgemental services provided to sex businesses will generate repeat and loyal custom in a somewhat alienating business world.

The trend then is toward increasing economic integration and social acceptability of adult businesses in Las Vegas. Businesses have also benefited from several high-profile lawsuits by the American Civil Liberties Union of Nevada regarding freedom of speech. Spurred by the recent economic recession, two proposals to increase taxes on adult businesses and legalize brothel prostitution in a red-light district downtown were discussed seriously by more local policy makers than in past years, although state legislators rejected both measures. At the same time, the line around acceptable sex is still strong. Businesses catering to the sado-masochism community have found it very difficult to get licenses. An upscale dungeon that opened in February 2008 was shut down six months later for applying through the wrong business license, though some believed the problem was that it was next door to a children's dance studio. Thus, while businesses are becoming further entrenched in economic institutions, social ambivalence still fuels resistance by some law makers.

41 'Sin City Chamber of Commerce' at <http://www.sincitychamberofcommerce.com/>.

54

While economic mainstreaming is a clear trend, social acceptability is not complete. On the one hand, the cultural changes discussed above have encouraged social acceptability of the sex industry. Sanders identifies distinct 'pull' and 'push' factors that have increased the social acceptability of sexual services.[42] 'Pull' factors provide endless opportunities to buy sex, including increased access through the Internet, travel, and tourism. Cultural changes drive what Illouz calls the 'pleasure saturated culture'.[43] The desire for pleasure has resulted, for some, in an outlook that sexual satisfaction is part of a healthy lifestyle, or even a 'right'. The draw to be 'self satisfied' for men of all ages has lead to an increase in the social acceptability of buying sexual services (in particular the acceptance of visiting lap-dancing bars as part of bachelor and stag parties and work or business engagements) and, to some extent, reduced stigma for those that do so. The cultural changes can be evidenced through the sheer proliferation and diversity of sex-markets: Harcourt and Donovan note at least 25 different sex markets, and there is evidence that in countries where prostitution is legalized there has been an increase in the provision of 'exotic' sexual services including bondage and discipline, submission, fantasy, the use of sex toys, and lesbian double acts.[44]

The 'push' factors refer to those personal circumstances that encourage men to seek out commercial sex. Age, stage of life, and stage or state of relationships, including unsatisfactory relationships, widowhood, and divorce drive men to seek out paid encounters either in addition to, or instead of, conventional sexual relations.[45] 'Push' factors are not only motivated by the desire for sex, but for emotional intimacy as part of a physical relationship. Sanders notes that clients who return to the same sex workers seek intimacy, emotional connections, and lasting friendships, in the context and safety of a commercial contract.[46] In the sex industry, as Bernstein notes, the marketing of 'the girlfriend experience' presents a product that satisfies the demands for an integrated social, emotional, and sexual exchange.[47]

---

42 T. Sanders, 'Selling Sex in the Shadow Economy' (2008) 35 *International J. of Social Economics* 704–16; T. Sanders, 'Male Sexual Scripts: Intimacy, Sexuality and Pleasure in the Purchase of Commercial Sex' (2008) 42 *Sociology* 400–17.

43 Illouz, op. cit., n. 18.

44 C. Harcourt and B. Donovan, 'The Many Faces of Sex Work' (2005) 81 *Brit. Medical J.* 201–6.

45 H. Ward et al., 'Who Pays for Sex? An Analysis of the Increasing Prevalence of Female Commercial Sex Contacts among Men in Britain' (2005) 81 *Sexually Transmitted Infections* 467–71.

46 T. Sanders, *Paying for Pleasure: Men Who Buy Sex* (2008).

47 Bernstein, op. cit., n. 11; A.K. Murphy and S.A. Venkatesh, 'Vice Careers: The Changing Contours of Sex Work in New York City' (2006) 29 *Qualitative Sociology* 129–54.

The turn towards social acceptability of commercial sex has helped promote the role of the female sex worker as a legitimate and valuable form of sexual labour in society. Although impossible to quantify, more women appear to be working in direct and indirect sexual labour. These workers are not just from poorer or less educated backgrounds. There are obvious 'push' factors for why women enter the sex industry: financial gain, as fewer well-paying jobs are available; low welfare benefits compared to the cost of living (especially for single mothers); and marginalization from the mainstream employment structure. According to a British government report, between August 2007 and July 2008, 5,514 people applied for 351 adult entertainment industry job vacancies that were advertised by the government's official job agency. These jobs, all legal, ranged from party planner; retail; non-dancing jobs in lap-dancing venues; dancers; adult chatline operators, models, warehouse packers, escorts, masseuse, topless TV channel presenters; web cam operators and performers; topless bar staff; nude butlers and cleaners; kissograms. Of the applicants, 59.1 per cent were male and 40.9 per cent female.[48]

Supply routes into sex work increasingly come from middle-class women with educated backgrounds.[49] Highly skilled mainstream jobs such as nursing already require bodily and sexual labour, and some workers see sex work as more profitable and convenient.[50] More recently, United Kingdom studies are showing that female students are a supply route into the sex industry. With rising tuition fees, mounting debt, and only low-paid unskilled work to top up student loans, students find a variety of different sex markets are accessible, financially beneficial, and require little commit-ment.[51] For middle-class and educated women (including students), the pull factors of the sex industry are making sex work a viable and attractive employment option with less social stigma. Indeed, as Agustín shows, there are groups of people in society for whom the sex industry is not a marginal but a mainstream work option.[52] For migrant workers who are limited by a lack of visa documentation, rights to work, formal qualifications. and fear of immigration police, the sex industry, like other informal unregulated economies, are one of a very few number of work options.

On the other hand, there is evidence of continued resistance to the social acceptability of both selling and buying sex. The 'whore stigma' persists

---

48 DWP Consultation, 'Accepting and Advertising Employer Vacancies from Within the Adult Entertainment Industry by JobCentre Plus' (2008).

49 Bernstein, op. cit., n. 11.

50 T. Sanders, '"It's Just Acting": Sex Workers' Strategies for Capitalizing on Sexuality' (2005) 12 *Gender, Work and Organization* 319–42; Sanders, op. cit., n. 36.

51 R. Roberts, T. Sanders, E. Myers, and D. Smith, 'Participant in Sex Work: Students' Views' (2010) 9 *Sex Education* (forthcoming); R. Roberts, S. Bergstrom, and D. La Rooy, 'U.K. Students and Sex Work: Current Knowledge and Research Issues' (2007) 17 *J. of Community & Applied Social Psychology* 141–6.

52 L.M. Agustín, *Sex at the Margins: Migration, Labour Markets and the Rescue Industry* (2007).

amongst countries where there is direct criminalization of sex workers, but also in regimes of legalization there is still evidence of stigmatization. Bradley notes the continued stigma attached to exotic dancing amongst women in the United States which affects their personal and public relationships.[53] The Nevada brothels are legal establishments where women work, yet being a 'sex worker' in the United States is still far from socially acceptable.[54] Despite the existence of unions and campaign groups throughout the world, the sex work labour movement has struggled to be effective in achieving legal change and rights.[55] In many countries, including the United Kingdom and United States, those who work as sex workers (even in legitimate businesses) have no employment rights. In the United Kingdom, there is no recognition of the job role 'sex worker', so individuals cannot register with tax authorities as legitimate workers, and are therefore exempt from benefits such as sick or holiday pay and pension rights. Some of this social ambivalence is fuelled by the radical anti-sex-work movement which takes the rigid position that sexual labour is violence against women, oppressive and wholeheartedly not an acceptable work option for women.[56] Equally, as Weitzer has succinctly argued, the exaggerated official and media concerns relating to trafficking into the sex industry has been responsible for myth-making about the everyday realities of sex work for many women, and the continued discourses around victimization and exploitation as the *only* experience in the sex industry.[57] These factors mean that there continues to be a social ambivalence about the selling and buying of commercial sex across Western countries.

TRANSGRESSION AND MAINSTREAMING

The mainstreaming of the sex industry produces contradictory impulses. On the one hand, it helps the industry to grow and maximize profits by drawing new demographics into their customer and supply base and tapping high-end

---

53 M.S. Bradley, 'Girlfriends, Wives, and Strippers: Managing Stigma in Exotic Dancer Romantic Relationships' (2007) 28 *Deviant Behavior* 379–406.

54 Hausbeck and Brents, op. cit., n. 13; B.G. Brents and K. Hausbeck, 'Violence and Legalized Brothel Prostitution in Nevada: Examining Safety, Risk and Prostitution Policy' (2005) 20 *J. of Interpersonal Violence* 270–95.

55 G. Gall, 'Sex Worker Unionisation: An Exploratory Study of Emerging Collective Organisation' (2007) 38 *Industrial Relations J.* 70–88; T. Sanders and S. Lopez-Embury, 'Sex Worker Organisation and Unionisation' in *Prostitution: Sex Work, Policy and Politics*, eds. T. Sanders, M. O'Neill. and J. Pitcher (2009); J. West, 'Prostitution: Collectives and the Politics of Regulation' (2000) 7 *Gender, Work & Organization* 106–18.

56 S. Jeffreys, *The Industrial Vagina: The Political Economy of the Global Sex Trade* (2008).

57 R. Weitzer, 'The Social Construction of Sex Trafficking: Ideology and Institutionalization of a Moral Crusade' (2007) 35 *Politics and Society* 447–75.

57

markets. It shatters preconceptions and age-old stereotypes about the types of people who sell and buy sex, through processes of upscaling, diversification, and gentrification. Sex work, for some, has become both a lifestyle choice and a potential work option. On the other hand, the adult sex industry has long relied on its transgressive nature to lure clients and to provide outlets for desire and sexual experiences that are pleasurable and exciting because they are beyond the bounds of mainstream culture. The element of titillation, surprise, and the unknown hold the mystique that cannot be eroded, otherwise the sex industry is no different from other leisure industries. The obvious irony of commercial sexual enterprises today is that their growth and successes with mainstreaming risks killing the thrill of participating in sexual communities that are absorbing and alluring precisely because they are taboo. There is therefore a fine line between the benefits of mainstreaming and the need to keep sexual enterprises just that little bit 'deviant' in order to keep the activities below the parapet of everyday consumption.

While the mainstreaming of the sex industry represents the liberalization of sexual culture, remaining social ambivalence produces contradictory regulations. In other words, the law both helps to expand and limits mainstreaming. Legal restrictions that seek to block mainstreaming often have an ironic function. They help ensure that sex businesses do not become so prolific that customers are saturated and lose interest in the experience that can be purchased. For instance, even in jurisdictions where brothels, sex shops, and lap-dancing clubs have a licence quota system, this operates to limit the number of sex businesses in any given locality. This, in turn, has the effect of keeping these businesses niche, specialized, busy, and profitable. Equally, anti-sex industry interests have the effect of raising the profile of lap-dancing activities and individual venues. Paradoxically, this eases the tension in commercial sex between mainstreaming and remaining taboo and tempting, allowing the best of both worlds for many segments of the commercial sex industry.

IMPLICATIONS FOR SEXUALITY AND SOCIAL ORDER

The sale of sex has always been a part of the commercial landscape in all epochs of civilization. In late capitalism, changing economic and social patterns have created the conditions that have allowed the sex industry to expand into mainstream economic markets. Neo-liberal policies designed to stimulate business and remove regulations have opened opportunities both for entrepreneurs and workers to capitalize on the growing markets for sex. Mainstreaming processes, led by economics, have to be understood in the context of neo-liberal policies, where the invitation to consume and commodify all aspects of social life are a powerful draw. Sexuality and intimacy have an important place in the market. As an array of sexual businesses are opening legally, they are increasingly integrated into mainstream business

58

associations, patterns of conducting business, joining or creating business associations, and marketing through mainstream channels and regulatory processes. The economic mainstreaming of sex businesses is not treated (very) differently in regulatory terms, or if they are, the requirements and restrictions are minimal and sometimes superficial. This has one significant disadvantage for the women who work in the venues: the sexualized nature of their working environment and their working conditions are not covered by health and safety laws, or checked by inspectors, and therefore there is little recourse to enforce better practices, standardized conditions or report exploitative employers and practices. Issues such as sexual harassment and poor employment rights are divorced from formal systems of regulation, rights, and protection. This has an effect on the ways in which women are open to exploitation in the workplace of sex businesses. Labour-market gender inequalities become everyday experiences for groups of women in this part of the service industry even as they, arguably, require more protection and attention to working conditions because of the very work they do. While these economic and labour market processes are becoming embedded, at the same time as there is an increasing acceptance of sexual commerce, there is also a backlash that drives deeper wedges between those for and against the industry, keeping alive the tired debates over 'exploitation' or 'work'.

What our comparative work is beginning to show is that increasing respectability accompanying economic mainstreaming has provided more legitimate work opportunities for women, who are the majority of the labour force, as sex workers. Women from the middle classes (and students) or at least not typically socially deprived status groups are entering the sex industries as workers. Men as consumers are accessing highly visible, normalized 'entertainment' in many different sex markets across the spectrum of indirect and direct sexual services. In between the seller and the consumer, all kinds of 'legitimate' businesses, including local and state officials, are benefiting and profiting from the mainstreaming of sexual consumption.

Yet, the economic mainstreaming of sexual commerce translates imperfectly into social or cultural mainstreaming. The sex industry has relied on and profited from its transgressive status. Reputations of 'red-light districts' are kept alive by their notoriety. Sporadic attention from the police maintains the label as an area of 'vice.' Inflated stories produced by the media attract voyeurs, vigilantes, the curious as well as those with intentions to purchase sex. The tainted windows of the lap-dancing bar, the shadowy suggestions posed by the female form, and the red carpets suggesting showbiz opulence are used to symbolize 'something different' and perhaps unobtainable in 'real' life. Therefore, the demand for sexual commerce is in many ways based on its marginalized and stigmatized status – an irony that is lost to those pushing prohibitionist policies in Europe and the United States.

This marginalized and stigmatized status creates casualties. For sex workers, at the level of their subjective identity, they are ostracized, live in

59

fear of the 'whore stigma', and cannot really go about sex work as a regular job without significant negative social impacts, which include criminalization, frequent experiences of violence, and little state protection. These consequences can have long-standing disastrous effects for those who gain criminal records, and are further barred from future job markets. The implications of stigma and criminalization essentially have a 'trapping' effect and produce more inequality for this group of women, as they are not treated as rightful workers in sex work and are ostracized from the mainstream labour market. For male purchasers, the new 'respectability' does not translate completely into acceptability of commercial sex as a healthy lifestyle option. Increasingly, 'demand' is highlighted as the root of immorality, criminality, and dangerous male sexuality and is becoming the new focus for punitive legislation, deterrence, and rehabilitation policies.[58] The control and regulation of certain types of sexuality and gender is highly implicated in these practices.

To conclude, the economic mainstreaming of sexual consumption has taken place in a context of the growth of the leisure industry in Western countries. This translates into accessible, visible, and potentially normalized sex markets. Despite this, the social and cultural acceptability of sex markets has not fully mirrored this mainstreaming. As a result, individuals who engage in the sex industry on either the supply or purchaser side continue to be regulated by social stigma and moralist attitudes that render the sex industries as culturally marginalized despite their increased social significance, economic profits, and little evidence of a dwindling in their popularity or place.

58 Sanders, op. cit., n. 46; J. Scoular, 'Criminalising Punters: Evaluating the Swedish Position on Prostitution' (2004) 26 *J. of Social Welfare and Family Law* 195–210; B. Brooks-Gordon, 'Clients and Commercial Sex: Reflections on Paying the Price: A Consultation Paper on Prostitution' (2005) *Crim. Law Rev.* 425–43; E. Bernstein, 'The Meaning of the Purchase: Desire, Demand and the Commerce of Sex' (2001) 2 *Ethnography* 389–420.

60

JOURNAL OF LAW AND SOCIETY
VOLUME 37, NUMBER 1, MARCH 2010
ISSN: 0263-323X, pp. 61–84

The Movement to Criminalize Sex Work in the United States

Ronald Weitzer*

Until recently, prostitution was not a prominent public issue in the United States. Law and public policy were relatively settled. The past decade, however, has witnessed a growing debate over the sex trade and the growth of an organized campaign committed to expanding criminalization. A powerful moral crusade has been successful in reshaping American government policy toward sex work – enhancing penalties for existing offences and creating new crimes. Crusade organizations have advocated a strict abolitionist orientation toward all forms of commercialized sex, which are increasingly conflated with sex trafficking. This paper examines the impact of this movement on legal norms and government policies. I argue that the moral crusade, and its government allies, are responding to the growth of the sex industry in recent years and to fears of its normalization in American society.

In November 2008, residents of San Francisco, California, voted on a ballot measure that would have de facto decriminalized prostitution in the city. The measure stipulated that the police would discontinue enforcing the law against prostitution. The measure failed, but was endorsed by a sizeable minority of voters – 42 per cent. Four years earlier, Berkeley, California voters had considered a similar proposal, with 36 per cent supporting it. As this paper will demonstrate, the San Francisco and Berkeley cases are entirely exceptional in contemporary America – where liberalization of prostitution policy is rarely discussed by political leaders let alone voted on by the public.[1] As a 1999 commission in Buffalo, New York, reasoned, 'since it is unlikely that city or state officials could ever be convinced to

* Department of Sociology, George Washington University, Washington DC 20052, United States of America
weitzer@gwu.edu

1 An exception is a bill in the Hawaii State Legislature in 2007, which would have decriminalized indoor prostitution and zoned street prostitution. The bill failed.

decriminalise or legalise prostitution in Buffalo, there is nothing to be gained by debating the merits of either'.[2]

Although some observers have documented a growing 'mainstreaming' or 'normalization' of the sex industry – especially regarding pornography and stripping, where there has been some spillover into mainstream media coupled with sheer abundance on the Internet[3] – prostitution remains beyond the pale in the United States. Indeed, prostitution is being increasingly demonized, marginalized, and criminalized as a result of the efforts of a robust moral crusade. The crusade initially targeted sex trafficking, but then expanded its targets to prostitution, pornography, stripping, and all other types of commercial sex.

The punitive trend may be viewed as a reaction to the increasing availability and mass marketing of sexual services and to what crusade and political leaders view as an alarming normalization of sex for sale. In other words, with the help of the Internet, the neo-liberal deregulation of commerce and flourishing of free markets has allowed the sex industry to expand as never before and on a global scale. Neo-liberalism also implies that individuals have the 'right' to engage in sexual commerce. I suggest that it is precisely this loosening of traditional sexual mores coupled with the unprecedented availability of a growing variety of sexual services that has created a huge backlash – in the form of a moral crusade that is attempting to stem the tide by pressing for laws that outlaw commercial sex work. This is part of a broader symbolic politics in which certain social forces have fought other signs of alarming 'permissiveness',[4] and have tried to impose a 'new respectability', one dimension of which Hunt describes as follows:

> 'New respectability' reflects the aspiring role of upwardly mobile women concerned to exhibit [independence from men which] produces a renewed sense of sex and sexuality as risk and danger … It finds expression in a preoccupation with the external danger of sex in general and male sexuality in particular … This in turn leads to a stress on women's stance as victim … The new respectability manifests itself most distinctively in preoccupation with sexual imagery and representation.[5]

I would extend the latter point to sexual commerce in general. In the United States, crusade efforts were latent in the 1990s but gained renewed vigour in

---

2 Prostitution Task Force, *Workable Solutions to the Problem of Street Prostitution in Buffalo, New York* (1999).
3 B. Brents and T. Sanders, 'Mainstreaming the Sex Industry: Economic Inclusion and Social Ambivalence', this volume, pp. 40–60; L. Comella, 'Remaking the Sex Industry: The Adult Expo as a Microcosm' in *Sex for Sale: Prostitution, Pornography, and the Sex Industry,* ed. R. Weitzer (2010, 2nd edn.); E. Jost, 'Making it Mainstream: Sexworkers as Characters' *Spread Magazine,* Winter 2008, 54–7.
4 D. Wagner, *The New Temperance: The American Obsession with Sin and Vice* (1997).
5 A. Hunt, 'The Purity Wars' (1999) 3 *Theoretical Criminology* 409, at 430.

62

the following decade because the advent of the Bush administration opened a uniquely favourable window of opportunity for crusade organizations to press their agenda. Developments during the Bush years are consistent with more general trends toward increased moral regulation in response to perceived social ills,[6] but it is also clear that the Bush administration radically altered the degree of state access and policy influence for social forces committed to amplified moral regulation.

This paper examines these developments, drawing on information from crusade groups, reports of government agencies, and relevant legislation. We shall see that activists have met with remarkable success in getting their views incorporated in government policy and law enforcement practices. In other words, the crusade is not confined to mere debate or sabre rattling, as it has attained a measure of success in criminalizing sexual services, manifested in new penalties, increasing arrests, and growing official demonization of commercial sex.

A MORAL CRUSADE PERSPECTIVE

A *moral crusade* is a type of social movement that sees its mission as a righteous enterprise to combat a particular condition or activity that is defined as an unqualified evil. Moral crusades have symbolic goals (attempting to redraw or bolster normative boundaries and moral standards) as well as instrumental ones (providing relief to victims, punishing evildoers).[7] Some are motivated by genuine humanitarian concerns and desires to help victims, while others are mainly interested in imposing specific mores on others, especially when conventional rules appear to be unravelling, thus creating anxiety about the erosion of normative boundaries or threats to a cherished way of life. Moral crusade discourse has three central characteristics:

- inflation of the magnitude of a problem (for example, the number of victims, harm to society), assertions that far exceed the available evidence;
- horror stories, in which the most shocking cases are described in gruesome detail and presented as typical and prevalent;
- categorical conviction: crusade members are adamant that a particular evil exists precisely as they depict it and refuse to acknowledge any grey areas.

By dramatizing the plight of traumatized victims, demonizing perpetrators, and exaggerating the extent of the problem, activists seek to alarm the public and justify draconian solutions.

6 Hunt, id.; Wagner, op. cit., n. 4.
7 S. Cohen, *Folk Devils and Moral Panics* (1972); E. Goode and N. Ben-Yehuda, *Moral Panics* (1994).

The crusade against trafficking and sex work in the United States (and some other nations) has been dominated by a coalition of the religious right and abolitionist feminists. Right-wing members include Focus on the Family, National Association of Evangelicals, Catholic Bishops Conference, Concerned Women for America, International Justice Mission, Shared Hope International, and numerous others. Feminist groups include the Coalition Against Trafficking in Women (CATW), Equality Now, the Protection Project, and Standing Against Global Exploitation (SAGE) – and the American movement is aligned with groups abroad such as the European Women's Lobby. The term 'abolitionist feminist' refers to those who argue that the sex industry should be eliminated because of its objectification and oppressive treatment of women, considered to be inherent in sex for sale. Mainstream feminist organizations, such as the National Organization for Women, have been far less active in this debate and have focused on other issues concerning women.

The religious and feminist coalition members may hold opposing views on other social issues, such as abortion, but they largely agree on sex work. The single-issue focus of most of these feminist groups – targeting the sex industry exclusively – trumps all other issues and explains their willingness to work with right-wing groups, in order to enhance the legitimacy of their campaign as a bipartisan left-right enterprise.

During the Bush administration (2001–2008), this crusade gained tremendous influence over policy making, successfully transforming the movement against sex trafficking into an official government project targeting all types of commercial sex. What is most remarkable about the resulting legal sanctions is how far they diverge from evidence-based policy. As I have shown elsewhere, almost all of the crusade's claims about trafficking in particular and sex work in general are either unsubstantiated or demonstrably false.[8] A crucial reason why this crusade achieved such remarkable success was the lack of a counter-discourse and lobbying by influential groups. On the few occasions when the movement's claims were challenged in public forums, those who voiced such opposition were either ignored or denounced as apologists for pimps and traffickers. This stands in contrast to some other vice contests, such as debates over drugs and abortion, where the claims of moral entrepreneurs have been more vigorously countered by advocates.

---

8 R. Weitzer, 'The Social Construction of Sex Trafficking: Ideology and Institutionalization of a Moral Crusade' (2007) 35 *Politics and Society* 447; R. Weitzer, 'Flawed Theory and Method in Studies of Prostitution' (2005) 11 *Violence Against Women* 934; R. Weitzer, 'The Mythology of Prostitution: Advocacy Research and Public Policy' (2010) 7 *Sexuality Research and Social Policy*.

The facts regarding sex trafficking are murky, but certain aspects are clear. We do know that relocation from one place to another for the purpose of selling sex has long existed. We also know that there are victims of coercive or deceptive enticement into the sex trade: people are transported to locations where they are pressured into prostitution. Reports from around the world indicate that coercive sex trafficking is by no means fictional. We also know that sex trafficking can be quite lucrative for the third parties involved. In fact, there are 'few other criminal activities in which the profit-to-cost ratio is so high'.[9] The most exploitative actors make huge profits off the labour of workers who accumulate little if any money of their own. In addition, some third parties act violently toward sex workers or demand sex from them, sometimes over a long period of time.

We do not know *how many* persons are trafficked across borders every year. The grand claims made by abolitionist groups that the magnitude of the problem is *huge* and *growing* are entirely unsubstantiated, but quite strategic. What do I by strategic? The size of a social problem matters in attracting media coverage, donor funding, and attention from policy makers. Moral crusades thus have a vested interest in inflating the magnitude of a problem, and their figures are typically unverifiable.[10] The anti-trafficking crusade claims that there are hundreds of thousands or millions of victims worldwide, and that trafficking has reached an 'epidemic' level. Such claims have been echoed by government officials in the United States and other nations. When specific figures are presented, they have ranged from 600,000 to 4 million.

Like the global numbers, domestic American figures have changed drastically in a short period of time. In 2000, the government claimed that 45,000–50,000 persons were trafficked into the United States annually – a figure based largely on one government analyst's review of newspaper clippings.[11] This dubious figure was cited in the landmark Victims of Trafficking and Violence Protection Act, 2000 (TVPA) as justification for the new law, which states unequivocally that 'Congress finds that … approximately 50,000 women and children are trafficked into the United States each year'.[12] The State Department's *Trafficking in Persons* report repeated the figure in 2002, but just one year later, the figure fell to 18,000–

---

9 P. Williams 'Trafficking in Women and Children: A Market Perspective' in *Illegal Immigration and Commercial Sex*, ed. P. Williams (1999) 153.

10 Goode and Ben-Yehuda, op. cit., n. 7, pp. 36–44.

11 J. Markon, 'Human Trafficking Evokes Outrage, Little Evidence' *Washington Post*, 23 September 2007. Strikingly similar to developments in the United States on the trafficking front, as described in this section of the article, is the British situation, which has also been coloured by moral panic and gross distortion of figures on the magnitude of trafficking. See N. Davies, 'Prostitution and Trafficking: The Anatomy of a Moral Panic' *Guardian*, 20 October 2009.

12 TVPA 2000, s. 102(b1).

20,000 (a 64–60 per cent decrease from 50,000) and the 2004 and 2005 *Trafficking in Persons* reports reduced the number further, to 14,500–17,500. Members of Congress and the Bush administration accepted these numbers uncritically and passed legislation based on the notion that huge numbers of people were victims of this newly-discovered 'modern form of slavery' – the favoured construct of this moral crusade.

Some agencies have questioned the figures. A General Accountability Office (GAO) evaluation disputed the prevailing estimates for their 'methodological weaknesses, gaps in data, and numerical discrepancies'. The GAO concluded that (i) 'country data are generally not available, reliable, or comparable', (ii) the 'U.S. government has not yet established an effective mechanism for estimating the number of victims', and (iii) the same is true for international non-governmental organizations (NGOs) working in the trafficking area.[13] The Justice Department noted the disparity between the official figures and the number of victims identified, which was attributed to either faulty figures or insufficient enforcement efforts:

> Most importantly, the government must address the incongruity between the estimated number of victims trafficked into the United States – between 14,500 and 17,500 [annually] – and the number of victims found – only 611 in the last four years [2001–2004] ... The stark difference between the two figures means that U.S. Government efforts are still not enough. In addition, the estimate should be evaluated to assure that it is accurate and reflects the number of actual victims.[14]

The 2008 *Trafficking in Persons* report by the State Department, for the first time, offered no specific number but instead used the fuzzy term 'thousands'.[15] The report also states that 1,379 trafficking victims were identified between 2001 and mid-2008, but this figure remains but a fraction of the number of persons allegedly trafficked into the United States during this time period (using the most conservative official figure: $14,500 \times 7.5$ years = 108,750).[16]

Crusade organizations and United States government agencies also claim that the number of trafficked victims is steadily increasing. A leader of the Polaris Project, for instance, claims that trafficking is 'fastest growing crime worldwide'.[17] Curiously, this claim contradicts the government's own numbers on both domestic and international trafficking, which steadily declined during the eight years of the Bush administration.

---

13 General Accountability Office, *Human Trafficking: Better Data, Strategy, and Reporting Needed to Enhance U.S. Anti-trafficking Efforts Abroad* (2006), especially 2, 10, 3, 14.
14 US Department of Justice, *Efforts to Combat Trafficking in Persons in Fiscal Year 2004* (2005) 4.
15 US Department of State, *Trafficking in Persons Report, 2008* (2009).
16 id.
17 Bradley Myles, Deputy Director of the Polaris Project, quoted in J. Iwasaki, 'Human Trafficking Increasing Worldwide' *Seattle Post-Intelligencer*, 4 August 2008.

66

Internationally, it is clear that sex trafficking has increased in *some* parts of the world, especially from the former Soviet Union and Eastern Europe. The break-up of the Soviet empire and declining living standards for many of its inhabitants has made such migration both much easier and more compelling than in the past. But an increase in trafficking after the demise of the Soviet Union does not mean that trafficking is growing now. Instead, it may have levelled off. A report by the International Organization for Migration points to this very possibility: the number of trafficked persons in south-eastern Europe that were identified and assisted remained virtually the same (declining slightly) between 2003 and 2004.[18]

Researchers have criticized the statistics proffered by activists, NGOs, and governments for their 'lack of methodological transparency' and source documentation,[19] for being extrapolated from a few cases of identified victims (who are unrepresentative of the victim population),[20] and for the lack of a standard definition of 'victims' as a basis for estimating the magnitude of the problem.[21] But these critiques have largely gone unheeded by Congress and the Bush administration. As a White House press officer stated, the issue is 'not about the numbers. It's really about the crime and how horrific it is. . . . How can we tolerate even a minimal number within our borders?'[22] In other words, when the numbers are challenged, officials respond that the numbers are not important. Yet, the government continues to cite the high numbers as justification for spending huge amounts of money funding abolitionist organizations that are conducting 'research' on the problem and on enforcement efforts to identify and rescue victims in the United States and abroad, efforts that have thus far paid few dividends relative to the expenditures.[23]

In a nutshell, *figures on the magnitude of the problem are totally unreliable*. Even general estimates are dubious, given the clandestine nature of the sex trade. There are several red flags: the official numbers have fluctuated radically over a short time period; relatively few victims of

---

18 International Organization for Migration, *Second Annual Report on Victims of Trafficking in South-Eastern Europe* (2005) 12. The numbers were 1,329 in 2003 and 1,227 in 2004.

19 L. Kelly, 'You Can Find Anything You Want: A Critical Reflection on Research on Trafficking in Persons within and into Europe' (2005) 43 *International Migration* 235, at 237.

20 G. Tyldum and A. Brunovskis, 'Describing the Unobserved: Methodological Challenges in Empirical Studies on Human Trafficking' (2005) 43 *International Migration* 17.

21 E. Gozdziak and E. Collett, 'Research on Human Trafficking in North America: A Review of the Literature' (2005) 43 *International Migration* 99.

22 Tony Fratto, quoted in Markon, op. cit., n. 11.

23 A. Farrell, J. McDevitt, and S. Fahy, *Understanding and Improving Law Enforcement Responses to Human Trafficking* (2008); M. Ditmore, *Kicking Down the Door: The Use of Raids to Fight Trafficking in Persons*, Sex Workers Project, New York (2009).

coercive trafficking have been located; and there is substantial slippage in how 'trafficking' is defined and how 'victims' are identified and certified as such.

1. *Complexities and grey areas*

Moral crusades paint problems in black and white, but the trafficking issue is full of nuances – complexities that are rejected by crusade leaders and by allied government agencies. One gray area is the issue of consent and intentionality. If the total number of trafficked persons is opaque, it is just as unclear how many individuals have been trafficked by force or deceit versus the number who have migrated with full information and consent regarding the type of work and nature of the working conditions. Crusade leaders typically lump these together or simply deny that anyone can consent to working in the sex industry.

Within the population of migrant women who have entered prostitution, there is a great deal of variation in their experiences of the migration process and complex relationships with intermediaries, ranging along a continuum. Migrants also hold diverse goals and desires, which need to be considered in relation to conditions in their home countries. As Julia O'Connell Davidson points out, even when migrants experience unpleasant or exploitative work-ing conditions in the destination locale, some consider this 'preferable to remaining at home, where threats to their security in the form of violence, exploitation, or straightforward starvation may be far greater'.[24] Laura Agustín concurs, describing both push and pull factors behind some migrants' actions:

> many people are fleeing from small-town prejudices, dead-end jobs, dangerous streets, and suffocating families. And some poorer people *like* the idea of being found beautiful or exotic abroad, exciting desire in others.[25]

This is not to romanticize sex work, but it serves as a useful counterpoint to the *victim* trope presented by abolitionist forces, which is challenged by a growing body of research:

- An investigation of immigrant Korean massage parlour workers in New York, for instance, concluded: 'invariably, the Korean women said they knew the kind of work they were expected to perform … The women had relative freedom of movement and had joined the sex business of their own free will … [They] had a lifestyle as prostitutes that did not fit the stereotype of the trafficked woman'.[26]

---

24 J.O. Davidson, 'Trafficking, Modern Slavery, and the Human Security Agenda' (2008) 6 *Human Security J.* 8, at 9.
25 L.M. Agustín, *Sex at the Margins* (2007) 45–6.
26 A. DeStefano, *The War on Human Trafficking: U.S. Policy Assessed* (2007) 88.

- A study of Vietnamese migrants working in Cambodia found that almost all of them knew that they would work in a brothel there and their motivations consisted of 'economic incentives, desire for an independent lifestyle, and dissatisfaction with rural life and agricultural labor'. After raids on the brothels by 'rescue' organizations, the women 'usually returned to their brothel as quickly as possible'.[27]
- In Australia, 'the majority of women know they will be working in the sex industry and often decide to come to Australia in the belief that they will be able to make a substantial amount of money ... Few of the women would ever consider themselves sex slaves'.[28]
- In Europe, research indicates that the women are 'often aware of the sexual nature of the work ... Many migrants do know what is ahead of them, do earn a large amount of money in a short time selling sex, and do have control over their working condition'.[29] One investigation of trafficking from Eastern Europe to Holland found that few of the 72 women interviewed were coercively trafficked and that a large number had previously worked as prostitutes:

> For most of the women, economic motives were decisive. The opportunity to earn a considerable amount of money in a short period of time was found to be irresistible ... In most cases recruiting was done by friends, acquaintances, or even family members.[30]

These are not isolated findings; other research shows that many migrants sold sex prior to relocating or were well aware that they would be working in the sex industry in their new home. One analyst concludes that, 'the majority of "trafficking victims" are aware that the jobs offered them are in the sex industry'.[31] Whether or not this indeed characterizes the majority, it is clear that traffickers do not necessarily fit the 'folk devil' stereotype popularized by the anti-trafficking movement. Some facilitators are relatives, friends, or associates who make travel arrangements, obtain necessary documents, provide funds, and otherwise assist with migration. Many of the Vietnamese women working in Cambodian brothels, for

---

27 J. Busza, S. Castle, and A. Diarra, 'Trafficking and Health' (2004) 328 *Brit. Medical J.* 1369; see, also, the identical findings in T. Steinfatt, *Measuring the Number of Trafficked Women and Children in Cambodia* (2003) 23–4.

28 L. Meaker, 'A Social Response to Transnational Prostitution in Queensland, Australia' in *Transnational Prostitution*, eds. S. Thorbek and B. Pattanaik (2002) 61, 63.

29 L.M. Agustín, 'Migrants in the Mistress's House: Other Voices in the Trafficking Debate' (2005) 12 *Social Politics* 96, at 98, 101.

30 J. Vocks and J. Nijboer, 'The Promised Land: A Study of Trafficking in Women from Central and Eastern Europe to the Netherlands' (2000) 8 *European J. of Criminal Policy and Research* 379, at 383, 384.

31 J. Doezema, 'Loose Women or Lost Women? The Re-emergence of the Myth of White Slavery in Contemporary Discourses of Trafficking in Women' (2000) 18 *Gender Issues* 23, at 24.

69

instance, had been recruited and transported by their relatives, including mothers and aunts.[32] These intermediaries have a qualitatively different relationship with migrants than do predators who use force or deception to lure victims into the trade.

In short, the evidence indicates that migration for sex work is a complex and diverse phenomenon. There are *several migration trajectories and diverse worker experiences*, ranging from highly coercive and exploitative to informed and conscious intentionality on the part of the migrant. Such complexities, nuances, and variations have been ignored or denied by abolitionist forces and by governments influenced by them.

CONFLATING TRAFFICKING WITH ALL OTHER SEX WORK

When a moral crusade achieves success with respect to its foundational objective, it may set its sights on other problems that it associates with its original *raison d'etre* – the phenomenon of 'domain expansion'. What began in the mid-1990s as a campaign against sex trafficking has steadily expanded over time. In addition, over time the focus of the crusade has shifted to 'the demand', that is, the customers, who are increasingly demonized and targeted for harsh penalties, as shown below.

1. *Targeting prostitution*

Religious conservatives have long denounced prostitution as perverse and sinful, a source of moral decay in society, and a threat to marriage because it breaks the link between sex, love, and reproduction. The anti-trafficking campaign has given these conservatives new opportunities to express these fears, which they do in their publications and websites and in the media. A government crackdown on prostitution ratifies the religious right's views on sex and the family. Some feminist crusade leaders also champion rather traditional views of 'proper' sexuality. The founder of CATW, Kathy Barry, does so in a remarkable passage in her seminal abolitionist manifesto, *Female Sexual Slavery*:

> We are really going back to the values women have always attached to sexuality, values that have been robbed from us, distorted and destroyed as we have been colonized through both sexual violence and so-called sexual liberation. They are the values and needs that connect sex with warmth, affection, love, caring ... Sexual values and the positive, constructive experience of sex *must be based in intimacy* ... It follows then that *sex cannot be purchased, legally acquired, or seized by force.*[33]

---

32 Steinfatt, op. cit., n. 27, p. 24.
33 K. Barry, *Female Sexual Slavery* (1979) 227, 230.

70

And another CATW leader, Janice Raymond, seems to agree, when she states that prostitutes' customers 'lack responsibility, intimacy, emotion' in their sexual behaviour.[34]

Yet, the core abolitionist feminist tenet is that prostitution is an institution of male domination and exploitation of women. CATW's website is unequivocal: 'all prostitution exploits women, regardless of women's consent. Prostitution affects all women, justifies the sale of any woman, and reduces all women to sex'.[35] It can never qualify as a conventional commercial exchange like other service work nor can it ever be organized in a way that advances workers' interests. As Laura Lederer insists:

> This is not a legitimate form of labour ... It can never be a legitimate way to make a living because it's inherently harmful for men, women, and children ... This whole commercial sex industry is a human-rights abuse.[36]

Abolitionist groups have fought for policies that target sex trafficking more than labour trafficking. A journalist sympathetic to the crusade nevertheless took issue with this exclusive focus on sex trafficking:

> To the dominant coalition ... the only slaves – anyway, the only slaves worthy of American attention – were prostitutes. And all prostitutes were slaves. Theirs was a circular logic that dumbfounded those who regularly aided real slaves, real prostitutes, and really enslaved prostitutes.[37]

Abolitionists were also intent on linking sex trafficking to prostitution.[38] The central premise is that *sex trafficking is inseparable from prostitution, and prostitution is evil by definition.* Not only are the two conflated, but activists also claim that 'most' sex workers have been trafficked.[39] Such linkage is a transparent attempt to lay the groundwork for the crusade's ultimate goal, that is, to eliminate the entire sex trade. Activist Donna Hughes, for example, calls for 're-linking trafficking and prostitution, and combating the commercial sex trade as a whole'.[40]

---

34 J. Raymond, 'Prostitution on Demand: Legalizing the Buyers as Sexual Consumers' (2004) 10 *Violence Against Women* 1182.

35 Available at: <www.catwinternational.org>.

36 Lederer, quoted in B. Jones, 'Trafficking Cops' *World Magazine*, 15 June 2002. Lederer was a leader in the anti-porn movement in the 1980s. Between 2001 and 2009, she was a senior advisor in the US State Department's Trafficking in Persons office. In 2009, she became Vice-president of Global Centurion, an organization fighting sex trafficking.

37 E.B. Skinner, *A Crime So Monstrous: Face-to-Face with Modern-Day Slavery* (2008) 289.

38 See, for example, M. O'Connor and G. Healy, *The Links between Prostitution and Sex Trafficking: A Briefing Handbook*, CATW and European Women's Lobby (2006); see, also, the article by CATW co-director Dorchen Leidholdt, 'Prostitution and Trafficking in Women: An Intimate Relationship' (2004) 2 *J. of Trauma Practice* 167.

39 D. Hughes, 'Accommodation or Abolition?' *National Rev. Online*, 1 May 2003, 1.

40 D. Hughes, 'Wolves in Sheep's Clothing: No Way to End Sex Trafficking' *National Review Online*, 9 October 2002, 2.

The American government has fully adopted the crusade's conflation of trafficking and prostitution. The State Department's website, 'The Link between Prostitution and Sex Trafficking', draws this 'link' boldly. The site proclaims that prostitution 'is inherently harmful'; that it 'leaves women and children physically, mentally, emotionally, and spiritually devastated'; that legal prostitution 'creates a safe haven for criminals who traffic people into prostitution'; and that prostitution is 'the oldest form of oppression'.[41] The site documents these notions with footnotes exclusively to writings by leading abolitionists, including Janice Raymond, Melissa Farley, Donna Hughes, and Gunilla Ekberg.[42] Some government officials privately questioned the crusade's depiction of prostitution,[43] but this internal questioning had no effect on the Bush government's official position that prostitution was an unqualified evil.

What is missing from this discourse is recognition that prostitution and trafficking differ substantively: prostitution is a type of labour, whereas migration and trafficking involve the process of relocation to access a market. Both empirically and conceptually, it is inappropriate to fuse the two.

The slippage between trafficking and prostitution is facilitated by demonization of the client. The identification of 'folk devils' is a staple of moral crusades, and this is certainly the case here.[44] The initial focus on traffickers has steadily expanded to include customers ('the demand'), who are seen as the root cause of trafficking. Some crusade members define both traffickers and customers as 'predators'. Melissa Farley declares that clients 'are not just naughty boys who need their wrists slapped. They could be more accurately described as predators'.[45] A recent report on clients of prostitutes in Scotland proclaims that 'prostitution is best understood as a transaction in which there are two roles: exploiter/predator and victim/prey'; the report advocates putting customers 'in the same category as rapists, paedophiles, and other social undesirables'.[46] Donna Hughes offers a blanket

---

41 US Department of State, 'The Link between Prostitution and Sex Trafficking' (2004) 1, available at <www.state.gov/documents/organization/38901.pdf>.

42 Gunilla Ekberg is now the co-executive director of CATW-International and is based in Brussels. Previously she was active in the successful campaign to criminalize clients in Sweden.

43 Skinner (op. cit., n. 37, p. 283) writes:
   But privately, Justice Department officials who actually dealt with victims were galled that the coalition expected them to find moral equivalency in the victimization of a $90,000-dollar-a-year call girl in Georgetown, who kept her own income and worked for herself, and a fourteen-year-old girl, raped fifteen times a day in a fetid trailer in a migrant labor camp.

44 Cohen, op. cit., n. 7.

45 Melissa Farley, quoted in A. Brown, 'Sex Industry in Scotland: Inside the Deluded Minds of the Punters' *Daily Record*, 28 April 2008.

46 J. Macleod, M. Farley, L. Anderson, and J. Golding, *Challenging Men's Demand for Prostitution in Scotland*, Women's Support Project (2008) 30, 27.

72

indictment: 'Men who purchase sex acts do not respect women, nor do they want to respect women'.[47] The very title of Hughes' report, *The Demand for Victims of Sex Trafficking*, seems to imply that customers are intentionally seeking trafficked 'victims'.

It is true that some clients are indeed predators, but the crusade's sweeping claims are caricatures. Research on customers cautions against gross generalizations: they vary considerably in background characteristics, behaviour, and motives for buying sexual services.[48] Some customers act violently and some seek out under-age prostitutes, but abusive clients appear to be in the minority.[49] In one study, only 8 per cent of arrested customers had a previous conviction for a violent or sexual offence.[50]

The focus on prostitution has had important policy outcomes in the United States. First, most of the enforcement efforts against trafficking have centered on prostitution cases, with much less attention to labour trafficking.[51] Since 2006, the Justice Department has created 42 task forces (multi-agency law enforcement units) responsible for identifying trafficking victims, but some enforcement agents equate sex trafficking with prostitution, as a recent assessment revealed: 'some local task forces have focused exclusively on prostitution, making no distinction between prostitution and sex trafficking'.[52]

Second, there has been a crackdown on 'demand'. The 2005 Trafficking Victims Prevention Reauthorization Act (TVPRA) authorized $25 million per year to be distributed to police departments for expanded arrests of those who 'purchase commercial sex acts' and other efforts against clients, such as funding the creation of john schools,[53] which are day-long rehabilitation programmes for clients, designed to educate arrested customers about the harms of prostitution and deter future offending. As of 2008, forty American cities had created such schools, which have also been introduced in Britain and Canada.[54] In just one city, San Francisco, more than 5,700 arrested clients passed through its john school between 1995 and early 2008.[55]

The 2008 TVPRA provides resources for additional enforcement. It contains funding for police data-gathering on the sex trade, studies of 'the

---

47 D. Hughes, *The Demand for Victims of Sex Trafficking* (2005) 7.
48 M. Monto, 'Prostitutes' Customers: Motives and Misconceptions' in Weitzer, op. cit., n. 3; T. Sanders, *Paying for Pleasure: Men who Buy Sex* (2008); J. Lowman and C. Atchison, 'Men Who Buy Sex' (2006) 43 *Canadian Rev. of Sociology and Anthropology* 281.
49 Monto, id.; Lowman and Atchison, id.
50 B. Brooks-Gordon, *The Price of Sex: Prostitution, Policy, and Society* (2006).
51 A. Farrell et al., *Understanding and Improving Law Enforcement Responses* (2008),
52 Women's Commission for Refugee Women and Children, *The U.S. Response to Human Trafficking: An Unbalanced Approach* (2007) 14.
53 TVPRA 2005, s. 204(1b, 1c)
54 M. Ohtake, 'A School for Johns' *Newsweek*, 24 July 2008.
55 id.

73

use of Internet-based businesses and services by criminal actors in the sex industry', and for dissemination of best practices for apprehending and prosecuting those who use the Internet for purposes of prostitution or trafficking.[56] This clearly sets the stage for increased arrests of persons who advertise sexual services online and who avail themselves of such services. Many local police departments around the country have increasingly monitored Internet postings in recent years, using them to arrest providers.

A third important outcome centres on eligibility restrictions for government funding. Activists successfully pressed the United States government to adopt a policy denying funding to organizations that were not sufficiently committed to eradicating prostitution. Today, to be eligible for United States funding, any foreign NGO working on the trafficking front must declare its opposition to prostitution and especially legal prostitution. This requirement was added to the 2003 TVPRA, and it applies to *any* funds or activities of the organization, including funds that come from sources other than the government. The State Department's policy is clear: 'no U.S. grant funds should be awarded to foreign non-governmental organizations that support legal state-regulated prostitution'.[57] This, despite the fact that the Justice Department had lobbied against the measure, questioning its constitutionality.[58] Furthermore, the ban applies to anyone, including Americans, who applies for funding to conduct research on trafficking.[59]

Similarly, the 2003 Global AIDS Act requires that any international organization working to curb AIDS must 'have a policy explicitly opposing prostitution and sex trafficking' if it wishes to receive such funding. This applies to American groups in so far as they work with or subcontract work to international organizations. Organizations that take no position on prosti-

---

56 TVPRA 2008, s. 237(c).
57 US Department of State, op. cit., n. 41, p. 2.
58 A letter from the Justice Department's Office of Legislative Affairs to Rep. James Sensenbrenner, chair of the Judiciary Committee in the House of Representatives (dated 24 September 2003), accepted that the government had the right to prohibit organizations from using government funds to promote prostitution, but opposed the prohibition on providing grants to organizations if they used *separate, non-government money* in support of prostitution:

> There is substantial doubt as to whether the Federal Government may restrict a domestic grant recipient participating in a Federal anti-trafficking program from using its own private, segregated funds to promote, support, or advocate the legalization or practice of prostitution. ... We believe that there is serious doubt as to whether that provision [in TVPRA 2003] would survive judicial scrutiny if challenged in court. In particular, we note that the prohibition on grant recipients using their own private, segregated funds to promote the legalization of prostitution, as opposed to the practice of prostitution, would be particularly vulnerable to legal challenge.

Because of these 'serious First Amendment concerns,' the Justice Department recommended that this provision be deleted from the Bill.
59 National Institute of Justice, *Solicitation: Trafficking in Human Beings Research and Comprehensive Literature Review* (2007) 4.

74

tution as well as those that favour decriminalization or legalization are thus ineligible for government funding.[60] Failure to do so results in summary denial of funding.

These funding restrictions cannot help but skew research and intervention in one direction, eliminating consideration of competing points of view and further privileging and institutionalizing the abolitionist perspective. In May 2005, 171 American and foreign organizations signed a letter to President Bush opposing the anti-prostitution pledge because they believe the policy interferes with promising interventions that require building trust with sex workers. Because of the restriction, several NGOs have declined to apply for government funding.

Legal prostitution systems are a prime target. CATW's mission is broad: to 'challenge acceptance of the sex industry, normalisation of prostitution as work, and to de-romanticise legalisation initiatives in various countries'.[61] Legalization is claimed to pose a symbolic threat to society, by giving the state's blessing to an institution that oppresses women, and legalization also allegedly increases trafficking, by removing the constraints on a formerly illegal and circumscribed enterprise. CATW's co-director, Janice Raymond, declares that 'legalized or decriminalized prostitution industries are one of the root causes of sex trafficking'.[62] And Linda Smith, director of Shared Hope International, testified in Congress that the government should 'consider countries with legalised or tolerated prostitution as having laws that are insufficient efforts to eliminate trafficking'.[63] Concerned Women for America claims that 'legalising prostitution does not remedy the problem of sex trafficking but rather increases it'.[64]

The state of Nevada is the only site in the United States where prostitution is legal and regulated by the government, and therefore has become a target of abolitionists. These brothels stand out as dens of iniquity ripe for criminalization. The groundwork for criminalization was laid in a recent State Department-funded investigation of Nevada's brothels by anti-prostitution activist Melissa Farley. Her report goes out of its way to demonize the state's legal brothels, and has been criticized by scholars who have studied the brothels for over a decade.[65] I describe Farley's report in

---

60 See N. Masenior and C. Beyrer, 'The U.S. Anti-Prostitution Pledge: First Amendment Challenges and Public Health Priorities' (2007) 4 *PLoS Medicine* 1158.
61 Available at: <www.catwinternational.org>.
62 J. Raymond, 'Ten Reasons for Not Legalizing Prostitution' (2003) 2 *J. of Trauma Practice* 315, at 317.
63 L. Smith, Testimony before Committee on International Relations, House of Representatives, Hearing on the State Department's *Trafficking in Persons Report*, 19 June 2002, 66.
64 Available at: <www.cwfa.org>.
65 K. Hausbeck, B. Brents, and C. Jackson, 'Vegas and the Sex Industry: Don't Make Assumptions about the Choices Women Make' *Las Vegas Rev. J.*, 16 September 2007.

some detail here because it was publicized and praised in the media, including the influential *New York Times*, and was given the stamp of credibility when it was published as an official State Department report. The report is saturated with wild claims based on anecdotes and flawed information, typical of Farley's writings.[66] First, Farley provides no evidence of trafficking into the brothels and relies instead on a few individuals' perceptions to make this connection:

> Women are trafficked from other countries into Nevada's legal brothels ... In Nevada, twenty seven per cent of our forty five interviewees [or just twelve individuals] in the Nevada legal brothels *believed* that there were *undocumented immigrants* in the legal brothels. Another eleven per cent said they were uncertain, thus as many as thirty eight per cent of the women we interviewed *may have known* of internationally trafficked women in Nevada legal brothel prostitution.[67]

Another way of reporting this 'finding' is that as many as 62 per cent did *not* believe that women were trafficked into the brothels, while the remainder either did not have an opinion or believed that there were undocumented immigrants, who are not necessarily 'trafficked'. Interestingly, Farley converts the *beliefs* of a *minority* into *evidence* of trafficking. Elsewhere, Farley writes that a few women in one brothel told her that women in another brothel had been trafficked from China. Instead of treating this as hearsay, Farley presents this is factual and calls the women who told her this story 'witnesses', lending their statements an aura of credibility.[68]

Second, Farley twists findings to fit her abolitionist orientation. In interviews with some workers at eight of Nevada's thirty legal brothels, she states, 'I knew that they would minimise how bad it was'.[69] If the respondent did not describe working in a brothel as 'bad', they were in denial, and Farley sought to penetrate this barrier: 'we were asking the women to briefly remove a mask that was crucial to their psychological survival'.[70] She also asserts that 'most' of the women working in the legal brothels had pimps, despite the fact that the women were 'reluctant to admit that their boyfriends and husbands were pimping them'.[71] And 'a surprisingly low percentage – thirty three per cent – of our interviewees in the legal brothels reported sexual abuse in childhood', a percentage that 'is lower than the likely actual incidence of sexual abuse because of symptoms of numbing, avoidance, and dissociation among these women' or discomfort discussing such experiences.[72] In citing research by Brents and Hausbeck that concluded that the brothels 'offer the

---

66 See the critiques of Farley's previous work in Weitzer, op. cit., n. 8.
67 M. Farley, *Prostitution and Trafficking in Nevada: Making the Connections* (2007) 118, 119. Emphasis added.
68 id., p. 120
69 id., p. 22.
70 id.
71 id., p. 31.
72 id., p. 33.

safest environment available for women to sell consensual sex acts for money',[73] Farley dismisses their findings by arguing that 'safety is relative, given that all prostitution is associated with a high likelihood of violence'.[74] Evidence that contradicts her position is summarily discounted.

What about legal systems in other nations? The State Department's own assessments appear to undercut the notion that legal prostitution systems are a magnet for sex trafficking. In its annual *Trafficking in Persons Report*, several nations where prostitution is legal (Australia, Germany, the Netherlands, New Zealand) were found to 'fully comply with minimum standards for the elimination of trafficking'.[75] Moreover, the 2005 *Report* reveals that the Dutch authorities report a 'decrease in trafficking in the legal sector', a finding confirmed by other analysts.[76] Rather than being a magnet attracting migrants into a country, it appears that legal prostitution may help *decrease* trafficking due to increased oversight. Moreover:

> it is the prohibition of prostitution and restrictions on travel which attract organised crime and create the possibilities for large profits, as well as creating the prostitutes' need for protection and assistance.[77]

As one analyst states:

> Traffickers take advantage of the illegality of commercial sex work and migration, and are able to exert an undue amount of power and control over [migrants] ... In such cases, it is the laws that prevent legal commercial sex work and immigration that form the major obstacles.[78]

In addition to potentially discouraging trafficking, legal prostitution can be organized in a way that enhances workers' safety, health, and job satisfaction – as seems to be borne out in several nations. These systems are not problem-free, but the evidence from these sites contrasts strikingly with the image proffered by the anti-prostitution crusade.[79]

73 B. Brents and K. Hausbeck, 'Violence and Legalized Brothel Prostitution in Nevada' (2005) 20 *J. of Interpersonal Violence* 289.
74 Farley, op. cit., n. 67, p. 20.
75 US Department of State, *Trafficking in Persons Report* (annual publication).
76 Transcrime, *Study on National Legislation on Prostitution and the Trafficking in Women and Children*, Report to the European Parliament (2005) 121. There has also been an overall decrease in prostitution establishments (brothels, window units) since legalization in 2000 due to increased government monitoring.
77 A. Murray, 'Debt Bondage and Trafficking' in *Global Sex Workers,* eds. K. Kempadoo and J. Doezema (1998) 60.
78 K. Kempadoo, 'Introduction: Globalizing Sex Workers' Rights' in Kempadoo and Doezema, id., p. 17.
79 The evidence for this is reviewed in Weitzer, op. cit., n. 8.

2. Targeting stripping and pornography

Domain expansion is broader than prostitution. Activists have pressed the government to criminalize 'the commercial sex trade as a whole',[80] and they have met with some success thus far. The key legislation on sex trafficking defines 'commercial sexual activities' as 'any sex act on account of which anything of value is given to, or received by, any person'.[81] One purpose of the 2005 End Demand for Sex Trafficking Bill was to 'combat commercial sexual activities' in general, because 'commercial sexual activities have a devastating impact on society. The sex trade has a dehumanising effect on all involved'. The bill targeted a wide variety of sex acts, such as lap dancing in strip clubs, legal brothel prostitution in Nevada, and pornography. Parts of the End Demand Bill were included in TVPRA 2005, which contains a section that repeatedly refers to the need to investigate and combat 'trafficking in persons and demand for commercial sex acts in the United States'[82] – effectively blurring the line between trafficking and commercial sex.

Donna Hughes's report on trafficking (funded by the State Department) includes sections on pornography and stripping.[83] Her report claims that 'the introduction of lap dancing has almost eliminated the distinction between dancing and prostitution', and also that women and girls are trafficked to perform at strip clubs (though she found only six cases of this in the United States during 1998–2005).[84] Other crusade members have made similar claims about strip clubs, which in the future may result in increased government surveillance or control. Hughes maintains that strip clubs are 'attractive to some criminals because they assume that since stripping is legal they will be less likely to be caught trafficking women into these markets'.[85] This, despite the overwhelming evidence that organized crime thrives under conditions where a particular vice is criminalized – amply demonstrated by drug, gambling, and alcohol prohibition – and tends to decline when it is legalized.[86] Organized crime may be reduced in legal prostitution as well. In Queensland, Australia, a government evaluation concluded that organized crime had been largely eliminated in the legal brothels, and in New Zealand, a government study found no evidence of criminal involvement in prostitution.[87] Elsewhere, organized crime may be

---

80 Hughes, op. cit., n. 40, p. 2.
81 TVPA 2000, s. 103(3); TVPRA 2005, s. 207(3).
82 TVPRA 2005, s. 201a.
83 Hughes, op. cit., n. 47. Hughes received $108,478 from the State Department to write this report: Attorney General, *Report to Congress on U.S. Government Efforts to Combat Trafficking in Persons in Fiscal Year 2004* (2005).
84 id., pp. 22, 26.
85 id., p. 22.
86 See, for example, the voluminous literature on Prohibition in the United States.
87 Crime and Misconduct Commission, *Regulating Prostitution: An Evaluation of the Prostitution Act 1999, Queensland* (2004) xii; Prostitution Law Review Committee,

more resilient in a particular vice sector, but the claim that it necessarily increases when prostitution is legalized, as abolitionists claim, is dubious.[88]

Pornography is also under new scrutiny. Most of the groups involved in the anti-prostitution crusade are equally alarmed by pornography, and they have begun to associate it with trafficking. In an article entitled 'Pornography as Trafficking', abolitionist icon Catharine MacKinnon equates the distribution of pornography with the trafficking of persons depicted in pornography:

> In the resulting materials, these people are then conveyed and sold for a buyer's sexual use ... Each time the pornography is commercially exchanged, the trafficking continues as the women and children in it are transported and provided for sex, sold, and bought again. Doing all these things for the purpose of exploiting the prostitution of others – which pornography intrinsically does – makes it trafficking in persons.[89]

The slippage between 'materials' and 'persons' is striking in this formulation. Conflation is even more conspicuous in MacKinnon's circular argument that 'the pornography industry, in production, creates demand for prostitution, hence for trafficking, because it is itself a form of prostitution and trafficking'.[90]

Pornography became widely available during the 1990s via video, cable TV, and the Internet. The expanding market of sexual material heightened anxieties within conservative and prohibitionist feminist quarters, whose leaders complained that the Clinton administration was ignoring the growing 'threat' to traditional values and/or to women.[91] Anti-porn groups had hoped that the inauguration of President Bush would result in a robust crackdown on pornography, but this did not materialize until his second term in office. Two years after Bush took office, a right-wing organization, Concerned Women for America, analysed the Justice Department's (DOJ) record to date, and complained that it was only targeting the most extreme kinds of porn:

> Until the DOJ vigorously and consistently targets the major hard-core porn producers and distributors of prosecutable but less deviant material, the industry will continue to make billions exploiting women, addicting men, exposing children, destroying marriages, and polluting the culture while laughing all the way to the bank.[92]

Report of the Prostitution Law Review Committee on the Operation of the Prostitution Reform Act 2003 (2008) 163–4.

88 Mary Sullivan, a leader of Australia's branch of CATW, claims that organized crime is 'inherent' whether prostitution is illegal or legal. M. Sullivan, *What Happens when Prostitution Becomes Work? An Update on Legalization of Prostitution in Australia* (2005) 4.

89 C. MacKinnon, 'Pornography as Trafficking' (2005) 26 *Michigan J. of International Law* 993, at 993, 1004.

90 id., p. 999.

91 Public Broadcasting Service, 'American Porn', *Frontline* television series (2006).

92 J. LaRue, 'DOJ Releases List of "Obscenity Prosecutions During This Administration"', Concerned Women for America, <www.cfwa.org>, 18 December 2003.

79

Attorney General John Ashcroft held private meetings with conservative groups in 2002 to assuage their concerns, and Attorney General Alberto Gonzales created a new Justice Department unit in 2005 (the Obscenity Prosecution Task Force), but anti-porn activists remained unsatisfied.[93] A 2007 letter to President Bush, signed by over fifty major players in the anti-porn movement, urged him to wage war on pornography. The letter writers were alarmed at the 'explosive increase' in the availability or pornography, which they associated with a host of harms. The letter argues that 'trafficking in women and children' is 'linked to the spread of obscenity' and that pornography 'corrupts children, ruins marriages, contributes to sex crimes against children and adults, and undermines the right of Americans to live in a decent society'.[94] The letter complains that the Justice Department has been lax in enforcing the obscenity laws, demands intensified prosecution of pornography cases, and asks Bush 'to make fighting obscenity one of your top priorities'. Two years earlier, one of the signatories, Patrick Trueman (former chief of the Justice Department's obscenity unit and now legal counsel for the Family Research Council), testified before Congress that 'pornography is closely linked to an increase in prostitution, child prostitution, and human trafficking ... Pornography is a powerful factor in creating the demand for illicit sex'.[95] And Donna Hughes asserted that the producers of pornography 'often rely on trafficked victims'.[96] These charges were made without supporting evidence.

It is clear that the perceived 'mainstreaming' or 'normalization' of pornography is the driving force behind activists' robust campaign to criminalize its production, distribution, and possession. As the leader of Morality in Media stated:

> if we could just send a message to people that this is not what sex is all about, we will have won more than half the battle. Whether you're a creationist or a Darwinist, sex is linked to something greater than masturbating to depictions of other people having sex. It's linked to a person. We have a capacity to love.[97]

---

93 'Justice Department Sets Sights on Mainstream Porn' *Pittsburgh Post-Gazette*, 11 April 2004.
94 'Appointment of New U.S. Attorney General and Other Matters Regarding Vigorous Enforcement of Federal Obscenity Laws', 10 September 2007. <http://www.moralityinmedia.org/obscenityEnforcement/Letter-Regarding-Appointment-of-New-U.S.-Atty-General_10Sep2007.pdf>. The letter was signed by, among others, Donna Hughes, Patrick Trueman, Morality in Media, Family Research Council, Concerned Women for America, Focus on the Family, American Family Association, American Decency Association, and Citizens for Community Values.
95 P. Trueman, Testimony, US Senate Subcommittee on the Constitution, Civil Rights, and Property Rights, Hearing on Obscenity Prosecution, 16 March 2005.
96 Hughes, op. cit., n. 47, p. 26.
97 Robert Peters, quoted in G. Beato, 'Xtreme Measures: Washington's New Crackdown on Pornography' *ReasonOnline*, May 2004.

Pressure from these individuals and groups helps to explain recent government actions regarding pornography. For the most part, the law has remained unchanged (the 1973 *Miller* decision – stipulating that local 'community standards' should be used to decide whether something is obscene – remains the cornerstone of pornography law),[98] but law enforcement has expanded. The Justice Department recently launched a new crackdown on pornography, including greater resources targeting adult pornography (previous practice centered on child porn).[99] The Justice Department also created a new unit (the Obscenity Prosecution Task Force) alongside the existing obscenity branch.[100] The head of the new unit, Brent Ward, was United States Attorney in Utah during the Reagan administration, during which he vigorously prosecuted distributors of pornography, attempted to impose new restrictions on strip clubs, prosecuted a phone sex company, and forced Utah's two remaining adult theatres to close.[101] Another major figure is Bruce Taylor, who served in the Justice Department's obscenity unit in the Reagan years, was a lawyer for the nation's premier anti-pornography group (Citizens for Decency through Law, founded in 1956), and was president of another anti-porn organization (the National Law Center for Children and Families). He is now the obscenity unit's senior legal counsel.[102] The appointments of Taylor and Ward were praised by right-wing groups that had pressed the Bush administration to launch a new war on porn.[103]

An intriguing arrangement is the link between the Justice Department and a leading anti-porn organization, Morality in Media (MIM). The Justice Department website contains a section, *What Citizens Can Do About Obscenity*, which encourages people to report 'hard-core pornography'. Since 2004, visitors who click on that icon are redirected to ObscenityCrimes.org, whose employees then conduct a review. This website is run by MIM, which received two large grants to fund the work of two retired police officers who review the complaints.[104] In the past few years, 67,000 citizen complaints have been passed from MIM to the Justice Department.[105] That the Department's website provides links to MIM appears to reflect a seamless convergence of interests with a very partisan organization.

---

98   This is in contrast to Britain, where recent legislation targets 'extreme pornography'. See F. Attwood and C. Smith, 'Extreme Concern', this volume, pp. 171–88.
99   'U.S. Attorney's Porn Fight Gets Bad Reviews' *Daily Business Rev.*, 30 August 2005.
100 US Department of Justice, 'Obscenity Prosecution Task Force Established to Investigate, Prosecute Purveyors of Obscene Materials', Press Release, 5 May 2005; R. Schmitt, 'U.S. Cracking Down on Porn' *Deseret News*, 15 February 2004.
101 'Nation's Porn Prosecutor Fronts War against Obscenity' *Salt Lake Tribune*, 26 February 2007.
102 Schmitt, op. cit., n. 100.
103 'Porn Industry Moans for Good Reason' at <www.cwfa.org>, 24 February 2004.
104 'Outsourcing Justice? That's Obscene' *Washington Post*, 15 July 2007.
105 'Federal Effort on Web Obscenity Shows Few Results' *New York Times*, 10 August 2007.

Whereas the Clinton administration prosecuted almost no cases involving adult obscenity, Bush launched several prosecutions. Between 2001 and May 2005, prosecution resulted in convictions of forty individuals and businesses, with an additional twenty indictments pending.[106] This record did not satisfy anti-porn activists. Former Justice Department official Patrick Trueman complained:

> The few cases that have been prosecuted involve extreme pornography, depicting violence, defecation, or animals. Most people have no interest in this stuff, and it's not the business the mainstream porn industry is in. By only pursuing extreme obscenity, the mainstream porn industry is given a green light. There's this perception that anything other than extreme pornography is legal, and it's not. The fact that it's not being prosecuted does not make it legal ... Most porn violates community standards; that makes it illegal, and it's easy to prove.[107]

Trueman went on to describe the dangers of mainstreaming:

> The mainstream porn industry has been left to do pretty much whatever it wants. Porn is now so pervasive that our college students don't even know how to date, because pornography has conditioned young men to believe that they're entitled to sexual services from women without the need for relationship. They're on such a steady diet of porn that they can't distinguish between love and sexual desire.[108]

In a nutshell, the trend in anti-porn enforcement under Bush can be characterized as both slow to materialize and less far-reaching than crusade activists had hoped for, yet greater than under the Clinton administration. Government anti-pornography efforts under Bush were less intensive than the major legal innovations and robust enforcement actions against prostitution and trafficking, but were nonetheless a significant part of the state's broad targeting of the sex industry in general.

Six months into the Obama administration, little has changed. Brent Ward remains in charge of the Obscenity Prosecution Task Force, and Justice Department prosecutors continued to work on cases inherited from the previous government.[109] In July 2009, a large coalition of anti-porn organizations, headed by the Alliance Defense Fund, requested a meeting with President Obama's new Attorney General, Eric Holder. Their letter to Holder illustrates, again, my argument that the current abolitionist crusade is a direct response to the perceived unravelling of traditional sexual mores due to the flourishing of sexual commerce and the alleged sexualization of the larger culture:

106 'Bush Administration Stepping Up Obscenity Prosecutions' *USA Today*, 4 May 2005.
107 Patrick Trueman, quoted in W. Laugesen, 'Pornography Crackdown' *National Catholic Register*, 22 April 2007.
108 id.
109 'Porn Prosecution Fuels Debate' *Politico*, 31 July 2009.

Since the advent of the Internet, illegal pornography has flooded homes, businesses, public libraries, and even schools. The results have been devastating to America. Pornography addiction is now common among men, women, and even many children. Children are creating cell phone pornography, in a new trend called 'sexting'. Pornography use is now a significant factor in divorce. Hotels, motels, cable and satellite companies, and other businesses are making tremendous profits by offering illegal, obscene pornography. America is becoming a 'pornified culture'. . . . We are compelled to write to you and ask for an expansion of the Administration's efforts against the scourge of pornography.[110]

The letter writers oppose both obscene material (that is, pornography that has been judged obscene by a jury) and the 'scourge' of pornography in general, including legal porn.

CONCLUSION

The evidence presented here shows that the dominant forces in the anti-trafficking, abolitionist crusade and their allies in the United States government are committed to a far-reaching attack on commercial sex – prostitution, strip clubs, pornography – all of which are associated with trafficking and 'sexual slavery'. A crackdown on, if not outright criminalization of, pornography and strip clubs becomes more palatable to mainstream organizations and moderate politicians if they can be linked to sex trafficking, that is, if they can be convinced that sex workers in these two sectors have been coerced and trafficked. Such domain expansion has been a gradual process. The initial, exclusive focus on trafficking was subsequently broadened as activists began to insist that all sectors of the commercial sex industry should be targeted for repression. Evidence of this domain expansion can be found in the areas designated for increased scrutiny in the End Demand Bill, the growing crackdown on domestic prostitution provided for in the 2005 and 2008 TVPRA, the requirement that those seeking government funding for their research or interventions on trafficking or AIDS sign an anti-prostitution pledge, and the Justice Department's increasing investigation of producers and distributors of adult pornography under the obscenity laws.

This moral crusade has succeeded, remarkably quickly, in transforming itself from social movement into a project of the United States government – becoming almost fully institutionalized in official discourse, legislation, and enforcement practices under the Bush administration. During this period, there has been an extraordinary osmosis between crusade and government ideology and policy initiatives. As I have shown here and elsewhere, the success of this movement is largely due to the convergence of interests and

---

110 Letter from Alliance Defense Fund to Attorney General Eric Holder, 15 July 2009.

organizational interpenetration between crusade groups and the Bush government, quite similar to the partnership between anti-pornography organizations and the Reagan administration in the mid-1980s.[111] The advent of a new government under President Obama is unlikely to alter the status quo, given how far-reaching the institutional investment in abolitionism has become. It is likely that right-wing political and religious forces will have less access to the state than under the Bush administration, but the laws, agency apparatuses, and enforcement machinery are likely to remain firmly in place for the foreseeable future.

111 Weitzer, op. cit., n. 8.

JOURNAL OF LAW AND SOCIETY
VOLUME 37, NUMBER 1, MARCH 2010
ISSN: 0263-323X, pp. 85–104

When (Some) Prostitution is Legal: The Impact of Law Reform on Sex Work in Australia

BARBARA SULLIVAN*

In Australia, prostitution regulation has taken a very different path from many other countries. Law reform has led to the opening of some significant new spaces for legal sex work, including the (very different) regulatory regimes established in two Australian states – Queensland (brothels legal if their owners are licensed) and New South Wales (most commercial sex businesses and some street prostitution decriminalized; no licensing regime). The main research question is: how has regulation impacted on the positive rights of sex workers? I argue that law reform has engaged a mix of neo-liberal and other approaches – not to increase personal or corporate freedom but as part of a practical strategy designed to control a range of social problems, such as police corruption and organized crime. Neo-liberal regulation of prostitution in Australia has always been deployed in tandem with other modes of regulation – including new criminal law and policing strategies, planning law, health regulations, and (of course) moral regulation.

INTRODUCTION

In Australia there has been a moderate opening of the space for legal sex work over the last three decades. Brothels and/or escort agencies have been legalized in a number of jurisdictions and street-based sex work has been decriminalized in New South Wales. This reform trajectory makes Australia similar to countries like the Netherlands and New Zealand and very different from countries like the United States and Canada (where most prostitution

* School of Political Science & International Studies, University of Queensland, QLD 4071, Australia
barbara.sullivan@uq.edu.au

The author wishes to acknowledge the following people for talk and feedback on an earlier draft of this paper: Chris Diamond, Janelle Fawlkes, Candi Forrest, Leslie Jeffrey, Elena Jeffreys, Maria MacMahon, Andrew Miles, Rachel Wotton, members of SQWISI and SSPAN.

85

remains illegal), Sweden and Norway (where prohibitions have been intro-duced on the purchase of sexual services), and the United Kingdom (where new policy approaches emphasize a welfare strategy designed to 'exit' women from prostitution). There is, however, no national uniformity in the changes implemented in Australia; as there are eight Australian states and territories, all with different approaches to prostitution law and policy, there has been no single/unified experience with prostitution law reform (despite claims to the contrary by radical feminist critics of the 'Australian experience').[1]

Until the late 1970s, the criminal law addressed to prostitution was similar throughout Australia; while the act of prostitution itself was not illegal, most prostitution-related activities were illegal – including keeping a brothel, living on the earnings of the prostitution of another, and soliciting in a public place for the purposes of prostitution. In Tasmania and South Australia the law still looks mostly like this. However, in other Australian jurisdictions significant changes began to be put in place from the late 1970s onwards. In 1979, New South Wales (NSW) decriminalized public soliciting for the purposes of prostitution; brothels were decriminalized in the 1990s and now operate (mostly) like any other business. Victoria, Queensland, the Northern Territory, the Australian Capital Territory and Western Australia have also changed their laws to allow for the operation of legal brothels and/or escort agencies (albeit using very different regulatory regimes from each other and from NSW).[2] However, a total ban on public soliciting for the purposes of prostitution remains in force in all these jurisdictions, making NSW the only state where (some) public soliciting is permitted.

The *reasons* why these legal changes were implemented in Australia are complex and numerous, underlining the importance of local political cultures and multiple/local deployments of power.[3] The main factors include the role of feminist movements in supporting law reform, including within the Australian Labor Party; the strength of sex worker advocacy groups in Australia;[4] *and* the application of neo-liberal measures designed to achieve a

---

1 See, for example, M. Sullivan and S. Jeffreys, 'Legalization. The Australian Experience' (2002) 8 *Violence Against Women* 1140.

2 For a recent discussion of the different legal regimes addressed to prostitution in Australia, see A. Quadara, 'Sex Workers and Sexual Assault in Australia', ACSSA Issues Paper No 8 (2008). See, also, T. Crofts and T. Summerfield, 'The Licensing of Sex Work in Australia and New Zealand' (2006) 13 *Murdoch Electronic J. of Law* 269.

3 B. Sullivan, *The Politics of Sex. Prostitution and Pornography in Australia Since 1945* (1997); J. Scott, *How Modern Governments Made Prostitution a Social Problem: Creating a Socially Responsible Prostitute Population* (2005).

4 This is partly an effect of the implementation in the 1980s and 1990s of health policies designed to combat HIV/AIDS in the sex industry; these utilized (and increased the importance of) peer outreach workers and sex worker organizations. However, the recent strength and vitality of the sex worker movement in Australia is also due to excellent leadership (see, for example, E. Jeffreys, 'Scarlet Alliance Brings Sex Worker Migration to Canberra' (2008) 28 *Aust. Feminist Law J.* 195.

better practical governance of the sex industry. In Australia neo-liberal strategies have been utilized in order to address a multitude of social problems often associated with prostitution, such as organized crime, police corruption, violence against women, the sexual exploitation of children, public health concerns (particularly around HIV/AIDS), and the amenity of inner-city neighbourhoods affected by street prostitution. In this context neo-liberalism should not be seen in terms of a normative project seeking simply to extend individual or corporate freedom. Neo-liberal governmentality involves 'a positive project' designed to address some of the practical problems that arise in governing states and their populations.[5] Moreover, as Barry Hindess has argued, while it is a neo-liberal ideal to rule through the free activities of autonomous individuals, liberals have also 'traditionally' taken the view that some individuals and populations do not possess the capacities which would allow them to be governed in this way.[6] So a 'liberal authoritarianism'[7] – directed at primitive or otherwise problematic subjects – may be part and parcel of neo-liberal government. Clearly, sex workers as well as men who pay for sex have been increasingly marked out for this sort of attention.[8] In Australia, neo-liberal concerns to improve the governance of the sex industry have led to the implementation of a range of different measures including: new criminal law (also decriminalization); legalization via regulatory change (licensing or registration of sex businesses); changes in policing strategies; and new public policies designed to improve the public health and/or the health and welfare of women. So describing the governance of the sex industry in Australia as 'neo-liberal' may, in fact, indicate very little about how the new governance regimes work, including their impact and consequences.

In this paper I am particularly concerned to explore the impact and consequences of law reform for women working in the sex industry. I examine the very different regulatory regimes addressed to prostitution in two Australian jurisdictions, Queensland (which licenses brothels but has no legal street work) and NSW (which treats brothels mostly like any other business and also has some legal street work). The paper utilizes published research, official reports, and twelve in-depth interviews conducted with sex workers, and other key informants, in Queensland and NSW during 2006–2009. The main question explored is: how has the mode of regulating prostitution in Queensland and NSW impacted on the positive rights of sex workers?

The term 'sex work' is *not* used here to imply a free choice by individuals to work, or not, in the sex industry. I assume that most paid work, including

---

5 B. Hindess, 'Neo-liberal citizenship' (2002) 6 *Citizenship Studies* 134; see, also, M. Dean and B. Hindess (eds.), *Governing Australia. Studies in Contemporary Rationalities of Government* (1998).
6 Hindess, id.
7 id.
8 See Sullivan, op. cit., n. 3; Scott, op. cit., n. 3.

sex work, involves varying degrees of coercion, exploitation, resistance, and agency.[9] Consequently, the term 'safety' is used to signify not a working life without danger, but the calculated management of the main risks associated with sex work.[10] The safety strategies available here will be individual, organizational, and policy based (including occupational health and safety policies overseen by state bodies). The criminal law in place will clearly impact upon the availability of these strategies in any specific context. The use of the term 'rights' in the research question signals attention to both the civil and labour rights of sex workers. The term 'capacity' is deployed to indicate the *constructed* nature of sex workers' safety and rights.[11] This paper argues that law and policy addressed to the sex industry has a significant impact on the making of safe (or not) working environments for sex workers, on their positive (civil and labour) rights, and on their capacities as both human beings and workers. These capacities include the ability to negotiate optimal working conditions, to seek advice and support (including from unions), and to obtain legal redress for injury or unfair treatment.

In the first two sections of the paper I briefly explore the history of prostitution in Queensland and the regulatory regimes put in place up to the present day via law, policy, and policing practices. The third section of the paper undertakes an exploration of the impact of the current regulatory regime on sex workers. The overall argument is that new possibilities for legal sex work have opened in Queensland over the last decade and that these have enlarged the positive rights and capacities of some sex workers, most notably those who work in licensed brothels. Workers in legal brothels have been able to receive some of the benefits of mainstream work environments. At the same time, however, deficiencies in the new regulatory regime mean that these workers do not enjoy 'good' working conditions. Also, workers occupied outside licensed brothels – including in (legal) private work and in illegal contexts such as the street, unlicensed brothels, and massage parlours – have seen a decline in their living and working conditions. The comparison with NSW draws attention to a number of key issues and suggests that the mode of regulation is an important factor determining the positive rights and capacities of workers in the sex industry. While the system is not ideal in NSW (see below), partial decriminalization offers some real advantages to sex workers, particularly in terms of positive rights.

9 B. Sullivan, 'Prostitution and Consent. Beyond the Liberal Dichotomy of Free or Forced' in *Making Sense of Sexual Consent*, eds. M. Cowling and P. Reynolds (2004) 127. Also, L. Jeffrey and G. MacDonald, *Sex Workers in the Maritimes Talk Back* (2006).
10 P. Pyett and D. Warr, 'Women at Risk in Sex Work: Strategies for Survival' (1999) 35 *J. of Sociology* 183; T. Sanders, *Sex Work: A Risky Business* (2005).
11 B. Sullivan, 'Rape, Prostitution and Consent' (2007) 40 *Aust. and N. Zealand J. of Criminology* 127.

A number of authors have explored the history of sex work in Australia.[12] From the early twentieth century through to the late 1970s, the law addressed to prostitution was very similar around Australia. While it was not illegal to practise prostitution, most prostitution-related activities were illegal including soliciting in a public place for the purposes of prostitution and owning or operating a brothel. However, there was no straightforward congruence between the law and the working lives of sex workers. In Queensland, despite the legal prohibitions, police deployed a policy of selective 'containment' in relation to prostitution.[13] While street work was heavily policed, some 'well run' brothels were allowed to operate with relative impunity although the workers in these establishments were required to submit to occasional arrest (so prosecution rates were maintained) and to undertake health examinations.[14] Levine has recently argued that the historical space permitted for brothels to operate in Queensland represented a local and colonial strategy for warding off social anxieties about prostitution: 'the aim was to diminish if not eradicate street walking in favour of the more easily controlled brothels'.[15] In Britain, she suggests, the opposite occurred; brothels were closed but police permitted some street prostitution.

In Queensland the regulatory regime addressed to prostitution has long included management via health law and policy. A Contagious Diseases Act, broadly modelled on a British Act, was introduced in 1868. This required prostitutes to undergo medical examination and to be incarcerated in a 'lock hospital' if they were found to be suffering from a sexually transmitted infection (STI). Levine argues that this legislation was initially aimed at working-class women in the state capital, Brisbane.[16] However, as a result of racial anxiety, it was also extended north into towns and regions with significant 'coloured' populations.[17] The aim was to stop sexual commerce across the racial divide. According to Levine, 'prostitutes represented (racial) degeneracy and excess, threatening the healthy growth of new world settler colonialism'.[18]

---

12 K. Daniels (ed.), *So Much Hard Work. Women and Prostitution in Australia* (1984); M. Arnot, 'The Oldest Profession in a New Brittania' in *Constructing a Culture: A People's History of Australia*, eds. V. Burgman and J. Lee (1988) 42; F. Frances, *Selling Sex. A Hidden History of Prostitution* (2007).

13 Sullivan, op. cit., n. 3.

14 id.

15 P. Levine, *Prostitution, Race and Politics. Policing Venereal Disease in the British Empire* (2003) 56.

16 id., p. 57.

17 id. The main targets were Chinese, Japanese, and Pacific Islander women. Levine says that indigenous women were not subject to the Contagious Diseases Act. They were, however, subject to 'protective' legislation that controlled all aspects of their lives and would have enabled both the health examination and physical removal of indigenous women engaged in sex work.

18 id., p. 236.

In the late-nineteenth and early-twentieth centuries, the Queensland Contagious Diseases Act was roundly criticized by Australian feminists; the laws were also resisted by some of the women incarcerated in the Brisbane lock hospital.[19] The Act achieved very little in terms of controlling the spread of sexually transmitted infection and clearly breached the civil rights of the women who were incarcerated without due process of law. It was not repealed until 1971 (when other coercive health regulations were already in place). The lock hospital in Brisbane was still in use in the mid 1940s and we can only guess as to how this fitted with the containment policies discussed above.[20] Certainly, the ability to remove women from street-based sex work and to enforce this with incarceration (without formal arrest or prosecution) would have been advantageous for police seeking to 'control' the industry. It would also have been advantageous for brothel owners whose businesses may have been threatened by street-based sex work. For brothels allowed to operate under the police containment policy, the threat of the lock hospital may also have been useful for controlling their workers, encouraging compliance with health examinations and occasional arrest by the police.

In 1959, Brisbane's tolerated houses of prostitution – some of which had operated openly for more than a century – were closed down by the Police Commissioner in an action widely reported in local newspapers. This was probably due, not to the success of any moral reform or campaign against police corruption, but to the collapse of long-standing criminal networks that organized the prostitution industry.[21] Police were central to the maintenance of this network and the brothels were apparently closed to prevent this coming to public attention. However, the policy of containment continued for almost another thirty years.

In the mid-1980s, in the declining years of a long-standing conservative government in Queensland, investigative journalists began to expose evidence of police corruption associated with gambling and prostitution rackets. This eventually led to the establishment of a wide-ranging official investigation – the Fitzgerald Inquiry – and resulted in the jailing of a number of high-profile figures including the former Commissioner of Police. Fitzgerald recommended a system of regulated/legal prostitution to prevent similar problems in the future.[22] The task of coming up with specific legal recommendations was given to the newly-formed Criminal Justice Commission (now the Crime and Misconduct Commission, the CMC). In a report published in 1991, the Commission recommended a system of licensed/legal brothels. However, the new Labor government of Wayne Goss declined this

19 id., pp. 130–1.
20 Sullivan, op. cit., n. 3, p. 48.
21 id., pp. 106–8.
22 Queensland Government, *Report of a Commission of Inquiry Pursuant to Orders in Council* (1989).

approach and instead introduced a range of new offences and tougher penalties for almost all prostitution-related activities.[23]

A NEW REGULATORY REGIME

In 1998 another new Labor premier, Peter Beattie, came to power in Queensland and he was a known supporter of prostitution law reform. A new act – the Prostitution Act 1999 – was soon passed and, albeit with some minor amendments, remains the cornerstone of the current regulatory regime in Queensland. The 1999 Act instituted a system for the licensing of owners and managers of brothels to be overseen by a new statutory authority, the Prostitution Licensing Authority (PLA).[24] Those who want to own or manage a brothel are required to apply to the PLA and complete an extensive police investigation of their background, associates, and financial situation. If this is successful, a significant annual licensing fees is payable (currently more than $10,000 per annum for owners). Also, the brothel premises are required to conform to local council planning laws. While local councils are not allowed to ban brothel businesses outright (except in small towns), brothels usually have to be located in industrial or commercial zones.

Under the Queensland Prostitution Act, the size of licensed brothels is limited to a maximum of five rooms for the provision of sexual services, and no more than eight sex workers can be rostered on at any one time. Brothels are not permitted to offer escort services (also called 'outcalls') or to serve alcohol. Advertising for staff is prohibited and all other advertising is both restricted and controlled by the PLA; licensed brothels can only advertise in printed publications (such as newspapers and telephone directories) and on-line. The advertisement is limited in size and cannot describe the ethnicity of workers at the brothel or the nature of any available sexual services. Within licensed brothels it is also an offence to provide or receive sexual services without a prophylactic (or to make an offer in this regard). The operation of the brothel also has to conform to regulations set out by the PLA and other state bodies, for example, in relation to occupational health and safety. Brothels have to be open to inspection by the PLA and (under certain conditions) police. To date there are only 25 licensed brothels in Queensland, a state with a population of four and a half million and a thriving tourist industry. This suggests that only a small percentage of sex work is presently being conducted in licensed brothels; the CMC has recently estimated this at 10 per cent.[25]

23 id., pp. 212–18.
24 See the Prostitution Licensing Authority, accessible at: <http://www.pla.qld.gov.au/default.htm>.
25 CMC (Crime and Misconduct Commission), *Regulating Prostitution. An Evaluation of the Prostitution Act 1999 (Qld)* (2004) xii.

91

Most, by far, of legal prostitution in Queensland is probably being carried out by private sex workers who work alone from their own premises or in outcall/escort prostitution; the CMC has recently estimated that outcall services constitute 75 per cent of the industry in Queensland.[26] Private workers are not subject to licensing and *can* legally provide outcalls. However, it is illegal for a private worker to work with another sex worker or to employ a receptionist; they may employ a licensed security guard and (since 2009) can maximize their safety by making phone contact with another person before and after a job. Advertising by private workers is restricted and subject to approval by the PLA. As with all sex workers in Queensland, it is also an offence for a private worker to provide or receive sexual services without a prophylactic (or to make an offer in this regard). Private workers do have some new protection against eviction by landlords; prior to 1992, landlords were required to evict sex workers or face criminal penalties themselves. Now, landlords are liable only when two or more workers are operating from the same premises (that is, an 'illegal brothel'). Moreover, under Queensland anti-discrimination law, sex workers operating legally have clear avenues of redress if they are evicted because they are sex workers. It is an offence to discriminate on the grounds of 'lawful sexual activity' and this specifically includes legal sex work (so it applies to both private workers and sex workers in licensed brothels).[27]

Under Queensland criminal law, unlicensed brothels, escort agencies, and all forms of street-based sex work are prohibited; they are also subject to heavy policing. Child prostitution, procuring, and living on the earnings of the prostitution of another (except where those earnings have been legally acquired) are also prohibited. A whole separate regulatory regime – attached to alcohol licensing – is addressed to stripping and lap dancing,[28] indicating a clear attempt to create and reinforce a boundary between 'erotic' activities (deemed *not* to be prostitution) and prostitution.

Since the early 1990s a significant amount of research has focused on prostitution and the conditions of sex work in Queensland.[29] There has also

---

26 id., p. xiii.
27 The Queensland Anti-Discrimination Commission gives two examples of situations where discrimination involving sex workers may be illegal: when a bank refuses credit when the occupation of an individual employed in legal sex work becomes known, despite a stable financial history, and when a real estate agent refuses to rent an individual private accommodation when the occupation is revealed (see <www.adcq.qld.gov.au/Brochures07/LSA.pdf>). There have been successful anti-discrimination cases pursued by sex workers in both Queensland and the Australian Capital Territory.
28 CMC, *Regulating Adult Entertainment. A Review of the Live Adult Entertainment Industry in Queensland* (2004).
29 F. Boyle, *The Sex Industry: A Survey of Sex Workers in Queensland, Australia* (1997); L. Banach, 'The Impact of the Law and Legislative Change Upon Sex Workers Health and Safety', unpublished PhD dissertation, University of Queensland (2001–10); Prostitution Licensing Authority, *Selling Sex in Queensland 2003* (2004).

92

been a number of high-level inquiries looking at the impact of the current regulatory regime.[30] From these and from interviews with key informants, it is possible to ascertain a great deal about changes in the situation of sex workers since the introduction of law reform and the new regulatory regime. The next sections of this paper discuss some of these changes – for brothel workers, private sex workers, and street-based workers.

WORKING IN A BROTHEL

As a result of the 1999 reforms, new spaces for legal sex work have opened in licensed brothels. This has been advantageous for sex workers in this sector who are now able to earn a living without fear of arrest, prosecution, heavy fines and/or imprisonment, and a criminal record for life. Brothels also offer the safest working environment for sex workers – as evidence from Australia and elsewhere in the world clearly demonstrates.[31] In brothels, sex workers are far less vulnerable to violence, including sexual assault, because of a number of proven safety measures including the presence of other staff, increased possibilities for screening clients (in reception areas), and the provision of alarms. Workers in brothels are also more likely to feel they are able to complain to police if problems do occur.[32] By law, the owners and operators of brothels are also required to maximize occupational health and safety for their workers; this compels attention to issues like the provision of adequate lighting, private rest areas for workers, and prophylactic equipment. Therefore, the opening of new opportunities for sex work in licensed brothels appears to have some clear benefits for sex workers particularly in terms of increasing positive rights such as health and safety.

Claims like this have recently been contested by Mary Sullivan[33] who has written about prostitution in the state of Victoria (where brothels have also been subject to licensing although not in exactly the same way as in Queensland).[34] Sullivan claims that public policy addressed to occupational health and safety in the sex industry ignores the bigger dangers of violence, including rape, which are 'an inherent part of prostitution'.[35] Occupational

---

30 CMC, op. cit., n. 25; CMC, *Regulating Outcall Prostitution. Should Legal Outcall Prostitution Services Be Extended to Licensed Brothels and Independent Escort Agencies?* (2006); A. Edwards, *Selling Sex; Regulating Prostitution in Queensland. A Report to the Prostitution Licensing Authority* (2009).
31 R. Perkins, *Working Girls. Prostitutes, Their Life and Social Control* (1991); P. Pyett and D. Warr, 'Women at Risk in Sex Work. Strategies for Survival' (1999) 35 *J. of Sociology* 183; B. Brents and K. Hausbeck, 'Violence and Legalised Brothel Prostitution in Nevada' (2005) 20 *J. of Interpersonal Violence* 270.
32 CMC, op. cit., n. 25, p. 51.
33 M. Sullivan, *Making Sex Work. A Failed Experiment With Legalised Prostitution* (2007).
34 See Crofts and Summerfield, op. cit., n. 2.
35 Sullivan, op. cit. n. 33, p. 282.

health and safety policies reflect gendered (male) interests and their main concern is to create a safe sex environment for 'male buyers' of 'prostituted women' and to make women responsible for this.[36] The language here clearly signals the author's prior commitment to a radical feminist analysis of prostitution. From the radical feminist perspective, prostitution is inherently violent and always involves rape.[37] It is not surprising then, that Sullivan is completely unimpressed by the regulatory regime in Victoria and public policy that attempts to minimize some of the risks associated with the occupation of sex work, including in legal brothels. She dismisses the active involvement of Australian sex workers over the last decade in the formulation of occupational health and safety policies addressed to the sex industry. In her discussion of 'rape and violence as occupational hazards',[38] she quotes extensively from radical feminist theory and avoids any address to research that often clearly contradicts her claims.[39] In the Queensland context, there is clear evidence of increased safety for workers in licensed brothels.[40]

This is not to suggest that employment in licensed brothels in Queensland is without any problems. It is clear that the regulatory regime has both advantages and some serious disadvantages for sex workers in brothels. In the first place, a new distinction has opened up between licensed and unlicensed (illegal) brothels which impacts particularly on workers in the latter. The criminal penalties associated with work in illegal brothels are now much higher than they were in the early 1990s. Consequently, while workers may continue to seek brothel employment because of its relative safety (particularly in comparison to street work), workers in unlicensed brothels are now more vulnerable to significant criminal penalties. The Queensland-based group, Sexual Service Providers Advocacy Network (SSPAN), which includes members who work in licensed brothels, has also recently claimed that certain 'types' of workers are not hired by licensed brothels; this includes older women, transgender, male, and drug-dependent workers.[41] So, as the number of licensed brothels is also quite small, the opportunities for legal employment in brothels in Queensland is actually quite limited.

This gives brothel owners some significant power. SSPAN has recently described Queensland's licensed brothels as 'oppressive work environments'.[42] There are a number of factors here. As in the state of

---

36 id., p. 264.

37 This sort of approach has been widely advocated by radical feminists. See, for example, S. Jeffreys, *The Idea of Prostitution* (1997).

38 Sullivan, op. cit. n. 33, pp. 281–327.

39 Perkins, op. cit., n. 31; Sanders, op. cit., n. 10; Jeffrey and MacDonald, op. cit., n. 9; Quadara, op. cit., n. 2.

40 CMC, op. cit., n. 25, pp. 69–70.

41 SSPAN (Sexual Service Providers Advocacy Network), *Submission to the Queensland Crime and Misconduct Commission* (2006).

42 id.

94

Victoria,[43] most sex workers are paid as independent 'sub-contractors' rather than as 'employees'. This means they do not have access to basic employment rights – such as sick leave, recreation leave or employer contributions to superannuation – and are responsible for paying their own tax. The latter also means applying for an Australian Business Number and conforming to the accounting requirements of tax law (which would be a challenge for most workers). The CMC has reported that most owners of licensed brothels have:

> contracts with individual workers which state that the worker is an independent service provider, that no relationship of employer/employee is created between the parties and that the sex workers is not subject to any control by the owner.[44]

Brothel owners claim this sort of contract reflects the actual organization of the work. They say that brothels charge clients a set fee for the rental of the room and that it is up to the client and the worker to negotiate the services to be provided without any involvement by management. However, both the CMC and sex workers have disputed this claim. The CMC says their researchers observed that in many cases the brothel receptionist, manager or licensee negotiates an overall fee for the room rental – and for 'extra' services – before the worker even meets the client.[45]

SSPAN also reports that, despite stressing the independent status of their workers, brothel owners and managers impose a wide range of controls on workers including 'the hours they can work, what they can wear to work and the prices they may charge for their services'.[46] Workers 'cannot even decide to whom they choose to provide sexual services' and workers who refuse to see particular clients or who 'commit other forms of "misbehaviour" in the brothel owners' eyes are subject to sanctions'.[47] Sanctions take the form of being given quiet shifts with fewer opportunities to earn money and even being removed from the roster altogether (which is effectively a dismissal without notice). Brothel owners will also threaten expulsion if workers decide to work shifts at another licensed brothel or if they conduct (legal) private work outside the brothel.[48]

As Murray has argued in relation to Victoria's licensed brothels, it is 'clear that women working in the legal sex industry are not supplying sexual services in their own right, on conditions and at prices they determine'.[49] So they have what the literature often describes as a 'false' sub-contracting

---

43 K. Murray, 'Labour Regulation in the Legal Sex Industry in Victoria' (2003) 16 *Aust. J. of Labour Law* 1.
44 CMC, op. cit., n. 25, p. 105.
45 id., p. 106.
46 SSPAN, op. cit., n. 41.
47 id.
48 id.
49 Murray, op. cit., n. 43, p. 338.

relationship or 'dependent self-employment' with brothel owners.[50] The designation of sex workers as sub-contractors has certainly undermined any potential for the unionization of workers in licensed brothels in Queensland. While at least one union has explored the possibility of recruiting sex workers, and the need for improved working conditions in licensed brothels, nothing has eventuated. It is also worth noting that, with the recent re-structuring of all employment in Australia (as more workers sign individual contracts and lose employment rights), the situation of sex workers may not be very different from some other workers. Sex workers are perhaps unique only in so far as they work in an industry without a history of employment rights; so there are no 'baseline' conditions to lose!

The CMC has recently commented that high licensing fees for brothels makes them 'different' from other businesses;[51] thus, by implication, they are less able than other businesses to 'afford' good employment conditions. But this simply calls attention to the hidden costs for sex workers of the regulatory regime put in place in 1999. The licensing regime and new institutional framework established under the Prostitution Act prioritizes the elimination of organized crime from the prostitution industry and the CMC has recently claimed this has been achieved in licensed brothels.[52] This achievement may carry some benefits for sex workers (although these should not be overestimated) but it has also had significant costs.[53] The long and expensive process for obtaining a brothel license in Queensland is beyond the means of most sex workers. So, under the current regulatory regime, it is unlikely that workers will be able to establish their own brothel businesses – and this includes small cooperatives of workers. Also, the regulatory regime established in 1999 has little capacity for addressing industrial issues inside brothels although, as suggested above, there are some significant problems here. One historical legacy of the illegality of the sex industry in Queensland is the absence of any established 'normal' working conditions (as exist for most other occupations in Australia).

This situation is compounded by the lack of sex worker 'voices' in decision making involving brothel regulation. Under the 1999 Act, a Prostitution Advisory Council was established that included a representative of sex workers. However, the Council was formally dissolved by the government in 2003 and many of its functions were transferred to the PLA. The Board of the PLA includes representatives of the police, the responsible

---

50 I am grateful to Chris Diamond and Fiona MacDonald for this point.
51 CMC, op. cit., n. 25, p. 106.
52 id., p. xii.
53 Sex workers regularly report that, like other workers, they want to be treated respectfully and have some control over their work. This could be achieved in an illegal/unlicensed brothel including those controlled by 'organized crime'. A Canadian sex worker activist told the author that one of the best places she had ever worked was in a brothel/massage parlour controlled by a motorbike gang.

minister, lawyers, and public health personnel; since 2003 it has also included two people who represent 'community interests'. However, there is no representation of sex workers. As Queensland has a (now) long-standing Labor government, the lack of any direct consultation with workers in the industry is both surprising and rather disgraceful.

In NSW, the situation of workers in brothels is better in many respects. As suggested above, the regulatory regime in NSW does not involve a licensing process although (like other businesses) brothel premises are subject to local council planning laws. So brothel operators do not have to be licensed, but their premises need council consent if they are to be immune from criminal charges associated with operating a 'disorderly house' of prostitution.[54] While there are some significant problems obtaining council consent (which means brothels are not really treated the same as other businesses),[55] the lack of a licensing requirement has enabled the development of a diverse range of prostitution businesses – including large and small brothels, escort agencies, private work, and so on – particularly in the City of Sydney. So sex workers in NSW may have a wider range of choices in relation to their work than their colleagues in Queensland. Most brothel workers in Sydney are employed as sub-contractors but there are also premises where workers are employees;[56] so there are choices available for workers in this regard. There are also (at least potentially) more possibilities for workers in NSW to develop their own brothel businesses or to work in small, cooperative arrangements with other workers; there are at least no licensing requirements or fees to limit this process. In the City of Sydney council area (which covers only the central part of the city), sex workers have received council consent to work in pairs in residential and mixed residential/commercial zones.[57] However, councils differ in their attitudes to prostitution businesses. Under state planning law, councils cannot prohibit land use for brothels but they can designate zones where brothels are permitted and prohibited. Many councils have moved to restrict brothels to industrial zones which effectively outlaws home-based businesses (including private workers) and many existing small brothels. As Red and Saul argue, the effect of this has been to force sex workers into large brothels.[58] In June 2007 this trend was exacerbated when the NSW government passed legislation which significantly enlarged the ability of local councils to close brothels operating without council consent. It is notable that evidence of the corruption of council

54 The NSW government has recently implemented a raft of new planning laws which have significantly increased the power of local councils over sex businesses: P. Crofts, 'Sex in the Dark: the Brothels Legislations Amendment Act 2007 (NSW)' (2007) 19 *Current Issues in Criminal Justice* 183.
55 Crofts, id.
56 Author interview with Andrew Miles in 2004.
57 Author interview with Andrew Miles in 2005.
58 E. Red and Saul, 'Why sex workers believe "Smaller is Better"' (2003) 6 *Research for Sex Work* 12–14.

97

officers responsible for planning decisions involving sex businesses has also recently appeared.[59]

In both Queensland and NSW brothel workers are also subject to oppressive and discriminatory regimes for health examinations.[60] They are effectively 'forced' (by regulation in the Queensland context, by common management practice in NSW) to undergo regular examinations for STIs. If these tests are not done, the brothel will not permit the sex worker to work. This occurs despite the evidence that Australian sex workers now have a very low incidence of STIs (lower than the general community) regardless of their geographic location or of the regulatory regime under which they work.[61] In Queensland, of course, sex workers in brothels are also required to use a prophylactic during any sexual activity.

So why are brothel workers in both NSW and Queensland subject to such onerous and compulsory health examinations? As suggested above, in Queensland, there is a long and continuous history of forced/compulsory health examinations of sex workers. According to the Crime and Misconduct Commission, this sort of practice in the present day is in the interest of 'ensuring a healthy society'.[62] However, given the state of our current knowledge about the incidence of STIs among sex workers – and the lack of compulsory testing for other workers vulnerable to infections, including doctors and nurses – this is clearly a problematic claim. However, it would seem to be part of the 'common sense' of Queensland political culture that sex workers *need* to be subjected to additional and regular health testing. The laws in this regard are rarely questioned and, indeed, are often used to reassure the Queensland public when amendments to prostitution laws are being proposed and debated. But why does this strategy 'work'? The answer here relates to deep assumptions about the nature of prostitution and about the sort of women (this is not the same for men) who do sex work. Our culture regards sex workers in two main ways – they are either sad victims (for example, of child abuse or of poverty and men's lust) or they are 'bad' women who are wilfully promiscuous and thus a danger both to themselves and the community.[63] These sorts of punitive and misogynist stereotypes tend to compromise the safety of all women working in prostitution and are probably one of the main reasons why the occupation of being a sex worker is so dangerous.[64] It is clear that the introduction of legal prostitution does not automatically wipe out these stereotypes. One way they are presently

---

59 'NSW Govt rules out brothel takeover' *ABC TV News*, 22 August 2007.
60 B. Sullivan, 'Working in the Sex Industry: The Re-organization of Sex Work in Queensland, Australia in the Wake of Law Reform' (2008) 18 *Labour and Industry* 73.
61 C. Harcourt, S. Egger, and B. Donovan, 'Sex Work and the Law' (2005) 2 *Sexual Health* 121.
62 CMC, op. cit., n. 25, p. 58.
63 Sullivan, op. cit., n. 3.
64 Sullivan, op. cit., n. 9.

being re-created, for example, is via the compulsory health testing of sex workers.[65] If the regulatory framework is not sensitive to the presence of such harmful stereotypes, and instead is actively involved in the representation of women sex workers as both vulnerable and pathological, then they will continue to have significant and detrimental effects on the lives of sex workers.

PRIVATE SEX WORKERS

Perkins and Lovejoy have recently published an extensive review of private sex workers in Australia.[66] In the Queensland context, private workers are somewhat freer than workers in licensed brothels. They tend to earn more than brothel workers because they retain the full fee paid by clients; they also have more control over their working hours.[67] Private workers in Queensland are not subject to mandatory health testing although, like brothel workers, they (and their clients) are required by statute to use prophylactics. Research suggests that private workers are more vulnerable to violence because they must work largely on their own if they are to work legally.[68] The advertising of their services is also subject to significant control by the PLA. Scarlet Alliance (the main national body of sex worker organizations) has recently commented on the 'broad scale police harassment and criminal prosecutions of private workers' in Queensland, particularly in relation to advertising.[69] Private workers have been prosecuted for as little as advertisements containing the word 'services' and some have been 'dragged to the police station in their sex work lingerie and charged with a criminal offence'.[70] This sort of action – by the PLA and police acting in concert – is clearly part of a broader campaign to bring private workers more directly under state control. Moreover, it is a campaign facilitated by the reforms put in place in 1999 and development of new forms of cooperation between the PLA and police. As suggested above, the main aim of law reform in Queensland was to eliminate illegal prostitution and, in particular 'organized crime'. In this context, illegal brothels, street-based sex work, and escort agencies have been subject to vigorous criminalization. But private workers are also seen as *potentially illegal* (because they are 'uncontrolled'). They may, for example, be tempted

---

65 For a discussion of how health programmes have led to the mistreatment of sex workers in other parts of the world, see B. Loff, C. Overs, and P. Longo, 'Can health programmes lead to mistreatment of sex workers?' (2003) 361 *Lancet* 1982.

66 R. Perkins and F. Lovejoy, *Call Girls: Private Sex Workers in Australia* (2007).

67 CMC, op. cit., n. 25, p. 83.

68 id., pp. 69–70.

69 Scarlet Alliance (Australian Sex Workers Association) and SSPAN, *Joint Submission to the Prostitution Licensing Authority Regulatory Impact Statement: Changes to the Fee Structure for the Prostitution Regulation 2000* (2006).

70 id.

to work in pairs and small groups (which can then be represented as 'organized crime'). Thus, much current policing has been focused on the entrapment of private workers by police(men) posing as clients and requesting two workers or requesting the provision of sexual services without a condom. Workers who agree to either of these proposals are liable to be arrested. It is notable that many of the cases that have come to court involve just two sex workers working together or a sex worker who engages a second person to monitor their safety. It is also worth remembering that historically, organized crime in Queensland has relied on – and been carried out by – police (see above). So any new regulatory regime – and perhaps especially one that aims to combat organized crime – should probably aim to *increase* the separation between sex workers, sex businesses, and police. The current laws clearly allow for some separation, via the PLA, but a great deal of police involvement in the regulation of prostitution (including private workers) continues, particularly via the monitoring of advertising by the PLA (which cooperates with the police).

STREET-BASED SEX WORKERS

The final group of workers to be addressed in this paper are street-based sex workers. It is widely acknowledged in the literature that these workers are more disadvantaged, more likely to be drug addicted, and more vulnerable to violence than the other groups of sex workers discussed above.[71] In Brisbane at least three street workers have been murdered in recent years. The regulatory regime introduced in 1999 has not addressed this problem in any concrete way, except by further increasing the penalties for public soliciting for the purposes of prostitution and intensifying police activity. New police powers in relation to 'moving on' street workers were introduced in 2006 and have been used against street workers in Brisbane. This sort of strategy is designed to deter all street work and encourage either exit or legal employment in the sex industry (although, clearly, legal employment will not be an option for many of the most vulnerable people involved in street work). The CMC has recently reported that the incidence of street prostitution has been 'significantly impacted' by 'current policing strategies' (which, it is claimed, support workers to leave the industry and target male clients) and by the use of new 'move-on' powers.[72] This police activity against street prostitution is evident in annual crime statistics released by the Queensland police service.[73] It is notable that arrests for public soliciting

---

71 Perkins, op. cit., n. 31; Perkins and Lovejoy, op. cit., n. 66; Harcourt et al., op. cit., n. 61; N. McKeganey and M. Barnard, *Sex Work on the Streets: Prostitutes and their Clients* (1996).
72 CMC, op. cit., n. 25, p. 81.
73 id., p. 79.

doubled between 2001/2 and 2002/3 and are now almost four times higher than before the introduction of the 1999 Prostitution Act.[74] Moreover, it is not likely that all or even most of those prosecuted for public soliciting are male clients or that sex workers feel 'supported' out of the industry by heavy policing tactics. The penalties for public soliciting have substantially increased since 1992. So, for street-based sex workers in Queensland, working conditions have positively declined since the introduction of law reform.

The situation in NSW is different. Public soliciting for the purposes of prostitution was decriminalized in NSW in 1979 and, while the law was amended in 1983 to prohibit soliciting within view of homes, schools, churches, and hospitals, this still leaves areas where soliciting is legal.[75] This reform is probably the main reason why fewer people are prosecuted for prostitution-related offences in NSW than in Queensland.[76] Also, as the NSW regulatory regime includes both a decriminalization of brothels and (some) street-based sex work, new possibilities for *safer* street work have opened; these bear directly on the lives and working conditions of some of the most vulnerable people working in the prostitution industry. For example, street workers can legally solicit for clients and then take them to the local 'safe-house brothel'. Two of these currently operate in East Sydney in areas adjacent to where street-based work is occurring and close to both health services and safe injecting premises. The safe-house brothels are privately owned premises and do not receive any public funding. They operate legally (that is, with council consent) in houses in a mixed residential and commercial precinct. Each safe-house brothel has four to five rooms available for short-term rental by street-based workers. The rental is cheap ($15 per half hour) and clients pay the management directly. The rooms have a bed, fresh linen, a bin, lighting, and a monitored intercom. There is a single entrance to the brothel controlled by the manager. There are also separate staff areas where workers can securely keep their belongings, shower, prepare food, talk to each other, and access notice boards with health and other information; outreach visits are made by a number of local health and welfare organizations. As in other legal brothels in NSW, the owners are required to provide safe-sex equipment to workers. A number of researchers[77] and service providers have confirmed the efficacy of safe-house brothels in terms of increased health and safety for street workers.[78]

---

74 id.
75 See B. Sullivan, 'The women's movement and prostitution politics in Australia' in *The Politics of Prostitution. Women's Movements, Democratic States and the Globalisation of Sex Commerce*, ed. J. Outshoorn (2004) 21.
76 S. Egger and C. Harcourt, 'A comment on John Scott, "Prostitution and public health in New South Wales"' (2004) 6 *Culture, Health & Sexuality* 439.
77 New South Wales Health Department, *The Health and Welfare Needs of Female and Transgender Street-Based Sex Workers in New South Wales* (2000).
78 This claim is based on interviews with health providers conducted by the author in 2006.

The regulatory regime in NSW also makes it more possible for street workers, to protect their civil rights. A recent article by Rachel Wotton is suggestive in this regard.[79] Wotton was an outreach worker with a sex-worker organization in Sydney. She describes a project undertaken with street-based sex workers in a suburban area with 'escalating' problems. The workers complained of police discrimination, contempt for workers, and not responding to complaints of crimes. Workers were being arrested for soliciting although they were not soliciting illegally under NSW law.[80] Wotton says:

> The police were predominantly arresting the women and not the clients. If clients were arrested they were given on the spot fines or a summons to go to a court while the women were taken to the police station and kept there for up to four hours.[81]

The workers were also often given unreasonably stringent bail conditions and many of them pleaded guilty just to get rid of these.

A pro bono lawyer was introduced and workers were encouraged to contest soliciting charges. One worker who stepped up for this had been charged with soliciting 'within view' of a church (even though the religious group had moved away). The sex worker was bailed but taken into custody again the next morning when she was seen having breakfast in the bail condition area. With the solicitor's help, and after four days in jail, the worker was eventually released and the charges were pursued into a higher court. Police then withdrew the charges. No more workers have since been charged with soliciting in this area. In the aftermath of the failed prosecution, workers obtained a commitment that police would 'take a more objective approach to policing of this area' and 'remain courteous and polite to the women just like they would with any other citizen'.[82] Police also agreed to undertake specific training and to produce a pamphlet which all police could use that described the law in this area and mapped the legal working area. Wotton says:

> Discussion has also taken place around the idea of identifying specific locations in this industrial area for workers and their clients to park, in order to do the jobs without causing any disturbance or offence for the surrounding community.[83]

In the United Kingdom there has recently been extensive discussion about the zoning of street prostitution. Van Doorninck and Campbell have made a cogent argument for the establishment of zones where street work is

---

79 R. Wotton, 'The relationship between street-based sex workers and the police in the effectiveness of HIV prevention strategies' (2005) 8 *Research for Sex Work* 11.
80 See, also, K. Edwards, 'Soliciting: What is the Go?' (1999) 24 *Alternative Law J.* 76.
81 Wotton, op. cit., n. 79, p. 12.
82 id., p. 13.
83 id.

tolerated (and workers are not arrested) as part of a multi-layered strategy to improve the safety and rights of street workers.[84] However, the experience of sex workers in NSW suggests law reform should be seen as an essential part of this rights-based strategy.[85]

CONCLUSION

So what can be said *generally* about the nature of prostitution regulation in Australia? In the first place, culture clearly matters as prostitution regulation in Australia has taken a very different path from many other countries. So we have not seen a shift from enforcement (punishment) to multi-agency regulatory responses designed to 'exit' women from prostitution, as has been described in the United Kingdom.[86] There *is* evidence of a shift towards a neo-liberal 'mainstreaming' of the sex industry, as Brents and Sanders describe in the state of Nevada in the United States.[87] However, this is more apparent in some Australian jurisdictions (for example, NSW) than in others (for example, Queensland). While we see some economic 'integration' of the sex industry, particularly in strategies designed to legalize or decriminalize brothels, this is also shot through with a deep and ongoing 'social ambivalence'[88] towards both prostitution and all parties who participate in selling and buying prostitution services. This is particularly evident in the regulatory approach adopted in Queensland where a new statutory authority has overseen the opening of legal brothels and the operation of an extensive licensing and monitoring system; so legal brothels are operated by 'mainstream' business people but are not treated as 'mainstream' businesses. Sex workers are also not treated like 'normal' workers (this is particularly evident in the requirements for health examinations). In NSW, although there is no licensing system and sex businesses have been 'mainstreamed' to a greater degree, there is obvious ambivalence expressed in the attitudes of many local councils which withhold planning consent from sex businesses.[89]

84 M. Van Doorninck and R. Campbell, ' "Zoning" street sex work: the way forward?' in *Sex Work Now*, eds. R. Campbell and M. O'Neill (2006) 62.

85 Ideally, of course, any decriminalization of street-based prostitution should also be combined with a range of harm minimization techniques (for example, safe-house brothels, injecting rooms, police liaison officers, and so on) as well as adequate funding of peer outreach and other services specifically developed for street-based sex workers (for example, sexual assault counselling, drug detoxification and rehabilitation programmes).

86 R. Matthews, 'Policing Prostitution Ten Years On' (2005) 45 *Brit. J. of Criminology* 877. See, also, the critique of this by J. Scoular and M. O'Neill, 'Regulating Prostitution. Social Inclusion, Responsibilization and the Politics of Prostitution Reform' (2007) 47 *Brit. J. of Criminology* 764.

87 See the article by B. Brents and T. Sanders in this volume, pp. 40–60.

88 id.

89 See Crofts, op. cit., n. 54.

103

In general, it can probably be said that prostitution regulation in Australia is very mixed. In the last three decades liberal and neo-liberal approaches have allowed for some opening of the space for legal prostitution. However, this is not primarily an attempt to increase personal or corporate freedom; it is part of a practical strategy (a new rationality of government) designed to control a range of social problems often associated with prostitution – including, most notably in Australia, police corruption, organized crime, and HIV/AIDS.[90] This mode of regulation operates in tandem with other approaches – including new criminal law and policing strategies, the creation of new government bodies responsible for the management of the legal sex industry, local council requirements, health policies, and (of course) moral regulation.[91]

But what does this all mean for sex workers? The above review of changes in the regulatory regimes addressed to prostitution in both Queensland and NSW suggests some advantages accrue to some workers in the wake of prostitution law reform. In Queensland, the range of legal sex work has opened (to include brothels) and this has led to both increases in safety and some new positive rights for legal sex workers. However, as indicated above, there remain significant problems with employment in licensed brothels, and private workers remain vulnerable to violence. Street workers remain extremely vulnerable to violence and to heavy legal penalties. In general then, it cannot be claimed that the new regulatory regime in Queensland has delivered major advantages to workers.

The comparison with NSW suggests that other modes of regulation deliver better outcomes for sex workers. Although significant problems are evident in NSW – particularly in relation to the impact of planning consent on private workers and small brothels – the absence of a licensing regime and the decriminalization of some street-based sex work allows more space for workers to choose between different types of employment. This moderates the power of sex-business operators and allows workers to organize in protection of their safety and rights.

90 See Dean and Hindess, op. cit., n. 5; also, Scoular and O'Neill, op. cit., n. 86.
91 On moral regulation, see R. Weitzer, 'Legalizing Prostitution: Morality Politics in Western Australia' (2009) 49 *Brit. J. of Criminology* 88.

JOURNAL OF LAW AND SOCIETY
VOLUME 37, NUMBER 1, MARCH 2010
ISSN: 0263-323X, pp. 105–24

Labours in Vice or Virtue? Neo-liberalism, Sexual Commerce, and the Case of Indian Bar Dancing

Prabha Kotiswaran*

Of late, the Indian state has adopted an abolitionist stance towards sex work and bar dancing. This article argues that although in the Indian state of Maharashtra, the judicial overturning of the ban against bar dancing has been celebrated by feminists as a triumph of women's right to livelihood over patriarchal demands of women's sexual morality, the judgment is predicated on a sharp distinction between morally 'good' and 'bad' female labour, namely, bar dancing and sex work. This is ironic given their striking sociological similarities and the stigmatization and levels of state abuse inflicted against both. The article considers the usefulness of the totalizing logic of neo-liberalism for explaining the increased judicial and feminist tolerance for bar dancing. The article argues that prospects for redistributive law reform for all sexual workers are dim unless the arbitrary legal distinctions drawn between markets in female sexual labour are overcome.

INTRODUCTION

Feminist scholars have grown increasingly dissatisfied with the state of the sex work debates, confined as it has been to the highly polarized positions between abolitionist radical feminists and sex work advocates. Of late, however, instead of striking the more familiar conciliatory middle ground between the two positions, feminist ethnographers of sex markets have started to outline the rapid changes in the economy of sexual commerce which extends well beyond transactional sex work and without necessarily

* School of Oriental and African Studies, University of London, Thornhaugh Street, Russell Square, London WC1H 0XG, England
pk5@soas.ac.uk

The author wishes to thank Jane Scoular, Teela Sanders, and Srimati Basu for their generous feedback on her article. Many thanks to Arundhati Katju and Chinmayee Chandra for their excellent research assistance.

105

implicating genital contact.[1] This, they argue, is a defining feature of late capitalism in the West, which has had effects on sex and sexuality more generally, including, they claim, the pornographication of culture, more liberal and egalitarian sexual attitudes, an acceptance of fleeting temporary relationships, an increasing commodification of intimacy and the heightened sexualization of work.[2] Moreover, studies of the micro-political economies of sex work reveal the various registers on which such changes have occurred, including the narrowing status differential between sex workers and their customers and the recreational ethic that informs the perceptions of both sex workers and their customers of the sex work transaction itself.[3] Even conventional forms of sex work conducted in brothels have not been spared such transformation. As Brents and Hausbeck demonstrate, legalized brothels in Nevada now use more mainstream business forms to market expanded skilled services and individualized touristic experiences to a broad range of audiences rather than rationalized sex acts.[4]

Feminists have thus documented shifts in the sex industry from modern industrial prostitution to post-industrial sexual commerce which, they argue, find their parallels in larger societal changes in the family form and the political economy.[5] For other feminists, however, an understanding of contemporary sexual commerce is located in an explicitly *cultural* study with a desire to 'leave behind' the conventional terms of the feminist discourse on sex work, as obfuscating and unable to appreciate the nuances of contemporary sex work.[6] While feminists have characterized this very turn to the cultural as constitutive of neo-liberal ideology,[7] I would suggest that a nuanced cultural appreciation of sexual commerce need not preclude feminist considerations of coercion and exploitation. In fact, I would argue that a materialist feminist approach is germane to the consideration of markets for sexual labour such as bar dancing. Moreover, there is every indication that female sexual workers in the Indian context themselves deploy the language of workers' rights. Under these circumstances, a post-colonial materialist feminist approach to female labour becomes not only desirable but politically essential.

1 L. Singer, *Erotic Welfare: Sexual Theory and Politics in the Age of Epidemic*, eds. J. Butler and M. MacGrogan (1993).
2 B.G. Brents and K. Hausbeck, 'Marketing Sex: US Legal Brothels and Late Capitalist Consumption' (2007) 10 *Sexualities* 425–39, at 426; Brents and Sanders in this volume, pp. 40–60.
3 E. Bernstein, *Temporarily Yours: Intimacy, Authenticity, and the Commerce of Sex* (2007).
4 Brents and Hausbeck, op. cit., n. 2, pp. 433, 435.
5 Bernstein, op. cit., n. 3.
6 L. Agustín, 'Introduction to the Cultural Study of Commercial Sex' (2007) 10 *Sexualities* 403–7.
7 R. Hennessy, *Profit and Pleasure: Sexual Identities in Late Capitalism* (2000).

Before it was banned, bar dancing took root in the west Indian state of Maharashtra, particularly its capital, Mumbai. Bar dancing was essentially where bars with a liquor permit and public entertainment license employed, in addition to waitresses, women who danced seductively, but fully clothed, in a group, to Bollywood film music on a stage before male customers who consumed liquor. Most customers, although not all, were middle-aged, married men.[8] A customer would shower the dancer he liked with rupee notes. In elite bars, he would repeatedly attract the attention of his favoured dancer until she gave him her number. As their liaison developed, the dancer would invoke in their friendship all the tropes of being the caring, domesticated wife, *but* with the additional promise of romance. The whole idea in the bar 'line' was to make the customer fall in love with the dancer and make him think she loved him too[9] thus postponing sexual intercourse for as long as possible while extracting gifts for herself and her family in the meantime.[10] Customers meanwhile tried to spend as little as possible before obtaining sexual services, measuring their payments in terms of sexual encounters.[11] A dancer was free to reject a customer she sexually disliked. This routine of seduction and deferred commodification led Mehta, a recent chronicler of life in Mumbai, to observe 'But dance bars are not really about prostitution, they are about courtship'.[12]

Going by the movie *Chandni Bar*,[13] a cinematic portrayal of bar dancers' lives in Mumbai, most exchanges between bar dancers and their customers hardly involved the highly stylized rituals that Mehta details. Instead, bar dancers flirted to increase customer spending at the bar. Many had regular customers, with whom they would limit interactions to dancing.[14] After the bar closed, bar dancers typically took bar-provided transport home rather than meet customers for sex work.[15] Bar owners supported the dancers' decision to refuse sex work with one dancer having reportedly broken a beer bottle over an unruly customer's head.[16] Where customers verbally harassed dancers, male co-workers, the bar owner, and other dancers intervened,

---

8 SNDT Women's University, Research Centre for Women's Studies and Forum Against Oppression of Women, *Backgrounds and working conditions of women working as dancers in dance bars* (2005) 31.

9 S. Mehta, *Maximum City: Bombay Lost and Found* (2004) 253.

10 id., p. 254.

11 id., p. 281.

12 F. Hariyanawala, '"I've seen politicians at dance bars"' *Mid-Day*, 17 April 2005, quoting Suketu Mehta.

13 *Chandni Bar*, directed by Madhur Bhandarkar, 28 September 2001.

14 SNDT, op. cit., n. 8, p. 26.

15 S. Ali, 'Mid Day's secret probe into dance bars' *Mid-Day*, 11 April 2005.

16 D. Bunsha, 'In step with the law' (2006) 23 *Frontline* available at <http://www.hindu.com/fline/fl2309/stories/20060519002404300.htm>.

making dancers feel safe.[17] As a study noted, 'It is this choice and space to negotiate that make the dance bars safer to work than other professions',[18] portraying bar dancing as a haven from sex work where dancers made the best of their objectification and control by men.[19] This hardly meant that bar dancing was not accompanied by sex work. An estimated 15 per cent of bar dancers also engaged in sex work[20] outside the dance bars and without their involvement. Although bar dancing offered the promise of an individualized experience, it was also undoubtedly a space for the collective male consumption of women's sexual performance which bolstered their patriarchal and class privileges. After all, female customers were not really welcome in these spaces.[21] Despite shoring their male privilege though, and in contrast to their portrayal by the ban's supporters as victims of female greed driven to financial ruin, customers in fact often displayed abjection[22] and a loss of social power that could only be recuperated in the market.[23]

Dance bars in Maharashtra are a relatively recent phenomenon with reportedly 24 dance bars in 1985–86 but almost 1,300 bars by 2005,[24] of which only 300 were properly licensed by the state. The industry employed 65–75,000 bar dancers[25] and directly or indirectly involved an additional 700,000 people.[26] A survey of 500 bar dancers revealed that none had been trafficked, only six were non-Indians[27] and that dancers were between 21 and 25 on average.[28] Almost 42 per cent were from communities which traditionally relied on sex work or dancing for sustenance. Some were daughters of mill workers who had lost their jobs with the closure of Mumbai's cotton mills in the 1980s.[29] A majority of them (86 per cent) had no other skills while 73 per cent were single earners,[30] with an average of nine dependents.[31] Even though bar dancers were not paid fixed salaries and

17 SNDT, op. cit., n. 8, p. 26.
18 id.
19 id., p. 31.
20 V. Kale, 'Securing and Safeguarding Rights of Stigmatised Through Social and Legal Action', paper presented at Workshop on Law and Social Movements, 26–27 June 2006, Bangalore, India.
21 'Shall we dance?' Mid-Day, 10 May 2005.
22 Mehta, op. cit., n. 9, p. 271.
23 id., pp. 279–80.
24 SNDT, op. cit., n. 8, p. 6.
25 S. Devasia, 'Bar workers, music sales will also be hit' Mid-Day, 6 April 2005.
26 A. Birai and A. Holia, 'Mr. Patil, this is why we need dance bars' Mid-Day, 14 April 2005.
27 SNDT, op. cit., n. 8, p. 6.
28 id., p. 9.
29 F. Agnes, 'State Control and Sexual Morality – The Case of the Bar Dancers of Mumbai' in Enculturing Law: New Agendas for Legal Pedagogy, eds. M. John and S. Kakarala (2007) 161.
30 SNDT, op. cit., n. 8, p. 12.
31 C.S. Bhattacharya, 'Dressed up with no place to dance – Curtain drops on Mumbai bars but girls still lie in hope' Telegraph, 15 August 2005.

bar owners kept 40 per cent of the gratuities,[32] given dancers' educational and skill levels, bar dancing was highly lucrative. In trendy bars, earnings equalled corporate salaries and a good dancer's daily income was twice that of a performer at a big New York strip club.[33] Some dancers even earned hundreds of thousands of rupees a night, the maximum reported figure being 900,000 rupees.[34] The next section maps the regulatory matrix governing an industry with only a small percentage of licensed dance bars.

REGULATING BAR DANCING

Dance bars were regulated by an elaborate labyrinth of licensing regimes relating to food, liquor, and public entertainment. Bar dancing, being a live performance, was also governed by the Dramatic Performances Act 1876, the public nuisance provisions of the Bombay Police Act 1951 (BPA), and Section 294 of the Indian Penal Code 1860 relating to obscenity.[35] In addition to substantial license and excise fee payments, dance bars paid the local police protection money on a regular basis.[36] Such rent-seeking practices meant that the police enforced the terms of licenses or invoked Section 294 or the BPA to raid dance bars when these payments were not made on time.[37] Bar dancers became a pawn in the struggle between the state and bar owners, the police being their biggest fear,[38] against whom they found support amongst co-workers, owners, and transporters. Meanwhile, bar owners challenged the state's prosecutorial efforts rendering Section 294 a heavily litigated provision under which courts held[39] that these performances were not obscene in themselves and that actual annoyance had to be caused to 'others' and not to male customers of sexual entertainment.

In 1998, this enforcement equilibrium was disturbed when the state increased the excise fee threefold overnight and raided a large number of

---

32 'Show must go on, so saris drape skirts in Mumbai bars' *Sunday Express*, 21 July 2002; 'Bombay's barmaids stage protest' *BBC News World Edition*, 20 August 2004.

33 Mehta, op. cit., n. 9, p. 248.

34 id.

35 Section 294 punishes anyone who performs any obscene act in any public place, or sings, recites or utters any obscene song, ballad or words, in or near any public place, with imprisonment for up to three months, or a fine, or both.

36 K.P. Babu, 'Cops protection for bars' *Mid-Day*, 9 April 2005; Agnes, op. cit., n. 29, p. 162; 'Dance bars, police raids and obscenity laws' *Asian Age*, 17 May 2005.

37 Agnes, id.

38 F. Agnes, 'Bar dancers and the issue of livelihood' *Asian Age*, 14 June 2005; 'Bar girls protest police harassment', *Deccan Herald*, 21 August 2004.

39 *State of Maharashtra* v. *Joyce Zee alias Temiko* (1973) ILR 1299 (Bom).; unreported judgment delivered by Justice Rege on 3 September 1984 in Criminal Application No. 782 of 1984; *Sadhna* v. *State* 1980 Cri L.T. 380 (Del); *Narendra H. Khurana* v. *Commissioner of Police* MANU/MH/0911/2003.

bars. As the tension between bar owners and the police mounted,[40] a newly formed bar owners' association[41] filed a writ petition in 2004 in the Mumbai High Court seeking protection from police harassment.[42] Yet, in the midst of this familiar judicial drama, something was different, for the deputy Chief Minister R.R. Patil declared it his personal mission to eradicate bar dancing. Although proposals were initially aimed at curbing the negative externalities of bar dancing by de-eroticizing bar dancing and micro-managing the physical space of the bars,[43] the provincial government ultimately banned bar dancing in March 2005. It cited the threat that most bar dancers, apparently foreign migrants, posed to state security,[44] the depravation of local youth,[45] the high levels of criminality in bar dancing,[46] and the public disorder and nuisance in neighbourhoods housing dance bars. Gender-based concerns that bar dancing offended the dignity of women and exploited them also emerged. Interestingly, the deputy Chief Minister and the Maharashtra State Women's Commission[47] repeatedly conflated bar dancing with sex work so that trafficking for sex work provided yet another justification for the ban. The ban took the form of an amendment to the Bombay Police Act 1951, with any violation being punishable by fine and imprisonment. However, conventional entertainment in drama theatres, the cinema, auditoriums, and sports clubs were exempt. Similarly, in the interests of art and tourism, dance performances were permitted in hotels with three stars or above, on the premise that both the management and patrons of these establishments were more sophisticated and would adequately police levels of obscenity.

Overnight, 75,000 bar dancers were jobless. The impact of the ban was dramatic yet predictable. The financial impact was the most palpable as many women who stayed on in the bars did waitressing or participated in the bar's orchestra, or stood in the bar while the music played.[48] They all had their incomes reduced to a fraction of what it was prior to the ban,[49] resulting in the sale of property, indebtedness, and reduced spending on nutrition, housing,[50] healthcare, and children's education. Interestingly, prices for sex work transactions fell to a third of what they used to be, presumably due to

40 Y. Naik, 'Mumbai dance bar ban this week: R R Patil' *Mid-Day*, 13 April 2005.
41 Agnes, op. cit., n. 29, p. 162.
42 id., p. 163.
43 'Bar raised for bar dancers' *Kolkata Times of India*, 29 July 2004, 10; A. Soondas, 'No cash & carry in Mumbai bars" *Telegraph*, 29 July 2004, 1 and 6.
44 Devasia, op. cit., n. 25.
45 'Maharashtra dance bars face the music' *Indian Express*, 31 March 2005.
46 '69% say YES to dance bars ...' *Mid-Day*, 16 April 2005.
47 D. Lokhande, 'Bar girls may get uniforms' *Mid-Day*, 22 May 2005.
48 SNDT Women's University, Research Centre for Women's Studies and Forum Against Oppression of Women, *After the Ban: Women Working in Dance Bars* (2006) 10.
49 id., p. 11.
50 id., p. 14.

an increase in the numbers of women selling sex.[51] There was an overnight change in the levels of abuse from both customers and the police.[52] Customers openly propositioned female employees in bars for sex; sexual harassment became more aggressive. Police harassment escalated as they demanded money, mocked women, and raided bars more frequently. The illegality of dancing thus immediately expanded the state's tolerated residuum of abuse, a term used by Duncan Kennedy to describe a situation where the legal system tolerates a certain level of abuse which is attributable to contestable social decisions about what abuse is and how important it is to prevent it, which in turn affects practices of abuse and social practices of both men and women, irrespective of whether they themselves are abusers, victims or bystanders.[53] As this tolerated residuum expanded, bar dancers recoded its effects in terms of a loss of dignity: 'First we used to have *izzat* (self-respect), now we have none.'[54]

Within three days of the announcement of the ban, bar owners, joined by bar dancers and several NGOs, feminist and otherwise, challenged the constitutionality of the ban. In April 2006, the Mumbai High Court overturned the ban, holding it unconstitutional for violating Article 14 or the equality clause of the Indian Constitution and for placing unreasonable restrictions on the fundamental right to practice a profession or carry on any occupation, trade or business under Article 19(1)(g). The government promptly appealed the decision and the case is currently pending before the Indian Supreme Court. Although the palliative effect of the High Court judgment for bar dancers remained merely symbolic, it was commendable in many respects. Unconvinced by the state's classification of dancing establishments according to their economic status, the High Court found no relationship between the classification and the law's purpose. If indecent dancing was the problem, the court reasoned, how could decent dancing be permitted in exempt locations but not the banned bars? Similarly, if women's exploitation was the target of the law, how could women be allowed to work in bars as waitresses and singers (*Indian Hotel & Restaurants Association* v. *State of Maharashtra* 2006, 136[55] hereafter IHRA) when they remained subject to exploitation?

The part of the Mumbai High Court judgment with the progressive 'charge' upheld bar dancers' right to livelihood as part of their right to carry on any occupation or trade. Fundamental for the court in considering the constitutional jurisprudence under Article 19, however, was the fact that dancing was not inherently pernicious and was therefore *res commercium*,

---

51 id., p. 20.
52 id., p. 13.
53 D. Kennedy, *Sexy Dressing Etc.: Essays on the Power and Politics of Cultural Identity* (1993) 137.
54 SNDT, op. cit., n. 48, pp. 23–4.
55 On file with author, also available at (2006) 3 *Bombay Cases Reporter* 705.

111

unlike sex work which being immoral, was *res extra commercium* (outside commerce). Dancing, the court noted, had an illustrious past since ancient Indian times, including in Maharashtra (IHRA, 191), so that, if bar dancing was harmful, then, Bollywood dancing would have to be banned. The question then was whether the restriction on bar dancing could amount to prohibition and if it was reasonable and in the interests of the general public. Here, the court held that the state had not discharged its burden of proving that the restrictions under the amendment met constitutional standards. The state's claims as to the immoral nature of dancing and any associated prostitution were negated by its poor enforcement of criminal law (IHRA, 196). Moreover, the state already possessed an adequate legal framework to target the negative externalities from bar dancing. The state had not used these appropriately, but had in fact, supported bar dancing for the past two decades, even issuing additional licenses and extending bar timings. Similarly, the court demonstrating a keen awareness of the gender bias operative in the state's ban was not convinced that bar dancing was against the public interest holding that women could not be effectively penalized for men's insatiable sexual needs (IHRA, 219) or the public consequences of liquor consumption (IHRA, 223). It reminded the state that many of the bar dancers were widowed, deserted or divorced and tried to earn a decent living for themselves and their families. That some may be exploited could not prevent others from pursuing a livelihood of their choice although they may have involuntarily resorted to it at times. The court also exposed the falseness of the dilemma posed by the state's ban that bar dancers stay poor rather than engage in an apparently unpalatable line of work. To quote from the judgment:

> Can a girl who may be semi-literate or even illiterate who may be beautiful, knows to dance or tried to dance [be] prohibited from earning a better livelihood or should such a girl, because of poverty and want of literacy be condemned to a life of only doing menial jobs? ... Inability of the state to provide employment or to take care of those women who had to take to the profession of dancing on account of being widowed, or failed marriages or poverty at home and/or the like cannot result in holding that their working for a livelihood by itself constitutes a threat to public order. There is no sufficient data to show that the women were forced into that profession and had no choice to leave it. (IHRA, 222–223).

The court also responded to the state's belated argument that women were trafficked into bar dancing by pointing out that dancers were not unique since waitresses, singers, and women in other jobs were trafficked (IHRA, 235–6). Nor was trafficking a part of the amendment's statement of reasons and objects but had only arisen during court arguments.

It was on these varied grounds that the court struck down the ban as violative of Article 19(1)(g). In a sense, the triumphant response of bar dancer organizers to the High Court judgment is understandable given its remarkable appreciation of the predicaments of working-class women and

112

for exposing the hypocrisy of the state's efforts to pose as the protector of societal morality. As Varsha Kale, the president of the Bharatiya Bar Girls' Union claimed, dancers were particularly appreciative of what she called the 'brakes' that the judgment placed on the deteriorating condition of bar girls who were subject to increased abuse from the police, criminals, and customers.[56]

A TALE OF TWO MARKETS IN REPRODUCTIVE LABOUR

As I have suggested, the Mumbai High Court judgment offered feminists much cause for celebration. It reined in the provincial government's hypocritical attempt to make bar dancers shoulder the burdens of protecting male morality against the backdrop of their systemic discrimination in the labour market, while itself failing to provide them with a viable livelihood. Further, the judgment had exposed the blatant effort of the provincial government to preserve elitist male spaces of sexual consumption in the name of high art over obscene, popular culture in the beer bars. Despite this apparent dismantling of gender and class hierarchies, however, the court's reasoning was fundamentally based on the notion that dancing was in and of itself a permissible activity, this being premised on the formal distinction between activities which were *res extra commercium* and *res commercium*. In this sense, the court, despite its proclivities towards a substantive analysis of women's livelihood options and the class inequalities this presumed, was essentially operating within a liberal legal framework so that the court ticked the boxes of constitutional law requirements rather than challenge more fundamentally the sharp distinctions drawn between sex work and bar dancing. Admittedly, it was not within the court's remit to address the constitutional status of sex work, but then, neither did it need to rule that sex work was *res extra commercium*. Although this article is less concerned with the implications of the court's judgment for sex work than for bar dancing, as I will demonstrate, whether consciously or not, sex work has been the fundamental point of reference for the provincial government, the High Court, and for feminists alike in configuring both the legal and normative status of bar dancing. In this context, the liberal legal rhetoric of the Mumbai High Court has significant implications for female markets in reproductive labour more generally. Significantly, however, one might query why even anti-ban feminists adopted a similar posture, leading them to treat in radically different ways two markets in female reproductive labour with such striking similarities. In this sense, the feminist characterization of the central question in the bar dancing debates as one of women's morality versus women's livelihood[57] is problematic, for not all labouring women were

56 Kale, op. cit., n. 20, p. 5.
57 Agnes, op. cit., n. 29, p. 170.

113

treated the same and the diktats of morality split the community of female sexual workers. Further, since the distancing of bar dancing from sex work was achieved only through the normalization of bar dancing itself, little attention was paid to the redistributive aspects of the relationship between bar owners and bar dancers, and between bar dancers themselves. Meanwhile, by affirming dancing as part of Indian culture, the status of the nation-state was consolidated while congealing the complex appropriation, historically speaking, by the patriarchal state of female sexual labour.[58]

As I have mentioned, sex work was the spectre that haunted the bar dancing issue. Consider the following structural similarities between bar dancing and sex work. Bar dancers, like sex workers, had entered dancing through other low-paying jobs traditionally held by women, to which they were likely to return after the ban. For relatively young girls from dancing communities like the *bedias*, the defloration ritual or *nath utarna* was the same prior to entry into bar dancing and sex work. Natal and marital families played a significant role in women's entry into bar dancing as in sex work. In *Chandni Bar*, the protagonist, when raped by her maternal uncle, is comforted by her friends at the bar who speak of parents, husbands, and lovers that compelled them to enter bar dancing and even transactional sex work. As the movie once again illustrates, bar dancers formed each other's support system that ultimately saw them through breakdowns in relationships with men and their own families. Bar dancers experienced similar levels of social stigma as sex workers so that respectable marriage was an unlikely exit option.[59] They often kept their work a secret from their family. Yet, like sex workers, they internalized the stigma attributed to their ill-earned money, hence their claim that the money from dancing never stayed with them.[60]

Bar dancers lived in the same urban residential spaces as sex workers, such as Foras Road or Congress House in Mumbai on the borders of Kamathipura, Mumbai's red light area; living in groups provided safety. Dancers, like sex workers, were aware that no girl their age made as much money as they did.[61] They viewed themselves as independent, without the desire to marry, earning an income with *izzat* or self-respect. Even where some dancers aspired to marriage, its fragility was always high on their minds, as with sex workers. Affective relationships were viewed as a threat to one's career in bar dancing, as in sex work.[62] At the same time that bar

---

58 S. Rege, 'The hegemonic appropriation of sexuality: The case of the *lavani* performers of Maharashtra' in *Social Reform, Sexuality and the State*, ed. P. Uberoi (1996).
59 Mehta, op. cit., n. 9, p. 255.
60 id., p. 270.
61 id., p. 256.
62 P. Kotiswaran, *Dangerous Sex, Invisible Labor and Other Stories of the Lumpen Proletariat: Rethinking the Regulation of Sex Work* (2011, forthcoming).

114

dancers viewed their work as lacking respect, they reclaimed some agency and dignity by asserting that they were in dancing out of need, not by force[63] and therefore not doing anything wrong.

Given these striking similarities in the abject labour performed by sex workers and bar dancers, it is no surprise that sex work became a central reference point in the controversy around the ban. The provincial government and many NGOs saw no difference between bar dancing and sex work in their threat to the patriarchal family. For the Deputy Chief Minister, R.R. Patil, bar dancers were whores in costumes, and Mumbai a city at risk of turning into a whorehouse.[64] The Maharashtra State Women's Commission meanwhile concluded that non-rehabilitated bar dancers would unconsciously slip into sex work.[65] NGOs like Prerna with an abolitionist stance towards sex work extended their analysis to support the ban.[66] The Dance Bar Virodhi Manch, a conglomerate of 24 NGOs, argued that bar dancing was merely a symptom of the basic disease of the trafficking of women and minor girls,[67] a position which found expression in the litigation. Even the provincial government belatedly sought to capitalize on the panic around human trafficking by raising the prospect of trafficked bar dancers and citing the influential American abolitionist organization, the Coalition against the Trafficking of Women. Despite the state's apparently feminist tone, its feminist pulse can only be discerned from the newspaper advertisements placed by the State Women's Commission prior to the passage of the ban that openly sided with the wives and children suffering abuse from alcoholic husbands and fathers,[68] rather than bar dancers earning 20,000 rupees a month. Sensing the dissonance in the state's concern with both women's morality and their sexual victimhood,[69] feminists openly accused it of using women's exploitation rhetorically without sharing the concerns of the women's movement, when bar dancing promoted women's livelihood and autonomy.

Meanwhile, anti-ban feminists had a complicated response to the ban. They, along with bar dancers, insisted that bar dancing was *anything but* sex work. Varsha Kale, claiming that no prostitution took place in bars, opined that what dancers did after hours was consensual adult business. Thus, bar dancing was a distinct activity,[70] which did not spur trafficking for sex work. Finally, if the ban proceeded, feminists argued that bar dancers would have

---

63 Mehta, op. cit., n. 9, p. 317.
64 A. Thakraney, 'Spoilsport or Mr. Clean?' *Mid-Day*, 17 April 2005.
65 Lokhande, op. cit., n. 47.
66 Agnes, op. cit., n. 29, p. 164.
67 SNDT, op. cit., n. 8, p. 1.
68 F. Agnes, 'Fundamental freedom and bar dancers' *Asian Age*, 4 October 2005.
69 SNDT, op. cit., n. 8, p. 30.
70 'Out of Tune', interview with Varsha Kale, president of the Bharatiya Bar Girls' Union conducted by J. Punwani, *Times of India, Bangalore*, 29 April 2005.

no choice but to enter that most abhorrent line of work, namely, sex work, an assertion that bar dancers agreed with.[71] These claims all visualized the street walker engaged in survival sex to feed her starving children when in fact the sex industry is as diverse and financially lucrative as bar dancing in its heyday. The on/off status of bar dancing viewed through the lens of prostitution persisted well into the bar dancing litigation, affecting the judiciary so that the fate of bar dancers essentially turned on whether bar dancing was sex work or not.

The initial constructions of bar dancing I have outlined were hardly static. As the ban escalated harassment against bar dancers, more actors joined the fray, and feminists were cornered into the problematic position of repeatedly insisting that bar dancers were anything but sex workers instead of challenging the more fundamental divide between moral and immoral women. Consider for instance, the post-ban actions of the Shiv Sena, the regional right-wing political party traditionally at the forefront of moral policing in the state. Despite its belated entry into the bar-dancing debate, the party's local female cadres with residents' associations forced the illegal evictions of bar dancers from certain North Mumbai neighbourhoods. Too terrified to resist, bar dancers had to leave without even collecting their rental deposits.[72] Condemning the evictions, anti-ban feminists like Kale and Agnes invoked the figure of the sex worker in a highly problematic way. Kale noted that 'as a practice, we never sided with prostitutes or bar girls who turned towards prostitution' while agreeing that the police were rightly fighting against immigrants and those involved in prostitution.[73] Agnes, meanwhile, indignantly noted that 'It is unjust. Commercial sex workers are allowed to live in peace as compared to the bar girls.'[74] Ironically, the Shiv Sena's pretext for evictions was that bar-dancer tenants were engaged in sex work. Not all anti-ban feminists however drew a bright line between bar dancers and sex workers, with the Forum Against the Oppression of Women upholding a woman's right to engage in sex work.[75] Ultimately, however, the inability to contest the predominant mode of argumentation and articulate bar dancers' own interests for the post-litigation phase meant that, despite the High Court victory, bar dancers continued to be harassed for doing sex work.

Attempts by the judiciary and feminists alike to delimit bar dancing from sex work went hand in hand with a logic of normalization. Bar dancing was, however, normalized not only in terms of the legitimate male need for *entertainment* satisfied in the past by indigenous traditions of female dancing

---

71 N.A. Bhuse, 'State may see huge boom in sex bars' *Mid-Day*, 13 June 2005.
72 'Bar girls: Women a target again?' *Cybernoon*, official website of *Afternoon Despatch & Courier*, 7 June 2007.
73 id.
74 id.
75 SNDT, op. cit., n. 8, p. 35.

but also in terms of women's *livelihood*. This normalizing discourse of bar dancing as livelihood came from many quarters, including the English media,[76] progressive Bollywood models and celebrities and movies like *Chandni Bar* which endorsed the region's dancing tradition as entertainment for different classes of men.[77] Other opinion makers recognized that where the corporate and media sectors thrived on the peddling of women's sexualized images, the ban amounted to hypocrisy by the city's elites. All this tied into Mumbai's image as a modern city with a liberal, cosmopolitan ethos that dissolved traditional hierarchies of Indian society like caste, religion, and linguistic differences. Consequently, the ban's proponents were portrayed as unsophisticated conservatives from the provincial hinterland.[78] Notably, the deputy Chief Minister was from Sangli, a rural albeit, prosperous district in Maharashtra.

Over the course of the litigation itself, the bar owners' association carefully constructed an image of bar dancers as employees with workplace protections and bar owners as paternal figures who provided them with a gender-segregated workplace and nightly conveyance for their safety thus ensuring bar dancers' modesty. Bar owners claimed that there was no physical contact between dancers and customers and that their clothing and dancing were modest, thus presenting bar dancing as dignified entertainment for the 'common man' unlike the discotheques where wealthy 'boys' and 'girls' wearing skimpy clothes engaged in drug and alcohol use and other immoral activities. This was meant to directly counter the state's attempt to exempt elite hotels from the ban.

As for feminists like Agnes, barely a decade ago they opposed women's beauty contests;[79] the Miss World beauty contest organized in Bangalore was criticized, for instance, for its objectification of women's bodies perceived to be a symptom of globalization.[80] Now, however, they viewed the objectification inherent in the highly sexualized atmosphere of the dance bar more pragmatically, to justify it as a means of livelihood for bar dancers and their dependent family members. Unlike beauty contests, where the invisible hand of global capital triggered opposition, in the case of bar dancing, the 'foreign hand', as feminists discerned it, lay in United States sanctions under the Victims of Trafficking and Violence Protection Act of 2000 against governments which took inadequate steps to tackle sex trafficking. Significantly, this deflection of the role of capital in women's objectification and commodification may be attributed to the fact that the predominant form of capital involved in bar dancing was domestic capital.

---

76 *Mid-Day*, op. cit., n. 46.
77 A. Mande, 'Men come here for recreation, not sex' *Mid-Day*, 14 April 2005.
78 Punwani, op. cit., n. 70.
79 Agnes, op. cit., n. 29, p. 164.
80 R. Oza, 'Showcasing India: Gender, Geography, and Globalization' (2001) 26 *Signs* 1067–95.

Just as the nation's cultural traditions of dance were affirmed by feminist and judicial discourse alike, the nation's entrepreneurs were less the focus of critical attention than global capital might have been. Consequently, instead of abolition, feminists called for the increased regularization of the working conditions of bar dancers with minimum remuneration and protections against sexual harassment by customers, unfair practices by employers, and abuse by the police.[81] This is true even of radical feminist organizations like the Bangalore-based Vimochana which has been vocally opposed to sex work but supports better working conditions for bar dancers.

Admittedly, normalizing bar dancing despite its inequalities may have been a strategic feminist move to delineate bar dancing from sex work so that ultimately, 'the emphasis had to be for a right to livelihood only through dancing and not beyond'.[82] Except that anti-ban feminists did go further to portray Mumbai as a recipient of male migrants for at least three hundred years who in turn needed entertainment[83] provided by women. Feminists invoked past Indian dancing traditions so that bar dancing simply became its modern manifestation. Except that now with globalization, they argued, the state's rulers wanted a 'new gleaming metropolis run by corporate capital – free of "slums" and "sleaze".'[84] Asserting poor men's rights to sexual entertainment necessitated the reclamation of their spaces of entertainment, namely, dance bars. In other words, male migrants' sexual needs were valorized as a response to the steadily ascendant neo-liberal logic seeking to reconfigure urban spaces in Mumbai but whose 'violence was hidden under the rhetoric of morality and progress'.[85] Thus, where in the context of sex work abolitionist feminists have been keen to interrogate male sexual need, in the case of bar dancing, feminists naturalized the male need for sexual entertainment. Any feminist contemplation of bar dancing as sexually exploitative for women[86] seemed marginal, although bar dancing is particularly open to running the radical feminist script of female sexual subordination involving the commodification of women's bodies with dancers themselves internalizing the eroticization of male domination.

NEO-LIBERALISM AND BAR DANCING: A THESIS REVISITED

In conclusion, could we theorize bar dancing as a relatively recent form of female sexual labour that has emerged under the shadow of neo-liberalism

81 SNDT, op. cit., n. 8, p. 36.
82 Agnes, op. cit., n. 29, p. 174.
83 SNDT, op. cit., n. 8, p. 5.
84 F. Agnes, 'Mumbai's bar girls and the question of morality' *Asian Age*, 14 April 2007.
85 id.
86 N. Rajan, 'Dance Bar Girls and the Feminist's Dilemma' *Economic & Political Weekly*, 10 February 2007, 471–4, at 472.

and shaped by it? After all, much contemporary feminist scholarship on sex work does precisely this. Irrespective of their ideological position in the sex work debates, both radical feminists[87] and sex-work feminists have increasingly highlighted the post-industrial transformation of Western sex markets. Indeed, the phenomenon of bar dancing exhibits some tell-tale signs of such a shift. For one, bar dancing took off in Mumbai in the 1980s when the city's cotton mills shut down and its economy starting de-industrializing, although it is arguable whether the city's economy was ever properly industrial to begin with.[88] At least some of the local dancers were daughters of mill workers rendered unemployed in the process. Customers flocking to these bars included poor, local, and migrant men, but also 'respectable' middle-class and wealthier men, including, politicians, industrialists, stockbrokers, diamond merchants, and bankers. Bearing testimony to the rising status of Mumbai as the nation's financial nerve-centre and its links with global capital, bar dancers lamented how their fortunes were linked to the stock market. For dancers, stock market losses translated into bolder demands from customers for sex upfront rather than a willingness to engage in the more elegant game of 'courtship'. Although fine-grained ethnographic studies of the sexual labour involved in bar dancing are necessary, such courtship even resembles Elizabeth Bernstein's useful concept of 'bounded authenticity' in the context of San Francisco's sex industry.

Moreover, the state's response although driven by a conservative sexual ethic, appeared neo-liberal in that it drew clear class-based distinctions between the so-called seedier bars, assumed to be a hub for prostitution while exempting wealthier locales for male consumption of women's sexual labour. As for the progressive judiciary and anti-ban feminists, they conveniently upheld the right to a livelihood within a liberal framework of rights by swiftly distinguishing it from sex work while eliding redistributive questions within the bar-dancing industry itself. Meanwhile, where feminists in an earlier decade were opposed to globalization and its commodification of women, they mobilized the very objectification of women in bar dancing as resistance to the state's neo-liberal attempts at ridding the city of nuisance and migrant 'others', when the labour of male migrants had been integral to the city's growth. Thus, viewing bar dancing as a form of female sexual labour shaped by neo-liberalism has some resonance, but for the two reasons that I will briefly allude to, I argue that it may not be the most useful framework to employ in a post-colonial setting like India.

The first of these reasons pertains to feminist claims as to the 'newness' of sexual commerce under post-industrialism. However, this assumes stages of

---

87 See, for example, S. Jeffreys, *The Industrial Vagina: The Political Economy of the Global Sex Trade* (2009).
88 S.K. Bhowmik, 'Making of a City' (reviewing A. Farooqui, *Opium City: Making of Early Victorian Bombay*) *Economic & Political Weekly*, 12 August 2006, 3506–7, at 3506.

development that the economy and family are thought to pass through, against the backdrop of which transformations in sexual commerce are charted. Some feminists have gone so far as to explicitly peg these aspects of national development to markets for sex work, characterizing south Asian markets as feudal and those of south-east Asia as modern-industrial.[89] The bane of post-colonial scholars for decades now has been to problematize such transition narratives of development. Elsewhere, I have problematized such assumptions of Western feminists in relation to the Indian sex industry.[90] Suffice it to say that received notions of the ideological coherence of neo-liberalism, its ability to generate real-world effects, and the causal relationship between the two all need to be queried in post-colonial contexts. This is already reflected in the varied senses in which the term neo-liberalism is used by Indian academics. Neo-liberalism is often used simply as a marker for the early 1990s when processes of market reform, including privatization and financialization, were initiated. At other times, neo-liberalism is deployed in a more 'productive' sense as responsible for transforming urban spaces of public consumption[91] or for the technologies of self-governance shaping precarious employment in the services sector.[92] Scholars have even argued that the space of non-corporate capital of which the bar dancing industry, run by entrepreneurial owner operators, would be an example, is subsumed within the logic of neo-liberalism.[93] This is because the neo-liberal logic of global capital is accompanied by the state's efforts to ensure hegemony by providing developmental and welfare services to those in the space of non-corporate capital (for example, peasants) for whom global capital has no use. Yet in other spheres, the valence of the shifts wrought by neo-liberalism is muted, as with the withdrawal of welfare-state safety nets, which are largely non-existent in the Indian context to begin with.

Specifically for south Asian sex markets, claims as to the newness, proliferation, visibility, and normalization of sexual commerce or of a shift from modern industrial prostitution may be premature. By this, I do not deny the major socio-economic transformations these markets have undergone, particularly, as a result of colonial rule where communities of dancing women found themselves transformed into proletarianized sex workers and, indeed, bar dancers.[94] Nor can one ignore how traditional courtesans have

---

89 K. Barry, *The Prostitution of Sexuality: The Global Exploitation of Women* (1995).
90 Kotiswaran, op. cit., n. 62.
91 S. Banerjee-Guha, 'Neoliberalising the "Urban": New Geographies of Power and Injustice in Indian Cities' *Economic & Political Weekly*, 30 May 2009, 95–107.
92 N. Gooptu, 'Neoliberal Subjectivity, Enterprise Culture and New Workplaces: Organised Retail and Shopping Malls in India' *Economic & Political Weekly*, 30 May 2009, 45–54.
93 K. Sanyal, *Rethinking Capitalist Development: Primitive Accumulation, Governmentality and Post-Colonial Capitalism* (2007).
94 J. Nair, 'From Devadasi Reform to SITA: Reforming Sex Work in Mysore State, 1892–1937' (1993) 1 *National Law School J.* 82–94; Rege, op. cit., n. 58.

once again refashioned their livelihood to partake of the transnational sexual economy and its diverse customer bases by using technology and cultivating a malleable cultural identity that projects both the fantasy of the modest, traditional courtesan and the savvy, cosmopolitan sexual agent.[95] Still, the extant sociology of sex work in India has promoted the stereotype of south Asian sex markets as predominantly involving brothel-based sex work with trafficked, enslaved sex workers.[96] In fact, brothel-based sex work accounts for only between 5[97] and 9 per cent[98] of the country's sex industry, which is otherwise widely dispersed and mobile,[99] particularly, in southern India where red-light areas are rare.

The second difficulty with using the lens of neo-liberalism to understand bar dancing is that it assumes a coherent national logic whereas in fact, as I will demonstrate, the state's logic varies considerably based on the issue at hand, the discursive frames shaping it, the scale at which the debate is taking place, and the modes of resistance deployed by women themselves. In other words, neo-liberalism has no a priori effect on how sexual labour comes to be regulated, for this is dependent on a disparate set of factors that operate to produce varied strands of national and provincial logics, often at odds with each other. I will briefly compare bar dancing and sex work to highlight my point. Sexual workers experience both forms of labour as abject and stigmatized with no money or respect.[100] Despite the ostensibly different regulatory spheres they occupy – the licensing regime in the case of bar dancing and criminal law in the case of sex work – bar dancers, and sex workers alike bear the brunt of police abuse due to this stigma. Not surprisingly then, both have been subject to the abolitionist legal agendas of the Indian state. Yet, in the case of bar dancing, abolitionism has been fuelled explicitly by a morally conservative agenda at the regional level, while with sex work, it has arisen from a more complicated matrix of factors, especially international abolitionism which has in turn been countered by

95 L. Brown, 'Performance, Status and Hybridity in a Pakistani Red-Light District: The Cultural Production of the Courtesan' (2007) 10 *Sexualities* 409–23.

96 *The Selling of Innocents*, produced by S. Jacobovici, E. Halpern, and W. Cobban, directed by R. Gupta, 25 November 1996; 'Slavery in Our Time' *New York Times*, 22 January 2006, s. 4; *Born into Brothels*, produced and directed by Z. Briski and R. Kauffman, 8 December 2004.

97 J. Sengupta and J. Sinha, 'Battling AIDS in India' (2004) 3 *McKinsey Q.*, available at <http://www.mckinseyquarterly.com/Battling_AIDS_in_India_1430>.

98 National AIDS Control Organisation, 'Targeted Interventions for Core High Risk Groups Under NACP III' (2007), available at: <http://www.nacoonline.org/upload/Publication/NGOs%20and%20targetted%20Intervations/NACP-III.pdf>.

99 S. Shah, 'Producing the Spectacle of Kamathipura: The Politics of Red Light Visibility in Mumbai' (2006) 18 *Cultural Dynamics* 269–92; Kotiswaran, op. cit., n. 62.

100 Ali, op. cit., n. 15.

HIV prevention efforts.[101] Correspondingly, note the remarkable difference in the images of sexual workers fostered by these abolitionist attempts, which are, in turn, determined by the existing feminist activist discourse on both issues. With sex work, an influential radical feminist position meant that the image of the sex worker oscillated between the enslaved victim and the sexual agent forced to do sex work under extraordinary constraints. Either way, she was free from all moral approbation as the male customer was held responsible through the criminalization of demand. With bar dancing, however, the dancer very much occupied the deviant position of an active, greedy sexual provocateur signified in the popular use of the term 'bar girl' and the pro-ban lobby's posing of the following query of Mumbaikars: 'Sweety and Savithri[102] – who will you choose?'[103]

The mobilizational patterns of bar dancers and sex workers also played some role in producing mixed legislative outcomes. Bar dancers operated within the realm of civil society by resorting to the courts, whereas sex workers have worked through the contingent spaces of political society carved out by groups whose lives are implicated in illegality.[104] Despite the existence of dance bars since the 1960s, bar dancers mobilized only in the late 1990s by protesting against poor pay and working conditions and their treatment as pawns during police raids. Leading up to the ban, the 5,000-member strong Bharatiya Bar Girls' Union formed in August 2004 and headed by a middle-class women's activist,[105] took up these issues. Generally speaking, however, the associational life of bar dancers was sparse and, consequently, organizational claims to representation weak, when compared to bar owners, who had as repeat players routinely litigated against the state under pre-ban laws, and anticipating the ban, had mobilized dancers for a similar challenge. In the event of a ban, then, with no political capital and some unstable support from feminists, litigation alongside bar owners became inevitable for bar dancers. This is not to suggest that their alliance was seamless, for the bar dancers' union restricted itself in pre-ban litigation to the conduct of police raids and in the post-ban phase to the lack of rehabilitation. Eventually, despite the successful outcome, litigation was not sufficient to quell the public backlash against bar dancers.

Meanwhile, sex workers in Kolkata mobilized in the early 1990s in the context of HIV prevention efforts but rapidly went beyond this restricted

---

101 J. Halley, P. Kotiswaran, H. Shamir, and C. Thomas, 'From the International to the Local in Feminist Legal Responses to Rape, Prostitution/Sex Work, and Sex Trafficking: Four Studies in Contemporary Governance Feminism' (2006) 29 *Harvard J. of Law & Gender* 335–423.
102 A traditional Indian name based on the mythical story of a loyal Hindu wife.
103 Agnes, op. cit., n. 29, p. 166.
104 P. Chatterjee, *The Politics of the Governed: Reflections on Popular Politics in Most of the World* (2004).
105 SNDT, op. cit., n. 8, pp. 7–8.

mandate to form the Durbar Mahila Samanwaya Committee (DMSC) for sex workers' empowerment which is today better characterized as a transformative social movement. Despite its political capital and possibilities for success in litigation, the movement has studiously avoided litigation choosing instead to pursue a range of legal strategies at the national, regional, and local levels, directed both towards the state and away from it in the form of self-regulation. Their articulation of workers' rights also goes beyond a mere right to livelihood as with bar dancers.[106] Sex workers and bar dancers have so far displayed solidarity with each other, leading to the intermingling of mobilizational vocabularies. To illustrate, by March 2007, Kolkata's sex workers, in support of bar dancers, had refashioned their annual conference as the All India Conference of Entertainment Workers, advocating a fundamental right to entertainment, including sexual pleasure and the social recognition of the entertainment industry.

While both mobilizational patterns have strengths and weaknesses, prospects for redistributive reform ultimately depend on whether female sexual workers are able to transcend the arbitrary legal regulation of bar dancing and sex work and the discourse of morality which has persistently 'stuck' to both sectors, albeit in different forms. Whether the underlying moral conservatism against bar dancing and the abolitionist wave in relation to sex work are a manifestation of the resistance to the cultural effects of globalization in a deindustrializing city like Mumbai is a hypothesis that remains to be tested. Gooptu has argued that in the aftermath of deindustrialization in a once highly industrialized city like Kolkata with a militant trade union culture, male workers compensate for the loss by adopting a conservative sexual ethic for women in their communities.[107] However, in the case of Mumbai, although several dancers were daughters of mill workers, supporters of the ban did not predominantly come from workers' communities or even the working class more generally, nor was their political support critical to the passage of the ban. This, of course, did not stop bar owners from presenting the ban as detrimental to the interests of working-class men. However, the argument that late capitalism has inaugurated a moment of dual regulation where poorer sexual entrepreneurs and consumers are penalized while their wealthier counterparts are enabled in their unregulated consumption of sexual services is not borne out in the case of bar dancing. If anything, despite precisely such an attempt by the provincial government to exempt wealthier establishments from the ban, NGOs and the judiciary were firmly opposed to such distinctions. Also, although the need for male entertainment found continual affirmation, bar

---

106 P. Kotiswaran, 'Introduction' in *Sex Work,* ed. P. Kotiswaran (2010, forthcoming).
107 N. Gooptu, 'Economic Liberalisation, Work and Democracy' *Economic & Political Weekly*, 26 May 2007, 1922–33, at 1932.

dancers framed their demands in terms of their livelihood rather than a sex radical right to pleasure. It is precisely with a view to the final legal resolution of bar dancers' demands that all eyes will soon be on the Indian Supreme Court as the bar dancing case comes up on appeal. Meanwhile, the feminist hope lingers that it will reverse the zero-sum game played by the patriarchal state so that the rights of one set of female reproductive labourers do not continue to be won at the expense of another.

124

JOURNAL OF LAW AND SOCIETY
VOLUME 37, NUMBER 1, MARCH 2010
ISSN: 0263-323X, pp. 125–44

Male Sex Work: Exploring Regulation in England and Wales

MARY WHOWELL*

Whilst sex-work policy in England and Wales claims gender-neutrality, local and national prostitution strategies primarily focus on female street-based sex workers. Men who sell sex are generally absent or inadequately considered in such policies, and measures to regulate commercial sex markets are rarely considered in terms of their impact on male working practice. Drawing on the Coordinated Prostitution Strategy *for England and Wales, this paper has two aims: first, to offer a gender-based critique of the current policy framework for England and Wales by arguing that sex-work policy is infused by a gendered understanding of sex work in which male identities are neglected or assumed deviant; and second to explore the notion that understanding sex work as it is performed locally is valuable when generating local and national policy. Informed by gendered readings of policy, social understandings of masculinity, and the (in)visibility of male sexual commerce this paper explores male sex work in the context of Manchester, England.*

INTRODUCTION: THE NATIONAL PROSTITUTION STRATEGY FOR ENGLAND AND WALES

Sex-work policy in England and Wales has been in flux for a number of years. In 2004, the most recent consultation paper on prostitution policy was published. *Paying the Price – A Consultation Paper on Prostitution* sought to elicit the views and knowledge of key stakeholders, agencies, and individuals who had an interest in, and understanding of, sex-work law and

*School of Criminology, Simon Fraser University, 8888 University Drive, Burnaby, British Columbia, V5A1S6, Canada
mewhowel@sfu.ca

I would like to thank Phil Hubbard, John Harrison, and Ian R. Cook for their helpful comments on earlier drafts of this paper.

practice.[1] The initial consultation produced 861 responses, the content of which were used to inform the subsequent White Paper and National Strategy document: *A Coordinated Prostitution Strategy and a Summary of Responses to Paying the Price*.[2] The *National Strategy* provides a policy framework for prostitution law in England and Wales.

When describing those involved in the selling of sex, it is stated in section 1.4 of *Paying the Price* that: 'this paper has adopted the phrase "people involved in prostitution" as the least value-laden alternative. This should be taken to mean *both men and women* unless otherwise specified.'[3] Yet throughout the consultation document, men are rarely mentioned. In addition, much of the literature on male prostitution goes seemingly unconsulted, despite *Paying the Price* often referring to literature pertaining to female prostitution. Perhaps the lack of attention to men can be attributed to the context in which the consultation arose. In the Home Secretary's foreword, it is suggested that the consultation was based on research commissioned by the Home Office into eleven Crime Reduction Programmes (CRPs), which aimed to reduce 'the number of young people and *women* involved in prostitution'.[4] This research was one of the key papers informing *Paying the Price* and the *National Strategy*. The absence of an explicit exploration of the needs of men who sell sex therefore appears to be a very visible, yet overlooked lacuna.

However, the failure of the Home Office to address male sex work in the *National Strategy* did not go unnoticed. It was noted in the *National Strategy* that 'respondents commented that *Paying the Price* provided scant information on male prostitution'.[5] The failure to address the absence of men at this critical stage – especially since the Sexual Offences Act 2003 made all sexual offences gender-neutral – can be considered neglectful at best, and at worst, dangerous. A policy vacuum has thus been created where the law states that all prostitution-related offences are gender neutral and yet the policy and guidance to enforce the law appears to apply only to women and young people.

Moreover, it could be argued that the policy direction the Home Office was going to take was clear from the image on the front page of *Paying the Price*, later used on the front cover of the *National Strategy*. The image depicts 'Ruth', a female, childlike figure stood in front of a door with broken glass windows, painted by an artist who had previously been involved in

---

1 Home Office, *Paying the Price: A Consultation Paper on Prostitution* (2004).
2 Home Office, *A Coordinated Prostitution Strategy and Summary of Responses to Paying the Price* (2006). See, also, B. Brooks-Gordon, *The Price of Sex: Prostitution Policy and Society* (2006).
3 Home Office, op. cit., n. 1, p. 12.
4 Home Office, *Tackling Street Prostitution: Towards a Holistic Approach* (2004) v. Emphasis added.
5 Home Office, op. cit., n. 2, p. 9.

126

prostitution. The image is undoubtedly of great emotional significance to the artist, and reflects her personal, damaging experiences of prostitution. Yet the use of this image is also seemingly indicative of the position that the Home Office was taking on prostitution, in both *Paying the Price* and the *National Strategy*: that it always and inevitably involves the exploitation of women and young people by men. The conflation of woman and girl in the image is also reflected in the policy approach of the Home Office, regarding adult consensual sex work as linked to child sexual abuse and trafficking.[6] Critically, the image is illustrative of the gender bias evident in Home Office policy, as men are demonized as dangerous abusers who damage women and young people through the purchase of sex.[7] This gender bias is dangerous, in that male sex-industry identities are all too often associated with deviance, danger, and exploitation, and only rarely does the male sex worker feature in policy discussion.

The aim of this paper is therefore twofold; first, it will outline the *absence* of male sex work in sex-work policy, as detailed through national policy documents. Secondly, it will draw on a localized case study of street-based sex workers in Manchester to explore how men sell sex on the ground, in order to explore the notion that understanding sex work on a local level is valuable when generating policy to be implemented in both a local and a national context. The data informing this paper was gathered as part of a PhD research project exploring the practice, performance, and regulation of male sex work in Manchester, England. Data collected included 28 interviews with 31 key stakeholders and 600 hours of participant observation with sex-work outreach projects. All names of places and people have been changed to preserve anonymity.

MALE IDENTITIES IN SEX WORK POLICY: MEN WHO BUY SEX

Although sex-work policy in England and Wales purports gender neutrality, men rarely feature in policy documents as sex workers. More commonly, masculine identities are the client/punter, pimp, trafficker, and rapist.[8] Men who buy sex are perhaps the most prevalent male identity cited in debates over policy, and are commonly the recipient of punitive intervention in the local context. Kerb crawling campaigns which 'name and shame' men, remove their driving licences, allocate fines, and send letters home have sporadically been implemented in geographically disparate areas across

---

6 Brooks-Gordon, op. cit., n. 2.
7 id.
8 'Walk in a punter. Walk out a rapist', *Crimestoppers* (2008), at: <http://www.crimestoppers-uk.org/media-centre/crime-in-the-news/may-2008–crime-in-the-news/walk-in-a-punter-walk-out-a-rapist>; Home Office, op. cit., n. 1; Home Office, op. cit., n. 2; T. Sanders, *Paying for Pleasure, Men Who Buy Sex* (2008).

England and Wales in recent years.[9] The client has become a much reviled identity, perpetuated through campaigns and media discourse as immoral and even dangerous. Kulick looks at how men who buy sex were pathologized in Sweden, and explores the differentiation between sexuality as behaviour (for example, buying sex) and sexuality as identity (for example, identifying as gay), arguing that men in Sweden who buy sex were 'making the transition from "temporary aberrations" to a "species".'[10] In this case, he concluded that the client was seen to embody and perform a deviant sexuality as opposed to a 'good sexuality, the morally comprehensible way to be'.[11]

'John schools', operational in the United States and in some parts of the United Kingdom, provide another example through which the client is demonized. Educators seek to alter the sexual behaviour of men who buy sex through presenting a particular radical reading of prostitution, which focuses on notions of abuse, entrapment, and violence. Some schools highlight risks of contracting STIs (constructing the sex worker as 'infected'), children exploited through prostitution (conflating adult sex work and child sexual exploitation), and one school in the United Kingdom even had the mother of a murdered street-sex worker and an ex-sex worker speak to those convicted of kerb crawling.[12] Not only is this ethically questionable, but the use of particular feminist rhetoric to radicalize debates on prostitution perpetuates the perceived deviance of male identities within sex industry discourse, which could potentially negate the needs of male sex workers through presenting prostitution only as a form of violence against women. In addition, the gendered notion of victimhood running through the *National Strategy*, and the emphasis placed on helping women exit sex work is problematic as it feeds on notions of female vulnerability, but fails to acknowledge the potential vulnerability of men.

In *Paying the Price*, clients of sex workers are described as 'users', a term suggestive of control and abuse. However, empirical research into off-street sex industries in the United Kingdom demonstrates that men do not 'use' sex workers in consensual adult transactions.[13] The 'user' is also constructed as 'diseased':

> While women on the street soliciting for trade is unacceptable to most communities, it is the nuisance caused by kerb crawlers that is usually the first concern. Every effort must be made to deter men from this activity, sending a clear message that it is seriously anti-social, that it fuels exploitation and

---

9 Sanders, id.

10 D. Kulick, 'Four hundred thousand Swedish perverts' (2005) 99 *GLQ: A J. of Lesbian and Gay Studies* 205.

11 id., p. 206.

12 R. Campbell and M. Storr, 'Challenging the kerb crawler rehabilitation programme' (2001) 67 *Feminist Rev.* 94.

13 T. Sanders, *Sex Work: A Risky Business* (2005); Sanders, op. cit., n. 8.

problematic drug use, and that going to prostitutes contributes to the spread of HIV/Aids[14] and STIs.[15]

This statement has been contested by sex-work organizations and academics, not only because of the suggestion that it 'fuels exploitation', but also, it is argued, because it has no empirical basis in terms of STI and HIV transmission rates.[16] Despite a number of empirical studies on men who buy sex, there is little evidence that the Home Office kerb-crawling initiative in 2007 (rolled out as part of the *National Strategy)* was based on representative or rigorous empirical research. Instead, men who buy sex were targeted through a series of campaigns in which posters, beer mats, and radio commercials were used to advocate the message 'Kerb crawling costs more than you think'.[17] Another campaign in 2008 targeted 'trafficking' in which any buyer of sex was called a 'rapist'.[18] This approach to changing the behavioural characteristics of social groups, that is, stopping men visiting female sex workers through what is essentially a form of 'moral bullying', is potentially dangerous and historically, comparable campaigns against other stigmatized groups have caused high levels of distress and even provoked vigilante attacks from local community groups.[19]

MALE IDENTITIES IN SEX-WORK POLICY: MEN WHO SELL SEX

Moving forward to consider male sex work itself, the *National Strategy* states that the government will provide:

> [G]uidance for local agencies on developing routes out of prostitution, including access to drug treatment, accommodation and a range of health services, and advice on education, training and employment ... [moreover] the government will work with projects providing services for male, transgender and transsexual prostitution [sic] to ensure that the guidance addresses the particular needs of these groups.[20]

It has been more than three years since the *National Strategy* was published, yet these guidelines remain phantasmagorical.[21] The failure to acknowledge

---

14 Capitalizations of AIDS is incorrect in the original Home Office (2004) publication.
15 Home Office, op. cit., n. 1, p. 67.
16 L. Cusick and L. Berney, 'Prioritising punitive responses over public health: Commentary on the Home Office consultation document Paying the Price' (2005) 25 *Critical Social Policy* 596; S. Kingston, 'Sexual abuse discourse: men who buy sex and prostitution policy', paper presented at 'Sex Work' research postgraduate conference, Leeds University, 22 January 2009; Kulick, op. cit., n. 10; United Kingdom Network of Sex Projects (UKNSWP), *Response to 'Paying the Price'* (2004), available at: <www.uknswp.org/UKNSWP_Paying_the_Price_response.pdf>.
17 Sanders, op. cit., n. 8.
18 *Crimestoppers*, op. cit., n. 8.
19 UKNSWP, op. cit., n. 16.
20 Home Office, op. cit., n. 2. p. 9
21 At the time of writing (August 2009) guidelines are yet to be produced.

129

men working in the sex industry demonstrates an unwillingness to acknowledge that men provide sexual services to both men and women.[22] Reasons for this omission have also been attributed to the failure of the Home Office to recognize the potential vulnerability of men in the sex industry, as Gaffney suggests:

> The [National] Strategy does not distinguish between the genders, yet there are clear distinctions within the literature between the experiences of young men and young women in prostitution. Young men selling sex are often perceived as 'delinquent' rather than vulnerable, so the needs of younger men selling sex tend to be unseen. The exploitation of young males is often ignored because of this societal failure to recognise their vulnerability. The [National] Strategy fails to recognise these differences or address these male specific issues.[23]

The reinforcement of the victimhood of women involved in sex work marginalizes that of men, which again results in the needs of male sex workers being lost in the midst of rhetoric.[24] In addition, the vulnerabilities of male and female sex workers are spatially contingent. There are clearly different risks attached to street work, indoor in-call escorting work, and pornography, but as in any job that involves contact with the public (for example, child-minding, social work, working in a petrol station or selling fish and chips), there are inevitably risks, which are assessed through policy and risk management. I am not suggesting that sex work is a 'job like any other', but as in most workplaces, there can be significant risks to health and safety if they are not managed appropriately. These risks are exacerbated by the indistinct legal status of sex work, with laws relating to prostitution being enforced sporadically and in different ways across different geographical areas. Indeed, one of the key points offered in wider, international literatures on prostitution is that the confusing and contradictory legal status of sex working can place sex workers in difficult and dangerous situations, as men and women are often unsure as to whether they are working legally or not.[25]

22 See 'I pay a man for regular sex' *Times*, 5 December 2007, available at: <http://women.timesonline.co.uk/tol/life_and_style/women/relationships/article2999703.ece>. It is important to note that published research on women who buy sex is very sparse.

23 J. Gaffney, 'A co-ordinated prostitution strategy and response to Paying the Price – but what about the men?' (2007) 6 *Community Safety J.* 27, at 2.

24 Brooks-Gordon, op. cit., n. 2; M. Whowell and J. Gaffney, 'Male sex work in the UK: forms, practices and policy implications' in *The Prostitution Strategy: Implications for Community Safety,* ed. J. Phoenix (2009).

25 P. Hubbard, 'Out of touch and out of time? The contemporary policing of sex work' in *Sex Work Now*, eds. R. Campbell and M. O'Neill (2006) 1; J. Lewis and E. Maticka-Tyndale, *Escort services in a border town: transmission dynamics of sexually transmitted infections within and between communities* (1999), Literature and Policy Summary, available at <http://web2.uwindsor.ca/courses/sociology/maticka/star/escortsummary.html>; J. Lewis and E. Maticka-Tyndale, 'Licensing sex work: public policy and women's lives' (2000) xxxvi *Can. Public Policy* 437; J. Lowman, 'Submission to the subcommittee on solicitation laws of the standing committee of Justice. Human rights, public safety and emergency preparedness' (undated), available at <http://users.uniserve.com/~lowman/>.

As yet, the Home Office has failed to provide the support it promised for agencies working with male sex workers in different environments. How sex is sold locally, and how local commercial sex scenes operate can provide important data to feed into debates surrounding sex work policy. The next section explores male street sex work in Manchester, where men selling sex on the street have developed particular methods of working, described here as *choreographies*. Through this analysis, it is possible to explore the strengths and limitations of policy which is operational in both local and national contexts.

MALE SEX WORK IN MANCHESTER: SETTING THE CONTEXT

The 2007/08 Manchester Prostitution Strategy identified four key areas where street-sex work is solicited and transacted in the city.[26] Three were areas of street-based female street-sex work, and the fourth, identified Manchester's 'Gay Village'[27] as an area of male street-sex work. Manchester houses one of the largest and most famous 'Gay Villages' nationally and internationally, and the Village itself has complex and interesting sexual histories and geographies. During the late 1900s, after industry had left the area now occupied by the Village, men seeking sex with other men commonly frequented the area in search of sexual excitement and anonymous erotic encounters. Abandoned warehouses and dark canal towpaths provided the necessary cover for public sex acts, and prostitutes, both male and female, were able to ply their trade from licensed premises, street corners, and along the canal towpaths. Although the growth of the Village into the cosmopolitan nightspot it now purports to be is regularly documented in the literature on gay commercial spaces,[28] prostitution and public sex are rarely considered in the historical context.

Notably, before Manchester's gay scene became marketed as 'one of Britain's friendliest, busiest and most welcoming',[29] the Village was a significant area of street sex work[30] and certainly up until the late 1990s, there were women working the streets and corners. Men have historically

---

26 Manchester City Council, 'Manchester Prostitution Strategy 2007/2008' (2007), available at: <http://www.manchester.gov.uk/egov_downloads/Appendix_1_Manchester_Strategy_2007.pdf>.
27 Known hereafter as 'the Village'.
28 J. Binnie and B. Skeggs, 'Cosmopolitan knowledge and the production and consumption of sexualised space: Manchester's gay village' (2004) 52 *Sociological Rev.* 39; B. Skeggs, 'Matter out of place: visibility and sexualities in leisure spaces' (1999) 18 *Leisure Studies* 213; I. Taylor, K. Evans, and P. Fraser, *A Tale of Two Cities: A Study in Manchester and Sheffield* (1996).
29 Marketing Manchester, 'Visit Manchester – gay and lesbian', at: <http://www.visitmanchester.com/gay-and-lesbian.aspx>.
30 Taylor et al., op. cit., n. 28.

131

sold sex from a number of the licensed premises in the Village, with one, the *Tally Ho!*[31] being known as a historical and current space of sex work. Men also previously worked from public toilets, notably those that belonged to the large bus station in the Village:

> The toilets at the bus station ten to fifteen years ago were absolutely an area where not only cruising and cottaging, but huge amounts of sex were being sold and the male sex workers would be hanging around there. There was a corridor going down to the toilets – it was like rent boy alley.[32]

The bus station was renovated in March 2002, and reopened as a large coach station, a well-lit, open-plan building, with 24-hour security. During the course of the area's regeneration, the women were gradually pushed out of the Village and into the 'out-of-the-way' streets surrounding Manchester's Piccadilly train station, and also to an industrial area north of the city centre. However, the men remained in the Village. According to sex-work project data, there are approximately 40 men working the streets of Manchester.[33] This number is reflected in PhD research conducted, where between January 2006 to July 2008 I encountered 41 men accessing or contacting the two sex-work projects I volunteered with. Excerpts from my research diary confirm that realistically, on a busy night there may be eight to ten working the street (perhaps reflecting that there were outreach project-arranged activities on), and at quieter times fewer than five. These men were typically aged between 18 and 25, many had unstable backgrounds, and were accommodated in temporary or hostel accommodation. The majority used either drugs or alcohol recreationally, fewer used drugs or alcohol problematically. Of these men approximately 40 per cent identified as straight, 20 per cent as gay, and the rest identified as bisexual or were questioning their sexuality; it is fair to say that the ways in which the men sexually identified was quite changeable. Despite Manchester City Council formally recognizing that men sell sex on the street and in licensed premises through the Manchester Prostitution Strategy,[34] there are few formal regulatory structures beyond the outreach services in place catering to the specific needs of male sex workers.

Although there is certainly a burgeoning literature on how sex work is practiced and performed,[35] the micro-politics of how and crucially where sex is solicited remain under-theorized. The performed actions that lead up to the

---

31 Not the real name of the premises.
32 Author interview with Charity Worker 1.
33 The Blue Room, *Practice Evaluation: Blue Wednesday*, unpublished Project Report (2008).
34 Manchester City Council, op. cit., n. 26.
35 E. Bernstein, *Temporarily Yours, Intimacy, Authenticity, and the Commerce of Sex* (2007); S. Oerton, and J. Phoenix, 'Sex/bodywork: discourses and practices' (2001) 4 *Sexualities* 387; A. Wilcox and K. Christmann, '"Getting paid for sex is my kick': a qualitative study of male sex workers' in *Sex as Crime*, eds. G. Letherby, K. Williams, P. Birch, and M. Cain (2008) 118.

sexual act itself (solicitation, kerb crawling, and negotiation of prices/ services on the street) that cause much tension in communities where sex is sold,[36] and are also subject to much scrutiny in policy, have rarely been considered in the academic literatures on sex work. Few scholars have looked to the embodied practices (solicitation, kerb crawling, walking, looking, states of dress/undress) which effectively sexualize the red-light landscape.[37] In this section, I will suggest that the tactics of solicitation used by men working the streets of Manchester's Gay Village effectively regulate the space through a performance of specific sexual choreographies operationalized 'in place' which, importantly, do not attract undue attention as being 'out of place'.[38] It is through the ambiguous nature of these choreographies that men are able to maintain and shape the beat. As a result, it is possible to argue that street sex workers effectively self-regulate the street space, and are *the* key players in regulating and shaping the local sex working scene.

1. *Ambiguity, sex working, and 'blending in'*

Walking for the purposes of soliciting sex, is an urban peripatetic practice that is commonly linked to practices of cruising,[39] yet rarely have the literatures on public sex and cruising been used to complement and enhance research into commercial sexual encounter. It has been acknowledged that sex is sometimes sold opportunistically through public sex environments,[40] and, as such, the processes through which men obtain partners when cruising for free sex is a useful lens for exploring practices of solicitation. Men working the streets maintain their ambiguous sexual identities as sex workers but at the same time are able to facilitate sexual transactions. As will be

---

36 M. O'Neill, R. Campbell, P. Hubbard, J. Pitcher, and J. Scoular, 'Living with the other: street sex work, contingent communities and degrees of tolerance' (2008) 4 *Crime, Media and Culture* 73; J. Pitcher, R. Campbell, P. Hubbard, M. O'Neill, and J. Scoular, *Living and Working in Areas of Street Sex Work* (2006).

37 K. Gregory, *The Everyday Life of Sex Workers in the Netherlands* (2005).

38 T. Cresswell, *In Place/Out of Place: Geography, Ideology and Transgression* (1996).

39 H. Bech, *When Men Meet: Homosexuality and Modernity* (1997); D. Bell, 'Fragments for a queer city' in *Pleasure Zones: Bodies, Cities, Spaces,* eds. D. Bell, J. Binnie, R. Holliday, R. Longhurst, and R. Peace (2004) 84; G. Brown, 'Ceramics, clothing and other bodies: affective geographies of homoerotic cruising encounters' (2008) 9 *Social and Cultural Geography* 915; L. Humphreys, *Tearoom Trade: Impersonal Sex in Public Places* (1970); M. Turner, *Backward Glances: Cruising the Queer Streets of New York and London* (2003).

40 A public sex environment is a public space used by men for sexual activity. Such spaces can include canal towpaths, swimming pools, beaches, cinemas, toilets, and a multiplicity of other spaces. See J. Gaffney, 'Guidelines for development of outreach work with men who sell sex' in *Manual: Tips, tricks and models of good practice for service providers considering, planning or implementing services for male sex workers*, ed. K. Schiffer (2002) 8.

explored here, this can be similar to the way in which men cruising for sex are able to solicit sexual encounter through subversive gestures. Cruising has been defined as:

> [A] moment of visual exchange that occurs on the streets and in other places in the city, which constitutes an act of mutual recognition amid the otherwise alienating effects of the anonymous crowd. It is a practice that exploits the fluidity and multiplicity of the modern city to its advantage. But cruising is not trans-historical – like everything else it is circumscribed by any number of social determinants and cultural and social specificities. And cruising is always site specific.[41]

I would extend this definition to be applicable in rural and suburban contexts rather than solely the urban although, as I shall discuss, the city does offer particular affordances and opportunities for cruising through its architecture and planning.

The Gay Village in Manchester is a bustling and busy space, catering primarily to the gay community, but the Village is also well used by heterosexual consumers. Although the area is mainly used in the evenings as a party and leisure space, during the day many of the pubs and bars open and serve food, coffee, and drinks. There are also other amenities, including several hairdressers, a doctor's surgery, takeaway shops, sex shops, a sauna, taxi firms, a large bus station, and the Lesbian and Gay Foundation (LGF), a regional charity catering to the lesbian, gay, and bisexual community in the north-west. There is a usually steady flow of people moving through the Village using these services and commuting between venues, day and night, all of which provides some cover for the men working the street:

> To the outside gazer you look like a person who's walking their dog, you look like a person who's walking home from a night out. They don't see you moving the circuit, only people who are also moving the circuit, going around in circles, waiting in a particular spot are able to recognise you doing that and if you are doing that, generally you are probably going to be looking for sex.[42]

Although this quote was taken from a discussion relating to public sex, it is equally applicable to sex work. Walking in and around the areas known for men selling sex is key to maintaining the 'beat'. Its role as a red-light landscape is thus (re)produced by the footsteps of those using it. For those who are aware of the beat, standing or walking along particular streets is a key factor in identifying men selling sex. Men can often be found walking around the Village in circuits or in venues offering similar commercial sexual opportunities. Walking for sex then is a useful strategy for those seeking sex in the city. By moving through the city in this quite mundane fashion, those seeking, and providing, sex are able to remain ambiguous and 'normal' in the landscape. Indeed, as Wunderlich suggests, walking (for whatever purpose) is 'an unquestioned form of movement through the city,

41 Turner, op. cit., n. 39, p. 9.
42 Author interview with Outreach Worker 5.

134

often unnoticed and not regarded in itself as being a particular singular or insightful experience'.[43]

The geographical mobility of sex workers, and the notion that the beat is constructed not only by police, residents, and outreach projects but by movement of sex workers and their clients, is well documented in the sex-work literatures,[44] yet the micro-politics of this performance largely remain ambiguous. But the reproduction of street space in Manchester through sexual choreography can clearly be seen in the words of a man who accesses the sex-work projects:

> Smith Street is for getting drunk, and then if you go along Richardson Street that's for picking up rent boys, and then sometimes outside the Blue Room[45] that as well, they [clients] drive down back alleys and wait there and then flash you when you walk past.[46]

Here the design and layout of the Village can be seen to provide affordances conducive to buying sex. The client is doubly concealed, first in a car, and secondly down a side street. To the passer-by, the client just looks like someone sitting in a car, perhaps picking up a friend or partner. When the client sees a man with whom he wants to engage walking past the car, he flashes his lights as a signal. To a passer-by this may seem unusual, but those simply passing through are unlikely to realize the intent. Like the traditional 'backward glance' used by men cruising for sex,[47] the subtlety of the intent to engage in commercial activity is masked by the fluidity and vibrancy of the urban spectacle; the bright-coloured lights of the bars on Smith Street, the hustle and bustle of (perhaps drunk) people moving between premises, the heady sounds of pop and dance music. The flashing of the car headlights from a side street could easily be lost as it is one of the 'fleeting and ephemeral moments, not intended to be captured' that constitute the fluidity of urban life.[48] It is the transient nature of the encounter that makes solicitation (by both sex worker and client) problematic to police effectively. The client has not solicited the sex worker in the traditional sense through

---

43 F.M. Wunderlich, 'Walking and rhythmicity: sensing urban space' (2008) 13 *J. of Urban Design* 125, at 126–27.

44 P. Hubbard and T. Sanders, 'Making space for sex work: female street prostitution and the production of urban space' (2003) 27 *International J. of Urban and Regional Research* 75; P. Hubbard, 'Community action and the displacement of street prostitution: Evidence from British cities' (1998) 29 *Geoforum* 269; S. Tani, 'Whose place is this space? Life in the street prostitution area of Helsinki, Finland' (2002) 26 *International J. of Urban and Regional Research* 343.

45 During the last 12 months of the fieldwork, the Blue Room, a creative arts based project for men who sell sex to men, took up residence in premises on Richardson Street and offered an outreach service from there.

46 Author interview with Sex Worker 4.

47 M. Turner, *Backward Glances. Cruising the Queer Streets of New York and London* (2003) at 9.

48 id., at 10.

kerb crawling, but has used the architecture and reputation of the street, and its position as a side street, to make his presence less visible than if he were on one of the main streets. The traditional sexual scripts of solicitation are rewritten through subversive notions: looking, making a subtle gesture (flashing the car headlights), and being strategically positioned within the red-light landscape. Traditional conceptualizations of kerb crawling as written through the National Strategy are thus largely redundant in this context.

Sex workers are also actively engaged in subversive methods of solicitation. One man I interviewed acknowledged that one of the key differences between the way in which men and women work could be attributed to identification and visibility:

> You could just give them a nod or give them a wave or a gesture 'come over here' or something. It's different to the girls. The girls will stand there and start moving their hips and do all this girly stuff but lads, you know, if guys are interested in picking up lads then they'll just stop anyway really, or you'll just give them a nod or something.[49]

Here the sex worker, as positioned within the red-light landscape, explicitly acknowledges the subtleness of solicitation; and how subversive gesture rather than any specifically sexual signal allows for the 'picking up' of a client. Similarly, stillness in spaces of sex work is also a strong (yet discreet) indicator that the men are selling sex. Atkins noted in his ethnography of public sex encounters that stillness of bodies in spaces of public sex can indicate commitment to a sexual encounter.[50] Just as in cruising areas then, the repetition of solicitation for sex contributes to the (re)creation of the commercial beat.[51]

Notions of waiting 'for business' also contribute to the 'anti-social' identities often mapped onto men working the streets, and one concern highlighted by the men themselves (but also by outreach workers) is that sex workers are sometimes blamed for incidences of street crime occurring in the area. This is perhaps partly due to the men 'hanging around' in the area, and because they have ambiguous identities, those not 'in the know' may be unsure of their intent or purpose in the Village. Moreover, solicitation constitutes more than being in the 'right' geographical spot at the right time, and ways of dressing are also a key component of sexual choreographies. It

---

49 Author interview 1 with Sex Worker 1.
50 M. Atkins, 'Objects that look: how is ambiguity of body and self maintained in the public sex encounter?', unpublished MA thesis, University of Manchester (2007); see, also, Brown, op. cit., n. 39.
51 See, also, on beats: N. McKeganey and M. Barnard, *Sex Work on the Streets: Prostitutes and Their Clients* (1996); S. Tani, 'Whose place is this space? Life in the street prostitution area of Helsinki, Finland' (2002) 26 *International J. of Urban and Regional Research* 343.

is well documented in the literatures that dress is a key performative factor in terms of identifying 'anti-social' bodies, sex-working or otherwise.[52]

The 'chav', stereotyped as a young person commonly involved in activities which could be considered 'anti-social', is increasingly commoditized across the sex industry. Internet escorts will pose in tracksuits and Burberry[53] to solicit custom, and 'chav' identities can be readily found in pornography. Here, I do not want to label the men who work the beat as chavs or scallies (even though a number of them may personally identify as such) but, rather, look at how certain elements of the chav or scally identity are threaded and drawn through their sexual choreographies when working the beat. In terms of street-based industries, one could argue that tracksuit bottoms and tops, hooded tops, trainers, and baseball caps are often worn by men working the streets anyway. The clothing is practical; it is warm, often waterproof, and comfortable for spending long amounts of time outside. This type of clothing is relatively accessible on the high street and also from a variety of different shopping outlets. It is also sold informally through networks of buyers and sellers who operate beyond the eyes of the taxman. Dressing this way also generates 'street-cred'. I can recall one man who accessed the sex-work projects altering his entire look and wardrobe so he could 'fit' in with the networks and gangs of young people who spent much of their time in public areas, engaging in street-based social activities. In doing this he also spoke of the sexual prowess it would give him to attract other 'hot scallies' with whom to engage in various sexual exploits. In terms of sex work practice, tracksuit bottoms with elasticised waists provide easy access in terms of removing and replacing clothing. When interviewed, the men spoke about the clothing as a key element of soliciting for business, 'if a lad is dressed up in trackkies, a lot of the punters will go for that lad. They like the straight-looking scally lads, you know that are always getting in trouble'.[54]

Entwistle has written on the implicit links between clothing and sexuality suggesting that, 'body adornment can be linked to sexual acts, give sexual pleasure, send out sexual signals, mark out sexualized identities'.[55] The clothing certainly marks the men out as sexually available when in spaces of sex work, and draws on particular elements of the chav or scally identity as erotic and sexualized. In this case, the desirability of the body is enhanced through clothing and the sexual, gendered social identity of the person wearing it and, crucially, its anti-social connotations. The hoodie is a symbol of anti-social behaviour as perpetuated through the media and hence of rough

---

52 For example, see K. Hayward, and M. Yar, 'The "chav" phenomenon: consumption, media and the construction of a new underclass' (2006) 2 *Crime, Media, Culture* 9.
53 Burberry is a designer brand with a trademark tartan, often worn by those identified as 'chavs' by the British media.
54 Author interview 2 with Sex Worker 1.
55 J. Entwistle, *The Fashioned Body* (2000).

and hard masculinities, as opposed to the 'cosmopolitan' and well-resourced gay man, so often portrayed through hegemonic forms of queer masculinity.[56] So although the men in the Village may or may not be involved in street related activity beyond sex work, they are often associated with the anti-social scally identity as this interview excerpt suggests:

> I: Do you think it is fair or unfair that sex workers are implicated in anti-social behaviour in the Village?
> R: [It] depends how you dress, but like I said, a lot of people dress in trackky bottoms and that, so yeah they will get tagged into the other side of it ... you look like you're going out looking for trouble really ... a bit rough and ready looking ... I suppose it that's probably one part of it, a bit rough and ready, scallified, it's just something to get their rocks off really.[57]

Through modes of dressing, the men present a hyper-masculinized, hetero-sexual, and anti-social identity through their appearance, which transcends hetero and homonormative boundaries. The choreography allows them to remain both visible and 'normal'. The complexity of performed gender and sexuality identities problematizes simplistic and monolithic readings of heterosexuality. Reiterating the work of Brown and Hubbard,[58] this sex-working performance offers not one reading of (hetero)sexuality but acknowledges the possibility for bodies to perform multiple and shifting (hetero)sexualities in varied spaces at different times. This has potential implications for policing, as an officer I interviewed commented:

> Male sex workers are hanging about street corners near the pubs and the gay community are concerned that they are making the place look a mess. They make it look unruly, unwanted, more seedy. They're disrespecting them because this is where they drink. This is the area they have created for themselves. So when people come through the Village and they see the young lad hanging round in a tracksuit they're not too keen on it. It looks threatening, you know they don't know whether they are a male sex worker or somebody waiting to rob them.[59]

The complexly performed identities of the sex workers as heterosexual, hyper-masculine, and potentially anti-social contributes to the complex way in which prostitution is policed in Manchester. It is problematic for the police to develop working relationships with the sex workers because of the ambiguity of their status, which is, in turn, exacerbated by the men often not wanting to admit their sex-working status to police because of the double

---

56 J. Beynon, *Masculinities and Culture* (2002); P. Johnson, 'Rude boys: the homosexual eroticization of class' (2008) 42 *Sociology* 65; M.S. Kimmel, 'Masculinity as homophobia; fear, shame and silence in the construction of gender identity' in *Theorizing Masculinities*, eds. H. Brod and M. Kaufman (1994) 213.

57 Author interview 2, with Sex Worker 2.

58 G. Brown, 'Urban (homo)sexualities: ordinary cities, ordinary sexualities' (2008) 2 *Geography Compass* 1215; P. Hubbard, 'Here, there, everywhere: The ubiquitous geographies of heteronormativity' (2008) 2 *Geography Compass* 640.

59 Author interview with Police Officer 3.

stigma of sex work and homosexuality. This is especially the case if the men would normally subjectively identify as heterosexual. This uncertainty in identifying sex workers is further complicated following reports of men masquerading as sex workers and robbing clients rather than providing a service in and around the Village. Yet it is exactly this sexual identity that clients of sex workers want to buy into:

> Yeah, it's more about control and aggression really. For most of them just the thought of having a scally, you know somebody who's macho or something, doing what they want.[60]

By adopting or performing a scally identity, the sex worker blends into the social scene of the Village by socializing with others who do not sell sex but could be identified as 'scallies'.

Also of note is how class – as expressed through particular and appropriate ways of dressing – was identified as a key factor in differentiating between which pubs sex workers use, and those they do not:

> Dress code has a big part to play in it. Going back a couple of years ago one of the bars on Smith Street had a really relaxed dress code. You could go in there with your Rockports[61] on. You could wear trackky bottoms and baseball caps and no one would bat an eyelid. And it was buy one get one free on the drink so on the outreach, we'd be straight to that bar and half the clients[62] would be at that bar. Now when the bar changed its dress code then obviously the lads stopped working in there. So just by changing the dress code it changed the clientele that was using the bar. So by stopping them going in in their trackkies, they then stopped the problem [of sex working] in that bar.[63]

Dress code, clientele, drinks prices and offers, ambience, the ability to 'fit in', and reputation all have an impact on which pubs the men use.[64] The *Tally Ho!*, for example, has had three sets of proprietors, yet the reputation of the pub as a 'rent boy joint' has remained. Also of note is the role that licensed premises can play in facilitating commercial sexual encounter. Although illegal gang activities can sometimes be attributed to this, seemingly less dangerous characters are also purported to be involved. Some stakeholders expressed concern over some of the door staff manning the licensed premises being involved in facilitating transactions:

> The regulars or the punters that go into the bars, in certain bars obviously the bouncer stands on the door, he will witness people and watch ... they'll have a nod that he's working or why don't you go and speak to him.[65]

---

60 Author interview Sex Worker 1.
61 Rockport is a brand of shoe.
62 In this case clients refers to the men accessing the sex work projects not the clients of the sex workers.
63 Author interview with Outreach Worker 2.
64 See, also, Binnie and Skeggs, op. cit., n. 28.
65 Author interview with Outreach Worker.

Through subtle gestures, movements, and looks, the transaction is enacted, but remains largely invisible to the outside gaze. As Turner puts it, the nod 'exploits the ambivalences and uncertainties inherent in the city'.[66] The extent to which the doormen across the Village are involved in arranging transactions is unknown, although there were suggestions from several interviewees that in the past there had been suspicions that doormen were 'running' some of the men. One interviewee suggested that when he was working in the Village during the late 1990s as a doorman and bar manager, there were doormen arranging transactions between clients and the men working the beat at the time:

> It's complicated and it's really hard to try and rationalize because there's so many different scenarios but the fact is that the door staff are organising and arranging transactions, either on or off the premises. Well I'm saying off because it's a case of they just go round the corner or they'll go to the sauna.[67]

In addition, several of those interviewed suggested that one establishment had a mattress that was available for rent above the bar area, although, as with much clandestine activity, reports of this were unconfirmed. The involvement of other actors across the red-light landscape problematizes the sex worker/client relationship and its negotiation across space; it also suggests that sex work is regulated by actors involved both directly and on the fringes of the commercial sexual exchange.

The crux of the argument is that subversive behaviour, mannerisms, glances, nods, and walking in and around particular spaces or places, when considered in conjunction with the affective properties of the Village environment (its buzz, vibrancy, colours, and hustle and bustle) allow for the discreet solicitation of business in the Village. Through the coming together of the myriad elements which constitute the Village and the choreographies of those seeking and selling sex, specific spaces of sex work are produced by men who sell sex. That men can sell sex on the streets and be relatively 'invisible' to the average passer-by is significant, because in much of the literature on female sex work, it is the visible presence of sex workers on the street which is of greatest concern to communities.[68]

In terms of how the Village is policed, police officers I interviewed suggested that sex workers were identifiable to some extent, but added that it was probably only those officers who spent time in the Village were able to recognize sex working behaviour. Interestingly some of the officers used conversational techniques to attempt to get men to identify:

---

66 Turner, op. cit., n. 47, p. 7.
67 Author interview with ex-Door Staff.
68 M. O'Neill and R. Campbell, *Walsall Prostitution Consultation Research: A Participatory Action Research Project. Full Report* (2004)' available at <http://www.safetysoapbox.co.uk/full_report.htm>.

It's a combination action, place and to a certain extent uniform as well, and if someone is standing around the Village for four hours, not making any attempt to sit down, have a drink, speak to people, if they are hanging around a certain area traditionally which used to be associated with them, before Richardson Street and it's giving a reason why they are in the Village for four hours not doing anything. Then you can kind of put two and two together and you can also mention Industry Street[69] to them ... they're acknowledging, you acknowledge that the pair of you know what you're talking about, which could probably open up a conversation to further on.[70]

The tactic used by this police officer avoids any mention of sex work, yet places the man in a position where he is potentially 'outed'. This is perhaps problematic in terms of social care, but also reflects issues around identity and ambiguity in male commercial sex. Despite the police making progress in identifying the men, how to develop working relationships with sex workers is another issue entirely; indeed it is possible that the embarrassment of being 'outed' would make the men less likely to engage. Some officers I interviewed suggested that when they identified the men, they would ask the men to 'move on' or 'go home'. This is awkward since a number of the men are street homeless, or living in temporary accommodation, and essentially many of the men will have few places they could move on to. Other officers suggested that they had developed relationships with the men to the point that intelligence could be exchanged. Yet interviews with men suggested that some felt apathetic towards the police, as they felt that 'all the police want is intelligence'.[71]

Male sex work is certainly less visible than female sex work in multiple media: in policy documents at local and national levels, which generally consider female sex work in more depth than male; academic and social research, where there has been more on female than male sex work; there is more social care provision aimed at female sex work, and more media attention is given to female sex work as opposed to male. It is therefore unsurprising that those officers I interviewed collectively suggested that they 'haven't got a great deal of experience with male sex workers'.[72] Yet there was consideration as to whether they should be treated in the same way as females:

When we've come across a male sex worker I think we'd probably treat them very similar and do a needs assessment very similar to what we'd do with a female sex worker. And you make a good point there ... are the needs of a male sex worker different to the needs to of a female sex worker and are the responses to male sex worker needs and female sex worker different?[73]

---

69 Industry Street is a public sex environment but it is also used by male sex workers to solicit commercial custom.
70 Author interview with Police Officer 4.
71 Author interview 2 with Sex Worker 1.
72 Author interview with Police Officer 4.
73 Author interview with Police Officer 1.

141

This issue is consistently raised by sex-work agencies working in the city. The Blue Room, a creative arts based project for men who sell sex to men in Manchester, is currently developing training packages for agencies and individuals who may work with male sex workers but are unsure as how to offer assistance and intervention in an appropriate way on a day-to-day basis.

What is clear from the section above is that the men sell sex discreetly, and the spaces in which they work are shaped by ways in which solicitation is performed through choreography. In Manchester, the message conveyed by those officers I interviewed was that the policing of prostitution was guided by 'priorities for the police, and resources'.[74] Thus, perhaps because of the relative invisibility of the men explicitly selling sex on the street, and the lack of complaints about male sex work received by the police and Village officials (as discovered through interview), spending police time and resources on enforcement activity may simply be unviable. It could be argued that Manchester City Council is actively addressing issues of male sex work in the city through their local prostitution policy, by addressing male sex work as a separate element within the strategy, and also by providing limited support and financial assistance to male sex-work projects. Yet it seems that in terms of how sex work is regulated on the ground, it is largely down to the men themselves and the networks in which they engage (door staff, licensed premises, clients, outreach projects). Hence it is possible to argue that local knowledge is important in terms of understanding sex work and how it is regulated. Understanding how local commercial sex scenes operate requires an understanding of not only how sex workers self-regulate, and also how they interact with formal bodies such as the police and outreach workers, but also less normatively considered bodies – for example, licensed premises and door staff – which contribute to the wider regulatory fabric of the red-light landscape.

CONCLUSION

What, then, can local, in-depth, empirical research contribute to debates over regulation and sex-work policy? First, let me be clear that the aim of this paper has not been to intimate that the absence of men in sex-work policy at the national scale is directly linked to their relative self-regulation at the local scale. It would be naive to transcribe policy in such a way, not to mention the fact that the Manchester case study is unique in and of itself, especially because of the Village and its affective properties which arguably facilitate choreographies useful for soliciting. However, there are three points worthy of consideration to be gleaned from the Manchester case

---

74 Author interview with Police Officer 4.

study, in terms of the value of local empirical research and its relationship to sex-work policy.

First, the research conducted in Manchester allows for the conclusion to be drawn that the ways in which men sell sex in Manchester are complex. Through the case study, the notion that place matters in the sale of sex is made clear. A further excavation of the case study would have demonstrated that history and locality matter in choreographies of sex work, as well as the presentation of bodies through dress and demeanour. The micro-politics of solicitation, in this case, allow for the notion of self-regulation to be employed; rather than top-down mechanisms shaping the beat, locally deployed networks are important in the regulation of prostitution in this context. Rarely does policy consider how sex work is operationalized and practiced on the ground, or the notion that spaces of commercial sex operating in different locales are shaped by different factors and networks. Perhaps it may be useful for those policies implemented in the local context to take account of local sex markets and how they operate, in order for policy and policing to be deployed in sensitive and appropriate ways.

Second, in terms of regulatory practice, this paper emphasizes the geographical mobility, agency, and regulatory capacity of sex workers, and the ability of sex workers to use spaces of sex work to facilitate commercial transactions. Here a geographical reading of sex work is useful: in short, place matters in street prostitution, as the Village offers particular afford-ances for solicitation. Key to this is that there are sites in the Village where different bodies come together (notably sex workers and clients), and through choreography, solicitation can be staged and sexual transaction enacted. Yet because of the affective properties of the surrounding environ-ment (its buzz, vibrancy, colours, and hustle and bustle) exchanges remain discreet. Through the intensities of place, spaces of sex work are produced and understanding this production of space will inevitably affect its regulation. That sex is sold in a diversity of street spaces remains uncon-sidered in national policy, and the micro-dynamics of localized spaces of sex work are not explicitly addressed in the local Manchester policy context either. This paper explores how the geography of the beat can impact on regulatory practice, which is worthy of consideration when implementing local policing structures.

Finally, perhaps the clearest conceptual theme running through the paper is one of invisibilities. The first half of the paper detailed the invisibility of men in sex-work policy and the second half considered the micro-dynamics of a male street beat in Manchester and how men could sell sex whilst remaining 'invisible' to the majority. The key point to emphasize here is that men do sell sex on the streets, as women do. Their service needs are not less, and are equally complex, especially in terms of performed sexualities and sexual practice. Offering readings of how men sell sex in local terms is one way of demonstrating, with the support of empirical evidence, that male sex work is worthy of consideration, that the needs of men should not be

143

negated, and that prostitution cannot be defined solely as the exploitation of women by men. The research presented in this paper can offer insight into street-based male sex working in Manchester, but multi-sited research with men who sell sex both on and off street, to men and women, should be conducted in order to explore fully the male street scene as it exists nationally. More than this, however, it is important to emphasize that the actions of sex workers and key regulators are not solely dictated by policy frameworks. The link between policy and practice is complex and fraught with contradiction and ideology. Policy is theoretically grounded through practice, yet it is difficult to assess how much a policy framework affects sex working in real terms, and how much local actors are able to break free from this.

In sum, this paper has offered a gendered critique of the current *National Strategy* for England and Wales, noting that male sex workers are conspicuous by their absence. Evident, however, in the case study of Manchester is that it is those extra-legal mechanisms of regulation – notably *choreographies* used by the men to solicit custom – that effectively regulate the street beat. Further explorations of this could contribute usefully to debates over regulation and policy. Thus, it is possible to conclude that although national and local policy frameworks dictate in macro terms how sex work is regulated, what happens on the ground is significant in local terms. Grounded empirical research is a key way of exploring how local commercial sex scenes operate, as the actions of individuals on the street have the opportunity to create and shape spaces of sex work. Thus, it may be useful for policy makers at national and local levels to consider the micro-dynamics of spaces used for street sex work so that appropriate policy interventions can be made.

JOURNAL OF LAW AND SOCIETY
VOLUME 37, NUMBER 1, MARCH 2010
ISSN: 0263-323X, pp. 145–70

Bellwether Citizens: The Regulation of Male Clients of Sex Workers

BELINDA BROOKS-GORDON*

Dangerous and discriminatory new provisions against sex workers' clients have repeatedly been put before parliament in England and Wales. Female ministers keen to punish clients of sex workers eagerly supported the Bill. However, while sex work has become a rights issue it is no longer just about women's rights. Diverse and multiple sexualities and working practices see gay, trans or bisexual workers selling sex to a diverse range of lesbian, gay, trans, and straight clients who may be able-bodied or disabled. This article critically examines the regulation of clients of sex workers, explores the current legislation against them, and reviews recent research evidence. The ideas that inform policy will be discussed along with the various policy approaches. The latest move to criminalize clients in the Policing and Crime Bill 2009 will be discussed along with the spectre of trafficking, used to scapegoat clients by a government which has undermined civil liberties and the fundamental concepts of a free society.

> *[A]nyone indulging in sexual activity is entitled to a degree of privacy especially if it is on private property and between consenting adults (paid or unpaid)*
>
> Mr Justice Eady[1]

INTRODUCTION

A re-run of the 1980s sex wars unfolded in United Kingdom parliamentary meetings over the Policing and Crime Bill 2009 last year when dangerous and discriminatory new provisions were introduced against sex workers'

* *School of Psychology, Birkbeck, University of London, Malet Street, London WC1E 7HX, England*
b.brooks-gordon@bbk.ac.uk

1 *Mosley* v. *Newsgroup Ltd* [2008] E.W.H.C. 1777 (Q.B.).

clients. The same uneasy alliance of separatist feminists and the religious Right that led to the calamitous Meese Commission in the United States was present but this time joined by female ministers eager to be seen to do something for women, mostly by punishing clients of sex workers. However, while sex work has become a rights issue it is no longer just about women's rights. Diverse and multiple sexualities and working practices see gay, trans or bisexual workers selling sex to a diverse range of lesbian, gay, trans and straight clients who may be able-bodied or disabled (see Whowell, this volume, pp. 125–44). These clients, as Mr Justice Eady pointed out, have rights too.

This article takes a critical look at the regulation of clients of sex workers. It will explore the current legislation against them, and provide a brief review of what is known about these men from recent research evidence. The ideology behind different views of clients that inform policy will be explored as I show how the various policy approaches, in Europe and beyond, impact on clients. The latest move to criminalize clients in England in the Policing and Crime Bill 2009 will be discussed along with the spectre of trafficking to show how this has been used to scapegoat clients by a government which has undermined civil liberties and the fundamental concepts of a free society.

CLIENT OFFENCES

Clients of sex workers are subject to the range of offences shown in Table 1. It is an offence in England and Wales[2] to loiter or solicit in a public place for prostitution. This includes any kind of tempting or alluring of sex workers in words, winks, glances, or smiles.[3] A street or public place includes any bridge, lane, or alley.[4] It is an arrestable offence to solicit from, or close to, a vehicle, either persistently or in a way to cause nuisance or annoyance. Loitering and soliciting were defined fifty years ago[5] and although these are 'nuisance' offences, the activity of waiting on the street is no different to waiting for a bus or a lift. Despite its presumed nuisance value, it is the commercial sexual activity that *follows* the waiting that is the substance of the offence. Similarly kerb-crawling[6] is the act of looking for someone and giving them a lift elsewhere There is therefore an interesting conceptual slippage between how the activity is defined, that is, by 'nuisance' and what is criminalized.

---

2 In Scotland the law is different; the Scottish Prostitution Act 2007 created an even more punitive legislative environment than in England and Wales.
3 See Release, *Sex Workers and the Law. Drugs, The Law and Human Rights* (2005).
4 A public place can be anywhere the public may wander, irrespective of their right to be there.
5 The Sexual Offences Acts 1956 and 1959.
6 The Sexual Offences Act 1985.

146

It is also an offence for any individual to have any sexual activity in a public lavatory, or to use threatening, abusive or insulting words or behaviour. For any of these offences, civil orders designed for anti-social behaviour (ASBOs) may also be applied[7] and breaching these can result in criminal charges. The most serious offence is of paying for sexual services from anyone under 18. The offence has a penalty of 14 years to life imprisonment. It is, however, questionable how easy this law is to police and gather intelligence on when consenting adults in the sex industry are increasingly alienated (by increasing criminalization) from the police services.

Table 1. Client offences

Offence	Maximum Penalties
Soliciting[8]	Fine
Kerb crawling[9]	Fine. Loss of driving licence, exposure to family and friends
Sex in a public lavatory[10]	Fine or 6 months sentence
Disorderly behaviour[11]	Fine
Anti-Social Behaviour Orders[12]	Ban on any behaviour, association, exclusion from any area, for between 2 years and life
Paying for the sexual services of anyone under 18[13]	14 years to life imprisonment

Patterns and trends of client offences

Historically, the purchase of sexual services was regulated through a variety of means in the civil and criminal courts, and also the canonical courts.[14] Offences have been constructed through history from Vagrancy Acts dating

---

7 See, generally, T. Sagar, 'Tackling On-street Sex Work' (2007) 7 *Criminology and Criminal Justice* 153–68; S. Collins and R. Cattermole, *Anti-Social Behaviour and Disorder. Powers and Remedies* (2006, 2nd edn.); E. Burney, *Making People Behave: Anti-social behaviour, Politics, and Policy* (2005).
8 Street Offences Act 1959, as amended by the SOA 2003.
9 Sexual Offences Act 1985 s.1(4).
10 SOA 2003, s. 71.
11 Public Order Act 1986, s. 5.
12 Crime and Disorder Act 1998.
13 SOA 2003, s. 47.
14 Where, for example, it was not illegal to buy or sell sex unless either the prostitute or the client was married in which cases, the act contravened the sacrament that marriage was believed to be, and it was tried in the ecclesiastical courts as fornication.

147

back to Henry VIII (1530–1), the recommendations of the Wolfenden Report, and subsequent Sexual Offences Acts (1956, 1959, 1967, 1985, and 2003). Prior to 2003, prostitution offences were minor, low-level offences. Table 2 shows the conviction rates for these offences. The main thing to note in these figures that the number of 'offences' are counted rather than individuals so that a large number of offences often pertains to a small number of individuals.

Recorded prosecution figures for street-based offences of soliciting show a reduction from the start of the decade and while soliciting offences peaked at 2,111 offences in 2002/03, they have since fallen year on year to a recent total of 1,071 recorded incidents in 2008/09, a fall in soliciting of 12 per cent from the previous year.

The catch-all term 'exploitation' also makes it difficult to disaggregate all the indoor offences, and prosecutions against consenting adult sex workers in indoor locations have traditionally been rare, so there is a mismatch between the low prevalence of the offences and government attention to them. Not surprisingly, there was a large rise in these offences from 127 to 186 with the implementation of the Sexual Offences Act (SOA) 2003, followed by a drop in the number of offences. A subsequent rise in 2006/07 accompanied the financial inducement provided to police following the Serious and Organized Crime Act (SOCA) 2005. The abuse of children through prostitution is linked to pornography in the way the offences are framed and counted, so it is impossible to disaggregate how many offences are for under-18s in prostitution and how many offences are for the possession or distribution of child pornography.[15]

Trafficking is the spectre through which political debates to criminalize clients are framed, yet the offence rate is low.[16] The total convictions for trafficking since it became a crime in The Sexual Offences Act 2003 amounts only to 207 recorded incidents. Because of the broad definition of trafficking in the SOA 2003 it is impossible to know how many of these offences are for serious (that is, coercive or violent) trafficking and how many were sex workers helping other or migrant workers with lifts or accommodation.[17] Estimates of trafficking vary: in 1999 the Metropolitan Police stated that 142

15 From a peak of 124 offences recorded in 2005/06 the number of offences fell to 110 in 2007/08. This drop by a fifth occurs at the same time as the increase in other convictions against consenting adult sex worker following the financial inducement for the police, court services, and the Home Office to prosecute adults in sex work. It has to be questioned whether the increased criminalization of adults in sex work results in worse relationships with the police and a concomitant reduction in intelligence and prosecution of under-age offences.

16 The logic of blaming clients for the unrelated behaviour of traffickers is flawed, however, and to blame respectful clients engaged in consensual commercial contracts is rather like blaming conscientious savers for the rapacious behaviour of City bankers.

17 483 HC Debs, col. 587W (19 November 2008).

148

Table 2. Prostitution offences in England and Wales 1997–2007/08[18]

	1997	1997/1998	1998/1999	1999/2000	2000/2001	2001/2002	2002/2003	2003/2004	2004/2005[19]	2005/2006	2006/2007	2007/2008	2008/2009	% change 2007/8 to 2008/9
Soliciting[20] purpose prostitution	–	–	1,107	973	1,028	1,655	2,111	1,944	1,821	1,640	1,290	1,215	1,071	–12
Exploitation Prostitution	131	142	215	138	129	129	127	186	117	153	190	184	175	–5
Abuse children prostitution or pornography	–	–	–	–	–	–	–	–	99	124	101	111	116	5
Trafficking for 'sexual exploitation'	–	–	–	–	–	–	–	–	21	33	43	56	54	–5

18 A. Walker, J. Flatley, C. Kershaw, and D. Moon (eds.), *Crime in England and Wales 2008/09, Vol. 1 Findings from the British Crime Survey and police recorded crime* (2009) Table 2.04.
19 The Sexual Offences Act 2003, introduced in 2004, altered the definition and coverage of sexual offences.
20 Data here includes exploitation of prostitution and soliciting, but not prostitution itself (which is not an offence) and because this activity includes that involving consenting adults, it is particularly influenced by police activity.

149

people had been trafficked, in 2000 the Home Office gave widely varying estimates of between 142 and 1,420 women trafficked into the United Kingdom. Incidents of trafficking for sexual exploitation dropped from an already low and declining rate.[21] At the same time, the government announced cuts in funding to the Metropolitan Police's human trafficking unit and budget cuts for Her Majesty's Court Service and probation (where the lack of increase for years represents a 25 per cent cut for the HMCS and probation service). This creates conflict of interests, when the prisons are full and budgets are being cut, for assets to be seized under the Serious and Organized Crime Act 2005 and divided up amongst these services.[22]

CHARACTERISTICS OF CLIENTS AND THEIR BEHAVIOUR

Criminalization of clients is a relatively recent phenomenon and in the Wolfenden Report,[23] street prostitution was characterized as a public nuisance while off-street prostitution was characterized as an issue of private morality which was not a matter for the criminal law. Most notably the behaviour was gender-specific with prostitutes being female and clients male. Current statutes dictate that prostitution is gender-neutral yet policy debates still use 'prostitute' to mean a female seller of sexual services and 'client' to refer to a male buyer of services, and government press releases use grotesque caricatures of abusive clients and abused sex workers. Yet one of the characteristics of a client's relationships with sex workers is its mundanity.[24] Legal cases, from that of Cynthia Payne to Max Mosley,[25] are characterized by the ordinariness from cups of tea with clients to luncheon vouchers of the daily routines of the sex industry. Sex workers illustrate the relational inter-dependence of sex workers and clients:

> Many ladies like me depend on their clients to be able to live and boosts the treasury's coffers too (I pay taxes, have my health checked) so what harm are we doing? It isn't always an easy job, but what is? At least I know I am valued by my gents and I value them.
>
> (Marcey, Respondent, 16 April 2008).

---

21 485 *HC Debs.* col 161 (4 December 2008).

22 Cuts of £22 million (2009–10) and £17 million (2010–11) to National Offender Management Service (NOMS) were also announced. Similarly, the Minister of Justice, Jack Straw, admits the budget will be reduced by £1 billion over three years (written answer to David Howarth MP, 483 *HC Debs,* col. 20W (17 November 2008).

23 *Report of the Committee on Homosexual Offences and Prostitution* (1957; Cmnd. 247; Chair, Lord Wolfenden).

24 For examples, see H. Kinnell and R.K. Griffiths, 'Male clients of female prostitutes in Birmingham, England: a bridge for transmission of HIV?', presentation to Fifth International Conference on AIDS, Montreal, Canada, June 1989; H. Ward and S. Day, *On The Game* (2007).

25 *Mosley,* op. cit., n. 1.

The NATSAL 2000 survey was a probability study of 11,161 men which showed that 4.2 per cent of the male population paid for commercial sex in the previous five years. This proportion rose from 2 per cent in 1990, and statistical analysis shows that the increase could be due to sampling error.[26] Outside London, 3.5 per cent of men had paid for sex in past five years, and only in London, the teeming metropolis (which also has the majority of the United Kingdom's male sex worker population), were proportions larger, at 8.9 per cent of men.[27] The men who had paid for sex in the previous five years were more likely to be aged 25–34, to be previously or never married, and to be resident in London. Given that the rate of divorce has increased, and the number of men who were previously or never married also increased, then this too, state the authors, could account for any increase between 1990 and 2000.[28] When the same question is asked over the past year, only 1.3 per cent of men reported paying for sex in the previous 12 months. Although women also pay for sex, the NATSAL survey omitted to ask women the question.

In an analysis of lifetime recourse to prostitution (LRP) in nine repeated representative cross-sectional surveys from 1987 to 2000, age-specific estimates of LRP were made. It was reported that 'There was no consistent increasing or decreasing trend over the years'.[29] The authors suggest it is possible:

> to reconcile the observed stability trend-wise, with the anecdotal evidence of increased recourse to prostitution. First, in the presence of population growth in the relevant age classes, one may find a higher absolute number of clients despite stability in relative numbers. Second, if anecdotal reports of the decreasing price of paid sex are true, existing clients may increase their buying frequency without a noticeable increase in LRP. Third, the increase in the number of clients may be due to men above the age range (17–45 yrs) covered in our study.[30]

26 See R. Weitzer, 'Flawed Theory and Method in Studies of Prostitution' (2005) 11 *Violence Against Women* 934–49.

27 In cities where overall rate of men paying for sex is high, a proportion of these are paying men for sex. H. Ward, C. Mercer, K. Wellings, K. Fenton, B. Erens, A. Copas, and A. Johnson, 'Who pays for sex? An analysis of the increasing prevalence of female commercial sex contacts among men in Britain' (2005) 81 *Sexually Transmitted Infections* 467–71.

28 Given what we know about social trends, for example, that the United Kingdom has an ageing population more generally with declining mortality rate, there is a tendency for wives to outlive husbands, divorcees take on average three years to remarry. Indeed, official projections from the Office of National Statistics suggest that 16 per cent of men born in 1964 will neither have married nor be in a cohabiting union by the time they reach their fifties, compared with 8 per cent of men born in 1946: this factor would lead to a projected increase in the client population.

29 A. Jeannin, V. Rousson, G. Meystre-Agustoni, and F. Dubois-Arber, 'Patterns of Sex Work Contact Among Men in the General Population of Switzerland, 1987–2000 (2008) 84 *Sexually Transmitted Infections* 557.

30 id., p. 558.

In a retrospective case note review study it was found that of 258 men who had paid for sex, three men had also been paid for sex.[31] Over half (51 per cent) had paid for sex abroad, 11 per cent paid somewhere else in the United Kingdom, 40 per cent in their own city, either on the streets or in saunas. The majority of the men (93 per cent) paid female sex workers and 4.3 per cent paid men for sex, others paid both. This was a clinic sample so the proportion of those paying for sex is likely to be higher than a general probability sample.

The prevalence of men who are clients of female sex workers varies across continents. In a study of 78 national household surveys, nine city-based surveys, and behavioural surveillance surveys in a total of 54 countries,[32] prevalence was lowest in Western Europe[33] with 3 per cent of men going to sex workers.[34] Other low-prevalence countries included Vietnam (3 per cent), the Caribbean (3–7 per cent), South Asia Pacific islands (3–5 per cent), and Latin America (2.5 per cent). In Cambodia it was 5–10 per cent, the United States and Australia, 6 per cent, Russia and Southern Africa, 7 per cent; West Africa, 9 per cent; and Eastern Africa,[35] 10 per cent. In China and Hong Kong it was 11 per cent; Central Africa, 15 per cent; and in Zimbabwe, 29 per cent. In Rwandan and Zambian truck drivers, prevalence was high at 47 per cent and 30 per cent respectively. Also in urban areas where incomes were higher, among men with high-mobility occupations such as migrant workers, police, military, drivers and truckers, more men paid for sex (25–30 per cent). In an exploration of patterns of lifetime payment for sex in a general population (in Switzerland), there was an age effect found with an increase in the younger age groups (17–30 and 31–45) which plateaued at 40 before declining.[36]

Client diversity

Clients of sex workers may be gay, straight or bisexual. They may be female, male or transgender. They may be single, married, divorced, or widowed. Approximately 25 per cent of men who paid for sex reported having sex with men.[37] As Laud Humphreys's classic study showed,[38] many heterosexually

---

31 T.M. Groom and R. Nandwani, 'Characteristics of Men Who Pay For Sex: A UK Sexual Clinic Survey' (2006) 82 *Sexually Transmitted Infections* 364–7.
32 M. Carael, E. Slaymaker, R. Lyerla, and S. Sarker, 'Clients of Sex Workers in Different Regions of the World: Hard to Count' (2006) 82 *Sexually Transmitted Infections* 26–33.
33 Aggragated data from nine countries.
34 This is the median figure, the mean was 3.5 per cent. Unless otherwise stated, subsequent means and medians are the same.
35 Data from six countries.
36 Jeannin et al., op. cit., n. 29.
37 Careal et al., op. cit., n. 32.
38 See L. Humphreys, *The Tearoom Trade: Impersonal Sex in Public Places* (1970).

152

married men have homosexual liaisons, and not only do gay men pay for sex but otherwise heterosexual clients pay for gay sex. Clients may also be able-bodied or disabled or with a sensory impairment. In research on communities with disabilities, it is apparent that men with physical and sensory impairments are a core group of clients who visit female sex workers and sexual surrogates.[39] One sex worker illustrates the reality of a disabled clients' experience:

> This week I saw a client with Spina Bifida. I had to lift him from his wheelchair, position him (not just dump him) on the bed, undress him, then later, redress him, and place him back in the wheelchair. I was lucky he only weighed 5 stone. Its one of the reasons why more than one lady on the premises can be a good idea.
>
> Penny, Respondent, 16 February 2008

Such insights into the client/sex worker relationship shows how the concepts of 'offenders' and 'victims' is a blurred or redundant concept when applied to the reality of many sex workers' and clients' lives. One sex worker described her clients thus:

> I wish the likes of Ms Harman[40] could meet with ladies like myself – this week alone I have helped a gent left with injuries after a major motor-cycle accident, a man unfortunate enough to have been born a dwarf, a nice fella who loves cross-dressing (and had nowhere to do it away from his wife – she would divorce him and deprive him of his family life if she knew of his preferences). Yesterday, I met again with a lovely gent – who was virtually a virgin at the age of 60+ when we met for the first time a year or so back.
>
> (Glenda, Respondent, 2008)

In a qualitative study on 50 indoor clients, Sanders[41] shows how relationships between male clients and female sex workers are not necessarily exploitative, damaging or disrespectful but that sexual and social scripts performed by male clients are normative and can be used to make sex work a responsible industry. She questions whether there are not economic, material, and social capital trade-offs in all relationships. Similarly, Earle and Sharpe[42] show how the same discourse exists in non-commercial and commercial sex. Analysis of police data on kerb-crawlers found clients to have a lower level of criminality than the general population with only 11 out of 518 men having a prior criminal record.[43] Kinnell[44] noted how violent

---

39 This is not necessarily just because they have an impairment, or because of discrimination in the social world. Like non-disabled men, they have unfulfilled sexual desires for a range of reasons. See T. Sanders, 'The Politics of Sexual Citizenship: Commercial Sex and Disability (2007) 22 *Disability and Society* 439–55.

40 Harriet Harman MP, Minister for Women and Equality.

41 T. Sanders, *Sex Work: A Risky Business* (2005).

42 S. Earle and K. Sharpe, 'Intimacy, Pleasure, and the Men Who Pay for Sex' in *Sex As Crime?*, eds. G. Letherby, K. Williams, P. Birch, and M. Cain (2008).

43 B.M. Brooks-Gordon, *The Price of Sex: Prostitution, Policy, and Society* (2006) ch. 4.

44 See, generally, H. Kinnell, *Violence and Sex Work in Britain* (2008).

153

men will adopt the 'client disguise' and mimic clients until they have manoeuvred a sex worker into a vulnerable position to attack her and that it is not unusual for serial predators to target sex workers just because they are easy to attack.[45] This has to be factored in whenever drawing retrospective assumptions from client populations, that is, it is not necessarily clients who are violent but the vulnerable situation in which sex workers operate which renders them vulnerable to violence from men who masquerade as clients, and also from the police and the community (including vigilantes).

EXPLANATIONS OF CLIENT BEHAVIOUR

While the Sexual Offences Acts 1985 explained the soliciting and kerb-crawling laws as public order offences,[46] public order has become a minor strand in current debates and two explanations of client behaviour have greater predominance: one is 'exploitation' and the other is 'consumption' of goods and services from the adult sex industry.

1. Client behaviour as exploitation

The perspective which holds that clients' behaviour is 'exploitation' regards the purchase of any type of sexual service as violence, that sex workers cannot consent and are thus 'exploited' by the client, and that prostitution is a symptom of patriarchal society. Those who argue from this perspective campaign for the prohibition of prostitution, and for the criminalization of clients in the belief that prostitution can be eradicated. The view is supported by few academics (for example, Farley and Raymond in the United States, Kelly in England, and Barry in Australia). The core claims of the exploitation hypothesis also proposes that all customers and traffickers are evil, and that sex work and trafficking are inextricably linked. While these claims have been shown to be exaggerated, unverifiable, or demonstrably false, the institutionalization of this discourse occurred in American policy making and practice under the Bush administration.[47] This was facilitated by the 'global gag rule', where the United States government had an abstinence and prohibition-led agenda which influenced many areas of sexuality research. Similarly, institutionalization of the prohibitionist stance occurred in official discourses in England and Wales[48] where passionate prohibitionist

---

45 id.
46 See, generally, H. Self, *Prostitution, Women, and Misuse of the Law* (2003).
47 R. Weitzer, 'The Social Construction of Sex Trafficking: Ideology and Institutionalization of a Moral Crusade' (2007) 35 *Politics & Society* 447–75.
48 For example, following the Government Strategy on Prostitution in January 2006, the Home Office launched a kerb-crawler 'marketing' campaign which is arguably a morality campaign; available at: <http://www.homeoffice.gov.uk/documents/paying_the_price.pdf?view=Binary>.

arguments manipulated debates and policy on sex work in the United Kingdom from the Sexual Offences Review in 1999 to gain supremacy between 2001–2008. It meant that essential services, advocacy, and advice on sexual health, HIV, and sex work were prevented and it affected all government funded research on prostitution between 2001–2008[49] in both the United States and the United Kingdom as many ideologically-driven but empirically unsound studies were published on abortion, sexuality, and prostitution in an agenda based on denial of choice.

2. Ideological underpinning of 'client as exploiter'

The exploitation hypothesis is informed by three strands of ideological thought. The first is the radical separatist lesbian feminism which argues that *all* heterosexual sex is exploitation.[50] The second is Marxist feminism, which argues that all work is exploitation, indeed, some of the ministers responsible for policy came from Marxist feminist backgrounds. The final strand is religious evangelism which argues that all non-procreational sex is wrong.[51] The uneasy alliance of separatist feminists and the religious Right that led to the calamitous Meese Commission are replicated in this alliance but with some important differences.[52] One is a critical mass of female parliamentarians eager to be seen to be doing something for women.[53] Another is the politicization of senior police officers who, using pseudo-scare tactics, have lobbied for more power,[54] and the vested interests of pressure groups influenced by American prohibition research and financially supported by

---

49 The rule was rescinded on 23 January 2009 by President Barack Obama.
50 A. Dworkin, *Intercourse* (1987); S. Jeffreys et al., *Love Your Enemy? The Debate Between Heterosexual Feminism and Political Lesbianism* (1981), see: <http://www.guardian.co.uk/lifeandstyle/2009/jan/30/women-gayrights>.
51 Many lobby groups are headed by separatists. The ideological and political alliance is interesting because the three groups take conflicting views on issues like abortion or same-sex partnerships.
52 Examples of this alliance included a new All-party Parliamentary Group on Prostitution chaired by ex-minister Fiona McTaggart, funded by a fundamentalist Christian anti-prostitution group. The first meeting was addressed by a radical separatist feminist from Sweden whose expenses were met by the Christian group.
53 Including Equalities Minister Harriet Harman, Home Secretary Jacqui Smith, Solicitor-General Vera Baird, Barbara Follet, ex-minister Fiona McTaggart, and Maria Eagle. These female MPs were fiercely loyal to each other, and Harman, in particular, was keen to regain feminist credentials after removing benefits from single parents in 1997 and later cutting pensions, moves which disproportionately affected women.
54 For example, Brain in T. Brain, T. Davis, and A. Philips, *National Strategy for Policing Prostitution: Guidelines for dealing with abuse and exploitation through prostitution* (1999).

155

the United Kingdom government. The POPPY Project, for example received £5.8m of public money.[55]

The perspective does not readily accept homosexual and transgender sex work, and the exploitation hypothesis was pursued through the argument that selling sex causes psychological trauma, but when explored empirically, the British Psychological Society (BPS) found that the reports upon which this was based on untested, unsubstantiated measures and application of unvalidated and unwarranted 'treatment'.[56] Yet the exploitation mantra gathered currency in a news media dependent on 'client journalism', and news agencies producing 'churnalism'[57] from government press releases and consultations which use trafficking rhetoric and inflated trafficking figures (which may also exploit migration fears and mask immigration statistics and practices).[58]

3. Clients as consumers in the sexual leisure industry

The second perspective in contemporary debates is that clients are consumers of goods and services in the (sexual) leisure industry (see Brents and Sanders, this volume, pp. 40–60). This is because sex work is work and exists as labour. While this perspective acknowledges that some sex workers are vulnerable, these vulnerabilities can either be designed out,[59] dealt with by stable housing, employment, and welfare support, or addressed in ways other than the criminal law. This perspective argues that sex work is specific form of labour which should be accorded the full rights and dignity accorded to other types of labour.[60] This perspective is supported by large studies

55 Charities Commission, *Accounts for Eaves Housing (incorporating Poppy Project)* (2008), available at <http://www.charitycommission.gov.uk/registeredcharities/ ScannedAccounts/Ends48/0000275048_ac_20080331_e_c.pdf>. Such funds enable it to lobby the government, to furnish the public with prohibitionist tools such as 'objector packs' against lap-dancing clubs, and to produce various reports which have been discredited by academics and medical practitioners. See T. Sanders, R. Campbell, M. O'Neill, B. Brooks-Gordon et al., 'A Response to "Big Brothel" by J. Bindel and H. Atkins, Poppy Project' (2008); Home Office, 'Prostitution' at: <http://www.homeoffice.gov.uk/crime-victims/reducing-crime/prostitution>.
56 The British Psychological Society, 'Memorandum of Evidence on The Criminal Justice and Immigration Bill (2008)', No. 388. Scrutiny Committee, Ninth Sitting (20 November 2007).
57 See, generally, N. Davies, *Flat Earth News* (2008).
58 Home Office, *UK Action Plan on Tackling Human Trafficking* (2007), available at: <http://www.homeoffice.gov.uk/documents/human-traffick-action-plan?view= Binary>.
59 T. Sanders and R. Campbell, 'Designing out vulnerability, building in respect: Violence, safety and sex work policy' (2007) 58 *Brit. J. of Sociology* 1.
60 It does not see all sex work as invasive because a) it can be non-contact (for example, sex chat lines), b) non-penetrative, such as bondage, domination, or many S&M practices, or erotic massage ('hand relief'), and that sex workers separate their sex work from the sexual activity they have with non-commercial partners in a variety of ways.

156

carried out by many independent academics and researchers[61] as well as by clinicians delivering sexual health services and medical research[62] and legal scholars.[63] A variety of different groups, including sex-worker groups such as the English Collective of Prostitutes, the International Union of Sex Workers,[64] and Xtalk campaign for sex work to be recognized as work, and for sex workers to be able to organize in order to make their working lives safer.[65]

This perspective argues that when prostitution is subject to the criminal law, it creates greater vulnerability. De facto criminalization makes sex workers vulnerable to exploitation and less likely to report any violence (irrespective of how or by whom perpetrated), access wider health or social services, and puts them, their families, and their partners at risk. When sex work is criminalized, sex workers are targeted by a variety of criminals and it starts a downward spiral into criminality and prison which inhibits exit from prostitution for those who wish to do other work.[66]

4. *Ideological underpinning of the client as in consensual commercial consumer*

The ideology of sex work as work is informed by traditional liberal principles (for example, J.S. Mill: 'over himself, over his own body and mind, the individual is sovereign') whereby it is not the place of the state to police personal morality. Just because some people disapprove of sex work or find

61 Kinnell, op. cit., n. 44; Brooks-Gordon, op. cit., n. 43; Sanders, op. cit., n. 41; Self, op. cit., n. 46; H. Self, 'Regulating Prostitution' in *Law and Psychology: Current Legal Issues* (eds.) B.M. Brooks-Gordon and M. Freeman (2006); Sanders and Campbell, op. cit., n. 59; V.E. Munro and M. Della Guista, *Demanding Sex: Critical Reflections on the Regulation of Prostitution* (2008); G. Scambler and A. Scambler (eds.), *Rethinking Prostitution in the 1990s* (1997); Ward and Day, op. cit., n. 24.

62 Ward et al., op. cit., n. 27; N. Jeal, C. Salisbury, and K. Turner, 'The multiplicity and interdependency of factors influencing the health of street-based workers: a qualitative study' (2008) 84 *Sexually Transmitted Infections* 381–5, available at: <http://sti.bmj.com/cgi/content/abstract/sti.2008.030841v1>; Ward and Day, op. cit., n. 24; M. Goodyear and L. Cusick, 'Protection of sex workers' (2007) 334 *Brit. Medical J.* 52–3.

63 See, for instance, A. Bainham and B. Brooks-Gordon, 'Reforming the Law on Sexual Offences' in *Sexuality Repositioned: Diversity and the Law*, eds. B.M. Brooks-Gordon, L.R. Gelsthorpe, M.H. Johnson, and A. Bainham (2004); Brooks-Gordon, op. cit., n. 43; J. Scoular and M. O'Neill, 'Social Inclusion, Responsibilization and the Politics of Prostitution Reform' (2007) 14 *Brit J. of Criminology* 2, available at: <http://bjc.oxfordjournals.org/cgi/content/abstract/azm014v2>.

64 International Union of Sex Workers, *Declaration of the Rights of Sex Workers* (2008), available at: <http://www.iusw.org/>.

65 id.

66 A number of 'think tanks' and policy fora, for example, Institute of Economic Affairs, Liberty, and Justice argue that not only does prohibition not work, but it makes the sex worker more vulnerable.

157

it distasteful, this is no basis for constraining freedoms in a liberal democracy. Sex work is the exchange of money for sex, and because there is nothing wrong with spending money, and there is nothing wrong with having sex, there is nothing wrong with paying for sex. In a modern context, between consenting adults, there is no philosophical difference between paid-for sex and any other sex between adults (casual sex, swinger sex, gay sex, unmarried sex, and so on).

The ideology is also informed by a historical socio-legal perspective showing how damaging alternative perspectives are to the safety of those in sex work, and how prohibition has failed historically. The law in its present form *creates* vulnerability, and the only solution to the problem of the disempowerment of those who choose to do the work is in empowering them to work safely. The ideology of sex as work is also informed by the peer-reviewed medical literature on harm-reduction and HIV,[67] queer theory, and the acceptance and respect of alternative lifestyles.[68] This ideology acknowledges same-sex and trans-sex work, and is underpinned by psychological and sociological empirical work showing the diversity of sex work.[69]

5. Tension between the two ideologies

The exploitation message gathered currency with a new generation of feminists and it provided a fertile climate for pressure groups to conflate sex work with exploitation, adultery, and trafficking; a parallel world where the mere act of being a client was thought to cause 'demand' for trafficking, and ordinary economic migration patterns were conflated as campaigners argued that the influx of migrants from eastern European states who, faced with discrimination and poor pay in other sectors, chose sex work over other forms of employment. Other studies, however, which were more methodologically sound showed sex workers in the United Kingdom to be motivated more by the flexibility of sex work for balancing childcare responsibilities, lifestyle choice, freedom, and the relatively high pay compared to other sectors. For example, Sanders's research showed that nearly half (48 per cent) of indoor workers had a degree or a nursing, caring, or teaching qualification.[70] And in more marginalized spheres, sex work can be a free choice or a rational 'resistance' and courageous choice in the face of poverty.[71]

---

67 These are: P. Aggleton, *Men Who Sell Sex. International Perspectives on Male Prostitution and HIV/AIDS* (1998); Ward and Day, op. cit., n. 24; Goodyear and Cusick, op. cit., n. 62.
68 See J. Weeks, *The World We Have Won* (2008); J. Weeks, 'Among Men in Britain' (2005) 81 *Sexually Transmitted Infections* 467–76.
69 Brooks-Gordon, op. cit., n. 43; Sanders, op. cit., n. 41.
70 Sanders, id.
71 See L. Agustín, 'Migrants in the Mistress's House: Other voices in the "trafficking" debate' (2005) 12 *Social Politics* 96–117; L. Agustín, *Sex at the Margins: Migration, Labour Markets and the Rescue Industry* (2007) ch. 5.

The two ideological positions give rise to four main policy responses and Table 3 shows the effect of each response. The prohibitionist approach underpins formal policy in Thailand and in many American states, such as New York.[72] The consequences of prohibition results in symbolic or status law, seen during the prohibition of alcohol in the United States. It also leads to institutional evasion, evidenced in England previously in divorce and abortion law.

While prohibition is a simple policy, easily understood by those who have to police it, many objectors argue that on pragmatic grounds it is a known policy failure.[73] It is impossible to enforce, as no-one has a vested interest in coming forward with evidence, and it gives rise to many other problems such as corruption in states where it is formal policy. Partial criminalization is another policy response with known failings. This intellectually incoherent policy was introduced in Sweden in 1999 under controversial circumstances, and despite independent evaluation of its incipient danger to street sex workers.[74] This policy response has poor support amongst academics[75] and some ministers.[76]

There is also the regulationist approach which accompanies legalisation in many parts of Europe such as Spain, Switzerland, Germany, and Austria. It is seen in differing forms in Nevada and the Netherlands, where partial regulation systems are in place and only those who are entitled to register can do so. This can result in a two-tier system (Netherlands) or allows brothels to operate but not street prostitution (Nevada, United States), which leaves those who work in brothels better off than in regions without them, but excludes those unable to work in brothels and leaves them much worse off. So regulationism, while vastly safer than criminalization or partial criminalization, is not as safe, effective or fair as either full legalization such as Switzerland or decriminalization.

Decriminalization has emerged as a step forward for change and empowerment in New Zealand. The Prostitution Reform Act 2003 (PRA)[77] decriminalized prostitution without 'endorsing or morally sanctioning it or its use'. It sought to safeguard the human rights of sex workers, promote their

---

72 Most notably seen in the New York moral crusade against escort agencies recently discussed in media coverage of the Eliot Spitzer case.
73 J. Meadowcroft, 'Prostitution' in *Prohibition*, ed. J. Meadowcroft (2008) 178–95.
74 Justis- og Politidepartmentet, *Purchasing Sexual Services in Sweden and the Netherlands* (2004).
75 For an exception, see R. Matthews, *Prostitution, Politics, and Policy* (2008).
76 A Ministerial group (including Vernon Coaker, Under-secretary at the Home Office and Barbara Follett, Under-secretary for Equalities) went to Sweden in January 2008 and returned saying that it was not the policy answer for England and Wales.
77 New Zealand Justice Ministry, *Report of the Prostitution Law Review Committee on the Operation of the Prostitution Reform Act 2003* (2008) available at: <http://www.justice.govt.nz/policy-and-consultation/legislation/prostitution-law-review-committee/publications/plrc-report/documents/report.pdf>.

Table 3. Policy responses to clients of sex workers and their effects

Character-ization	Response	Aim	Policy	Effect
Exploiter	Prohibition	Eradication	Criminalization of clients and criminalization/'rehabilitative penalties' of sex workers.	Institutionalized evasion. Symbolic law. Corruption. Witch-hunts. Increased danger and death of street sex workers. Blackmail of sex workers and clients of sex workers. Distrust of police, intelligence breakdown. Industry goes underground. Proliferation of pimping. Increased imprisonment > including family breakdown (sex workers and clients). Hard to exit as criminalization traps sex workers into prostitution.
Exploiter	Partial criminalization	Containment	Criminalization of clients/decriminalization of sex workers.	Confusion. Incoherent legal framework. Impossible to police (as star witnesses won't testify). Danger to sex workers, as clients more nervous on streets. Blackmail of clients. Distrust of police. Effectively creates criminalization.
Customer	Regulation	Containment of street work. Labour and human rights/harm reduction	Decriminalization of sex workers, clients, brothels, safety or tolerance zones for street sex workers. Full labour regulation similar to other service sector work including site inspections of premises. Licensing of brothels.	Partial containment of street work. Less danger and fewer deaths of street workers. Better health and safety for indoor workers. Bad brothels/businesses closed down. Better condom use. Creates two-tier system if not all allowed to register.
Customer	Decriminaliza-tion	Self-governance. Full labour and human rights/harm reduction.	Decriminalization of both sex workers and clients, brothels. Premises subject to same regulations as other service sector work.	Empowerment of sex workers. Best health and safety of sex workers. Improved ability to exit sex work. Best cooperation with police. Least violence. Best harm reduction.

160

health and safety, contribute to public health, and prohibit under-18s in prostitution. The new law led to improvements in the health, safety, and human rights of sex workers. A rigorous five-year evaluation revealed that over 90 per cent of sex workers felt they had legal rights under the PRA, and more than 60 per cent felt they were more able to refuse sexual services. Prior to the enactment of the PRA, the industry's illegal status meant sex workers were open to coercion and exploitation. The impact of the Prostitution Reform Act 2003 in New Zealand shows that decriminalization reduces violence, gives greater empowerment of workers, and better cooperation with police against attempts at coercion. The PRA empowered sex workers by removing the 'taint of criminality' so they can take more control of their employment relationships, especially those with clients. Such deregulation is part of the richer historical tradition of feminist concern for those in the sex industry espoused by social reformer Josephine Butler and her 1869 campaign which led to the repeal in 1883 of the Contagious Diseases Acts. To be workable, policy on sex work has to be based not on moral authoritarianism, but on sound psychological and legal principles and robust evidence that respects the civil liberties and human rights of both sex workers and clients.

CONTEMPORARY POLICY PROPOSALS IN ENGLAND AND WALES

The Policing and Crime Bill 2009 contains provisions for a new offence of paying for sexual services with someone subjected to force, threats or deception; punitive measures against loitering and soliciting including the forced 'rehabilitation' of sex workers; and closure orders for indoor premises.[78] Downing Street argues it will 'protect vulnerable groups, particularly women and children by tackling demand for prostitution'; 'prevent low level crime and disorder taking root in our communities by tightening controls around lap dancing clubs'; and 'strengthen our ability to fight serious and organized crime through improved recovery of criminal assets and improved international judicial co-operation.'[79] The stated purpose is the prevention of violence, abuse, and trafficking into prostitution, yet to date there have been no provisions which explicitly address violence.

The Bill comes a short time after harsh sanctions were imposed on sex workers, and those who pay them, in the Sexual Offences Act (SOA) 2003. The Sexual Offences Act was followed by the consultation, *Paying the Price*, in July 2004[80] and the Home Office, *A Coordinated Prostitution*

78 The Policing and Crime Bill will amend the SOA 1959 and SOA 2003.
79 See <http://www.number10.gov.uk/Page17673>.
80 For a critical analysis, see B. Brooks-Gordon, 'Clients and Commercial Sex' (2005) *Crim. Law Rev.* 425; also, K. Soothill and T. Sanders, 'Calling the tune? Some observations on Paying the Price: a consultation paper on prostitution' (2004) 4 *J. of Forensic Psychiatry and Psychology* 1–18, at 15.

Strategy[81] which controversially[82] recommended tackling the 'demand' for prostitution with punitive measures against clients.

The Bill reintroduces provisions removed the previous year from The Criminal Justice and Immigration Bill 2008 (c. 123–125). Following significant concerns expressed,[83] the clauses on prostitution were withdrawn from the Bill[84] to return in the Policing and Crime Bill 2008 (following a lamentably short eight-day deadline for comments) and before the results from the Home Office review, *Tackling the Demand for Prostitution: A Review* (2008) were published. The Bill contains provisions 'aimed at reducing the demand for prostitution and shifts the focus of enforcement from those working as prostitutes to those that pay for sex'.[85]

1. *Criminalizing payment for sex*

The most controversial part in the new Bill is the strict liability offence of 'paying for services of a prostitute subjected to force, threats or deception' (c. 13). It will be irrelevant whether the client 'is, or ought to be, aware that C has used force, deception or threats' [c. 13(2)b]. The creation of a new offence would criminalize virtually all clients because of the broad definitions of 'gain'. All prostitution is for gain, otherwise it is just sex. For the purpose of this section, 'force' includes psychological means including exploitation of vulnerability (s. 53a, 5.4). This could be broadly interpreted to mean forced by economic 'vulnerability', and that could include the majority of sex workers as all economic situations and poverty is relative. Strict liability means that prosecutors would not have to prove that a client knew that the sex worker they paid was 'trafficked' or 'pimped'; prosecutors would simply have to show that money changed

---

81 Home Office, *A Coordinated Prostitution Strategy* (2006) available at: <http://www.homeoffice.gov.uk/documents/cons-paying-the-price/>

82 The Strategy is examined in Brooks-Gordon, op. cit., n. 43.

83 Not least the Safety First Coalition (which includes members of the church, the RCN, medical consultants, National Association of Probation Officers (NAPO) and the Trade Union and Professional Association for Family Court and Probation Officers, drug and prison reformers, anti-rape and anti-poverty organizations, residents from red-light areas, sex workers, sex-work projects, disability rights groups), the International Union of Sex Workers, and others working in harm-reduction programmes. There was concern that broadening the definition of persistence would increase the vulnerability of sex workers and would also result in net-widening, drawing more women in particular into the criminal justice system.

84 During passage of the Bill, medical service providers, academics, and sex-worker advocates provided evidence to the House of Commons and House of Lords and received considerable support from a number of politicians, and parliamentarians (including John McDonnell MP, Evan Harris MP, Lord Faulkner, Baroness Stern, Baroness Howe, Baroness Miller).

85 Home Office, *Policing and Crime Bill Explanatory Notes* (20 May 2009).

hands.[86] Thus the proposals would criminalize the majority of clients and create a situation similar to that of Sweden where it is more dangerous for sex workers.

The proposals would mean that the clients who currently contact the police if they have concerns about a sex worker's situation would not do so for fear of being criminalized. If a woman had been coerced into working, escaped and continued to work in sex work for herself, the proposals would criminalize her clients. The Police Federation have argued that it would be impossible to police because clients and sex workers in consenting contractual relationships won't testify against each other. Any acts involving those who cannot consent are already illegal[87] and critics argue that the Home Office should focus on helping sex-working women to bring charges against any violent man or women (who sometimes also rob them) to justice rather than bringing in dangerous new laws because prosecuting clients is a diversion from prosecuting violent men.[88] For sex workers, this provision would render them liable to many of the inchoate offences in English law such as incitement, accessory, and procurement (and thus make them more vulnerable in law).

Given that 25 per cent of men who pay for sex have sex with other men, to criminalize male clients of male sex workers would return to pre-Wolfenden days of criminalizing same-sex activity in private, just because money changes hands. It would be an infringement of civil liberties and natural justice. For disabled groups, the European (case) law ruling that defines one's sex life as the most intimate part of one's private life means that, for disabled clients (men and women) paying a sex worker sometimes to lose their virginity or for the first non-medical touch in their lives, it conflicts with European Human Rights Law.[89]

2. Loitering and forced rehabilitation

There is an amendment to the offence of loitering and soliciting in clause 15 and the term 'common prostitute' is substituted by the word 'person'. Any loitering behaviour (to sell sexual services) taking place on two or more occasions in any period of three months is redefined in clause 15 as 'persistently'. Such infrequency can only be described as occasional.[90] This is accompanied by compulsory and forced 'rehabilitative penalties' in clause

---

86 People convicted under the new law would face a fine of up to £1,000 and receive a criminal record.
87 There are already numerous offences against kidnap, rape, trafficking, and so on.
88 L. Longstaff, 'Accused: British Legal System That Fails to Protect Women' *Tribune*, 15 February 2008.
89 *Niemitz* v. *Germany* (1993) 16 E.H.R.R. 97.
90 In practice, persistence is currently interpreted as two or more occasions of soliciting in the same evening.

16 in an amendment to c. 57 of the Street Offences Act 1959. This means that anyone can be arrested for waiting for clients on the street if they do it twice in three months. They would then have to attend three meetings with a supervisor approved by the court in order to (a) address the 'causes of the conduct constituting the offence, and (b) find ways to cease engaging in such condition in the future' by compulsory rehabilitation order under section 1(28) of the Street Offences Act 1959. The rehabilitation period will be six months and failure to comply would result in a summons back to court and 72-hours imprisonment. This clause changes the whole tenor of the law on this issue from public order to morality and reintroduces a system that failed after the Sexual Offences Act 1959.[91] The provisions in the Bill (and much of the media discussion)[92] drew on extrapolations from limited evidence from street-sector samples,[93] which form a small part of the sex industry,[94] and applied this to all sections of the industry. Yet the majority of sex work is based indoors.[95] Compulsory rehabilitation schemes, rather than helping to address complex and diverse needs, penalize vulnerable people, including clients with disabilities and street-based sex workers.[96] The research evidence also shows that rehabilitation schemes for complex needs should be voluntary. Coercion into rehabilitation is not an appropriate or effective way to deliver treatment. Linking service provision with the criminal justice system can have a negative impact on the relationship of trust between project staff and service users.[97] This clause further disenfranchises vulnerable clients and sex workers by repeating the rehabilitation period (of six months) if the conviction is not spent.

3. Soliciting and kerb crawling (re)defined

Clause 18(1) creates a new single offence of soliciting to replace kerb crawling in a street or public place and persistent soliciting on foot. The new clause removes the need for persistence, making kerb crawling or soliciting punishable on the first occasion. Because it also removes the requirement for

---

91 In evidence to the Criminal Law Revision Committee 1984 the Metropolitan Police said that 'cautions and charges' appeared to have little deterrent effect and it was observed that the 'women had no desire to receive a lecture from members of the social services with less experience of life than themselves'. It also reintroduces imprisonment for a prostitution offence, paras. 5.16 and 5.23. See Self, op. cit., n. 46, p. 275.
92 Clauses 15–17 are expanded versions of clauses that the government removed from the previous year's Criminal Justice and Immigration Bill.
93 Weitzer, op. cit., n. 47.
94 Estimated by most studies to be no more than 10–15 per cent of the entire industry.
95 Sanders, op. cit., n. 41.
96 J. Pitcher, R. Campbell, P. Hubbard, M. O'Neill, and J. Scoular, *Living and working in areas of street sex work: from conflict to coexistence* (2006).
97 R. Campbell and M. O'Neill (eds.), *Sex Work Now* (2006).

164

kerb crawling to cause annoyance or nuisance to others, this means that anyone could be charged for asking a sex worker for information or stopping to ask directions. If one sex worker spoke to another about a client who wished to see both of them, both sex workers could be criminalized. The provision would therefore severely affect sex workers' and clients' right to association. This is a recycling of the Shelton Bill which sought to remove persistence but was filibustered out of parliament in 1990 following recognition that it would cause more vulnerability and herald in a new 'sus' law for police to stop Irish or immigrant men, or anyone the police want to stop for any other purposes.[98] Enforcement against kerb crawlers results in greater danger to sex workers as they are removed from usual forms of support, and have less time to negotiate safer sex, prices, and terms.[99] The government strategy on prostitution of January 2006 resulted in police clampdowns against kerb crawlers in cities which made things more dangerous for street workers and ended in the murder of five young women in Ipswich during November and December 2006.[100] Legal groups also argue that this 'will have no tangible effect on the sort of crime that really does affect our communities (violent crime and crimes against property). Critics argue that it will further distort policing methods, crime figures, and ultimately undermine confidence in the criminal justice system.[101]

4. *Police powers to close premises associated with prostitution*

A new civil order is put forward in clause 20 to close premises used for activities 'related to certain sexual offences'. These closure orders could be applied retrospectively and on the hearsay evidence of one person. The provision would give the police enormous power to seal premises on suspicion (that is, without any proof) that activities related to specified prostitution (or pornography) offences have happened or may happen, and can be issued regardless of whether an offence will be committed.[102] An officer can use reasonable force to enter premises if necessary to effect the

---

98 Sir William Shelton proposed The Sexual Offences Bill 1990, a private members bill for the removal of 'persistence' in kerb-crawling legislation. The Bill was, however, talked out by Ken Livingstone who recognized the removal of 'persistence' would be less safe for sex workers and could provide a Trojan horse with which to bring in a new 'sus' law to use against Irish, Black, or immigrant people whom the police might want to charge for other purposes. See B.M. Brooks-Gordon and L.R. Gelsthorpe, 'Prostitutes' Clients, Ken Livingstone, and a New Trojan Horse' (2003) 42 *Howard J. of Criminal Justice* 437–51.

99 See Brooks-Gordon, op. cit., n. 43.

100 If the kerb-crawler client is convicted, a fine is imposed, which if unpaid could lead to loss of liberty through imprisonment. This happens for one incident that causes no nuisance or annoyance to anyone, in pursuance of a legal activity. Policing kerb crawling like this is open to abuse by the current system of target-led policing.

101 Release, *Response to Home Office Proposals* (2008).

102 Home Office, op. cit., n. 85, para. 122.

165

notice, and close premises altogether, to owners and residents, for up to three months, with an extension made at any time before the end of the period.[103] The penalty is a level 5 fine (currently £5,000), imprisonment for 51 weeks or both. Closure orders are made through civil proceedings but breach of them is a criminal offence. This represents a blurring of the lines between civil and criminal proceedings. The provisions in the Police and Crime Bill 2009 are incoherent and dangerous, and will result in more, not less 'exploitation'.[104] These proposals on clients are in conflict with empirical evidence showing how sex work could be made less 'problematic' to the law.[105]

5. 'Supply' or 'demand'?

The government argued that 'paying for sex fuels the demand for trafficked women' but there is no evidence either way to state whether sex markets are demand-driven or supply-led. Indeed, the government's targets of 50 per cent of students in higher education, coupled with the increase of students in the sex industry (given its flexible hours, relatively high pay, making it work that many students choose to do while doing their degree), could equally be used to show that the government is fuelling supply. The Equalities Minister Harriet Harman was responsible for cuts to lone parent benefits in November 1997, so that if lone parents (the majority of whom are women) go into sex work through lack of money to bring up their children, then this has helped to fuel supply in the sex industry. A newspaper ban put forward by Ms Harman on sex workers' advertisements and the Newspaper Society made it harder for sex workers to advertise and reach clients themselves, and this could 'fuel' the demand for go-betweens, that is, pimps. The Equalities Minister maintained that tackling domestic violence is a priority but made the financial situation harder for women who wished to escape a violent partner with her reduction of these same benefits. Violence is often used as the excuse for greater state intervention in sex work, yet more violence occurs in marriage, but no attempt has been made to criminalize marriage, so questions have to be asked about the focus on clients.

103 id., para. 132.
104 At a public meeting in Parliament on 25 November 2008, the Safety First Coalition told how it had been inundated by women who had been raided, arrested, charged, and face imprisonment for running safe, discreet premises where no coercion was taking place with anti-trafficking legislation used to justify these raids.
105 See, for example, J. Scoular, J. Pitcher, R. Campbell, P. Hubbard, and M. O'Neill, 'What's anti-social about sex work? Governance, discourse and the changing representation of prostitution's incivility' (2007) 6 *Community Safety J.* 11.

Impressions that the sex industry is rife with trafficking have been used by the government to justify punitive proposals against sex workers' clients. The Home Office and ministers have repeatedly stated that 4,000 people had been trafficked into prostitution in the United Kingdom in 2003 at any one time.[106] Requests under the Freedom of Information Act finally produced the Home Office 'internal audit' in which the 4,000 figure was constructed. It is apparent from the flawed methods and unsubstantiated assertions that the figures are not supported by any credible evidence and that the figures were fabricated.[107] And some corners of the press have had to retract large figures of trafficking previously published.[108]

The official report on trafficking from the police operation Pentameter 1 shows that despite 55 forces hunting for them, only 88 people were trafficked. If it is accepted that 80,000 work in the sex industry,[109] then only a tiny proportion, 0.11 per cent of people in the sex industry, were trafficked.[110] A subsequent operation, Pentameter 2, found 167 trafficked people, which is still only 0.21 per cent. The people found in Pentameter 1 and Pentameter 2 in 2007 were the result of over 1,337 raids of more than 1,300 premises targeted by the police as likely to be abusive. Less than a fraction of 1 per cent of people in sex work were found to be trafficked (and some of these were not in the sex industry but in domestic service).[111]

Trafficking is used as the reason to punish clients and enforce the prohibition of sex work. The 'rescue industry' offers a dehumanizing view of

---

106 Joint Committee on Human Rights, Twenty-Sixth Report, *Legislative Scrutiny: Equality Bill* (2008–09) HL 169, HC 736, available at: <http://www.publications.parliament.uk/pa/jt200506/jtselect/jtrights/245/24507.htm>.

107 R. Dubourg S. Farouk, L. Miller, and S. Pritchard, 'People Trafficking for sexual exploitation' in *The impact of organized crime in the UK: revenues and economic and social costs*, retitled *Organised crime: revenues, economic and social costs, and criminal assets available for seizure*, eds. R. Dubourg and S. Pritchard (2004).

108 S. Butterworth, 'Open Door: The readers' editor on the studious reader's approach to "studies"' *Guardian*, 8 December 2008 (retracting figures talking up the percentage of women 'trafficked', it states that 'the article should not have made the claim. In doing so it (unintentionally) misled readers' into thinking that trafficking figures were higher than otherwise). Available at: <http://www.guardian.co.uk/commentisfree/2008/dec/08/prostitution-open-door>.

109 This is not an unproblematic mathematic, see L. Cusick, H. Kinnell, B. Brooks-Gordon, and R. Campbell, 'Wild guesses and conflated meanings: Estimating the size of the sex worker population in Britain' (2009) 29 *J. of Critical Social Policy* 703–19.

110 J. Avenell, 'Trafficking for sexual exploitation: a process review of Operation Pentameter', Home Office Research Report 7 (2008), available at <http://www.homeoffice.gov.uk/rds/pdfs08/horr07b.pdf>.

111 See <http://www.homeoffice.gov.uk/about-us/news/pentameter-2> and <http://www.publications.parliament.uk/pa/cm200708/cmhansrd/cm080715/text/80715w0010.htm>.

migrants in the sex industry, the vast majority of which do not want to be rescued. There are many grassroots rebellions against the rescue industry.[112] The United States-led neo-conservative 'war' against prostitution looked like a puritanical 'white woman's burden',[113] and policy on trafficking in England and Wales does not acknowledge that migrants can exercise choice, that the decision to leave one's origin country in order to seek a better life shows control over one's life, as an active post-colonial agent.[114] Distortion also comes in the misleading term 'sexual exploitation' instead of 'sex work', and in some reports there is confusion between those in prostitution and those sexually abused in domestic service.[115]

It has been suggested that inflated trafficking figures could be used by a government to mask migration figures. Migration increased from the start of this century from the accession states of Europe, and it occurs for many labour markets including agricultural, retail, and service-sector work. It is possible to appreciate the motivations of sex-work migrants such as transvestite workers escaping police violence in Serbia[116] or young gay-sex workers from Poland, where the conservative Prime Minister has subscribed to the stamping out of homosexuality. Indeed the government has been criticized by the Royal Statistical Society for manipulating the presentation of migration figures.[117] The Policing and Crime Bill proposals, however, are also put forward in the wider context of erosion of civil liberties whereby the 'mission creep' of laws brought in for one purpose are used against citizens in everyday life.[118] The conflict of interest inherent in asset seizure in particular[119] undermines civil liberties and fundamental concepts of a free society.[120] Such seizure of assets

---

112 See <http://www.empowerfoundation.org/> and <http://www.rhrealitycheck.org/blog/2008/08/07/sex-workers-iac-listen-us>.

113 N. Rothschild, 'Prostituting Women's Solidarity: The UK government's call to British women to help combat "sex trafficking" amounts to a crackdown on immigration' *Spiked*, 27 November 2008, available at: <http://www.spiked-online.com/index.php?/site/article/5973/>.

114 Agustín, op. cit. (2007), n. 71.

115 For example, see C. Zimmerman, M. Hossain, K.Yun, B. Roche, L. Morison, and C. Watts, *Stolen Smiles* (2006).

116 B.M. Brooks-Gordon, 'State Violence Towards Sex Workers' (2008) *Brit. Medical J.* 337:a:908 doi:10.1136/bmj.a908.

117 See <http://www.rss.org.uk/pdf/Home_Office_Press_Office_RSS_President_to_Chair_of_Authority.pdf>; <http://www.telegraph.co.uk/news/newstopics/politics/2977230/Home-Office-accused-of-burying-bad-news-over-immigration.html>; <http://www.dailymail.co.uk/news/article-1057116/Home-Office-apologises-Minister-accused-hijacking-spin-free-immigration-briefing.html>.

118 C. Pantazis, 'The Problem of Criminalisation' (2008) 74 *Criminal Justice Matters* 10–12.

119 On 17 November 2008, judges spoke out against the conflict of interests inherent in courts' funding reliance on court fines.

120 The obscure common law offence of 'aiding and abetting misconduct in a public office' was used to arrest Damian Green MP. He was questioned for nine hours and his homes and Commons office were searched after he was arrested on 27

provides a real motive for the persecution of those in commercial sexual relationships, for the flimsy cover of inflated trafficking statistics, and the way an increasingly powerful police state will fund itself.

7. Politics, press, and public opinion

Katherine Raymond, special advisor to Home Secretary David Blunkett from 2001 to 2004, helped prepare the Green Paper *Paying the Price*, and subsequently stated that the government 'forensically examined the prostitution laws', and asked for people's views on legalized brothels and local authority sponsored red-light districts. The results however were not welcomed by a Downing Street fearful of a hostile media response. In 2006 Raymond wrote:

> brothels, giving women a safer place to work, should be made legal, and subject to licensing conditions [and] ... red light zones have their problems. But their existence can help reduce crime, and enhance women's safety.[121]

It is a reflection of modern governance that even when public support is high for the right policy, fear of media reaction creates the wrong one.

An IPSOS Mori poll found that 59 per cent of people (six out of ten) feel 'prostitution is a perfectly reasonable choice that women should be free to make'. The survey, commissioned and funded by the Ministry for Women and Equality, shows two-thirds of the public to be pro-choice and pro-sex work.[122] The support for legalization has been called 'massive'.[123] There are no groups of active sex workers who support the prohibitionist stance and criminalization of clients.[124] It an irony that a Ministry set up to help women is strongly supporting measures that stigmatize women and provide (mainly male) police with enormous power over (mainly female) sex workers' lives and property under the pretence of protecting them from the mythical monsters that are their clients.

November 2009. Mr Green had been given information about migration leaked by a member of Home Office staff. The case is highly unusual and it illustrates the degree to which the erosion of civil liberties and fundamental freedoms has occurred, and the sensitivity of the Home Office about its migration policies.

121 See K. Raymond, 'Brothels and safe red light areas are the only way forward' (2006), available at <http://www.guardian.co.uk/commentisfree/2006/dec/17/comment.politics3>.

122 IPSOS Mori (2008), available at <http://www.equalities.gov.uk/pdf/Attitudestowardsprostitutionsurvey%20June2008.pdf>. The findings come despite the use of 'push-polling' questions, the fact that only women were mentioned, and derogatory stereotypes, words, and imagery were used, and mentioned only heterosexual prostitution and not same-sex or trans workers.

123 'Massive support for legalisation of prostitution' *Politics.co.uk*, 27 November 2008, available at: <http://www.politics.co.uk/news/opinion-former-index/policing-and-crime/massive-support-legalisation-prostitution-$1251359.htm>.

124 I. Dunt, 'Prostitutes United' *Politics.co.uk*, 8 September 2008, available at: <http://www.politics.co.uk/analysis/policing-and-crime/feature-prostitutes-united/-$1239427.htm>.

169

CONCLUSION

To pay for sexual services is not in and of itself a crime in England and Wales. The offences on the statute book that relate to an adult sex worker's clients and broad definitions mean that the provisions lack clear purpose for workable policy and recognition of clients of sex workers as entitled to the same civil and human rights as other citizens. Provisions on sex work have suffered from a flawed consultation process,[125] a misdirected remit, and unsustainable assumptions.[126] Policy has been marred by divisions in perspectives and by a conservative approach to 'abstinence' as well as the de facto criminalization of sex workers' clients. New provisions, which if implemented could change the whole tenor of the law from nuisance to prohibition in a raft of punitive proposals and interventions, would be damaging and dangerous. Sex workers' clients are bellwether citizens[127] and their broader criminalization represents repression in otherwise neo-liberal times. Where the erosion of their liberties start, others follow[128] and it is an indicator of how the state may yet treat the rest of society.[129]

125 Brooks-Gordon, op, cit., n. 43.
126 Home Office Ministers and the Equalities Minister are already linked to organizations carrying out flawed and unethical research practices. As a result, government policy on prostitution is built on sensationalist studies that are inaccurate, see Butterworth, op. cit., n. 108.
127 This has already been seen in the laws around DNA sampling.
128 The Metropolitan police were ordered to destroy DNA samples collected and held unlawfully from kerb crawlers prior to the Police and Criminal Justice Act 2001.
129 The expansion of the DNA database to include innocent people was ruled unlawful in December 2008 by the European Court of Human Rights. The progression was a logical and predictable erosion of civil liberties.

170

JOURNAL OF LAW AND SOCIETY
VOLUME 37, NUMBER 1, MARCH 2010
ISSN: 0263-323X, pp. 171–88

Extreme Concern: Regulating 'Dangerous Pictures' in the United Kingdom

FEONA ATTWOOD* AND CLARISSA SMITH**

This article begins with an exploration of section 5 of the recent Criminal Justice and Immigration Act 2008, otherwise known as the 'Dangerous Pictures Act' which outlaws the possession of 'extreme images', and the Rapid Evidence Assessment belatedly used to justify the legislation. We then examine the claims of the growth, dissemination, and widespread availability of material which 'glories in sexual violence' and its putative 'effects'. This current crisis over the meanings of pornography highlights the rhetorical function of the conceptual discourse of 'pornographication', its links to problematic figurations of the consumer or viewer of explicit materials, and how the identification of 'extreme' pornography has given voice to a range of anxieties about media spectacularization of the body. We end by arguing that opposition to the legislation is not just a matter of protecting personal freedoms or refusing to recognize the existence of harms; instead, we propose that academics will need to question the very parameters on which the impulses to legislate are based.

INTRODUCTION

Pornography is often central to debates about sex and, as Henry Jenkins notes, is also:

> at the center of the controversy surrounding any new media as the public adjusts to the larger shifts in the ways an emerging medium shapes our relations to time and space or transforms the borders between public and private.[1]

* Faculty of Arts, Computing, Engineering and Sciences, Sheffield Hallam University, City Campus, Howard Street, Sheffield S1 1WB, England
F.Attwood@shu.ac.uk
** Centre for Research in Media & Cultural Studies, David Puttnam Media Centre, University of Sunderland, St Peters Campus, St Peters, Sunderland SR6 0DD, England
clarissa.smith@sunderland.ac.uk

1 H. Jenkins, 'Porn 2.0' (2007), at: <http://henryjenkins.org/2007/10/porn_20.html>.

Online pornographies increasingly provide a key site for moral, political and legal debates about sex and regulation, condensing a range of fears about the dangers of sex and technology around the connection of body and screen and about 'dangerous pictures'.[2]

Since the 1990s, the primary focus of these fears has been on the child victims of porn, or of paedophiles lurking online, and on cyberporn and cybersex addicts, expressing the dangers of the Internet as a violent and disturbing 'sea of sex'.[3] More recently, this focus has shifted to include a concern with 'extreme' pornography and its users. In a recent issue of this journal, McGlynn and Ward welcomed legislation criminalizing 'extreme' pornography, but their argument rested on the unsupported assertion that 'pornography can nurture real injustice and ruin real lives',[4] and on a dangerously old-fashioned view that forms of culture that fail to 'make our society a kinder, more compassionate or more human place'[5] necessitate legal intervention, a test with clear implications beyond 'extreme' forms of media text – indeed, their critique lumps together online rape fantasy sites and *Playboy* magazine. Other academics have been more critical of the legislation, particularly those with expertise in media production, consumption, and regulation and in various forms of extreme media.[6]

The twenty-sixth Criminal Justice and Immigration Act received Royal Assent on 8 May 2008 and became law in England and Wales on 26 January 2009. Part 5 of the Act specifically outlaws the possession of any image if it is both 'extreme' and 'pornographic' and:

> portrays, in an explicit and realistic way, any of the following—
> (a) an act which threatens a person's life,
> (b) an act which results, or is likely to result, in serious injury to a person's anus, breasts or genitals,
> (c) an act which involves sexual interference with a human corpse, or
> (d) a person performing an act of intercourse or oral sex with an animal (whether dead or alive), and a reasonable person looking at the image would think that any such person or animal was real.[7]

2 Z. Patterson, 'Going on-line: Consuming Pornography in the Digital Era' in *Porn Studies*, ed. L. Williams (2004) 105–23.

3 Y. Akdeniz, *Sex on the Net: The Dilemma of Policing Cyberspace* (1999); T. Craig and J. Petley, 'Invasion of the Internet Abusers' in *Ill Effects: The Media Violence Debate*, eds. M. Barker and J. Petley (2001, 2nd edn.) 186–201; A. Hamilton, 'The Net Out of Control – A New Moral Panic: Censorship and Sexuality' in *Liberating Cyberspace: Civil Liberties, Human Rights and the Internet*, ed. Liberty (1999) 169–86.

4 C. McGlynn and I. Ward, 'Pornography, Pragmatism, and Proscription' (2009) 36 *J. of Law and Society* 327–51, at 327.

5 id., p. 349.

6 See, for example, 'Memorandum submitted by Dr Clarissa Smith et al. (CJ&I 341)', Criminal Justice and Immigration Bill Committee (2007), available at: <http://www.publications.parliament.uk/pa/cm200607/cmpublic/criminal/memos/ucm34102.htm>.

7 Criminal Justice and Immigration Act 2008 (c4) Part 5, available at: <http://www.opsi.gov.uk/acts/acts2008/ukpga_20080004_en_9>.

The history of this law may not be well known to readers of this journal but its specific provisions regarding 'extreme' pornography have their genesis in the sad case of Jane Longhurst, a teacher asphyxiated by Graham Coutts in 2003 in a 'sex game' he claimed went wrong. During his trial the prosecution described Coutts's habitual use of pornographic internet sites featuring sexual violence. Following the trial, the victim's mother, Liz Longhurst, called for a ban on such sites and gathered a petition of 50,000 signatures to support it. Two MPs, Martin Salter and David Lepper, lent their voices to the campaign along with the moral crusading group MediaWatch UK and various British newspapers. All suggested that, while the websites did not cause Coutts to murder Jane Longhurst, they had 'normalized' his perverted view of sexual pleasures. Existing law, in the shape of the Obscene Publications Act 1959, was, they argued, unable to deal with the specific threat posed by the availability of the 'deeply abhorrent' materials online. As Home Office Minister Vernon Coaker put it:

> Such material has no place in our society, but the advent of the internet has meant that this material is more easily available and means existing controls are being bypassed – we must move to tackle this.[8]

In 2005, the Home Office, under the then Home Secretary Charles Clarke, began a consultation process inviting interested parties to make their representations regarding the desirability of legislation against 'extreme pornographic imagery'. Julian Petley has chronicled[9] the responses to the consultation and the subsequent misrepresentation of those responses which allowed Coaker to claim that, 'the vast majority of people find these forms of violent and extreme pornography deeply abhorrent'.[10] Petley points out 'a clear and substantial numerical majority opposed the proposals'.[11] However, opponents of the legislation were predominately individuals whereas supporters were drawn from organizations such as the 'police forces, moral entrepreneurs and groups representing women, children and religious interests'.[12] Supporters' arguments for legislation centred on the ways in which the internet facilitated access to pornographic materials such that they required special controls. In particular, the police were vociferous in the need for additional legislation and that its remit should go even further than that proposed:

> In our opinion acts of coprophilia (excrement, urination) within pornograph [sic] are examples of the total degradation of the person subject of such acts. It

---

8 'Cracking down on violent pornography', 30 August 2006, available at: <http://www.homeoffice.gov.uk/about-us/news/violent-porn-outlawed>.

9 See various articles available at: <http://www.indexoncensorship.org>.

10 'Victory for victim's mum in crackdown on web sex violence' *Daily Mail*, 30 August 2006.

11 J. Petley, 'To the censors, we're all Aboriginals now' *Spiked*, 2 July 2007, at: <http://www.spiked-online.com/index.php?/site/printable/3556/>.

12 id.

is our view that such acts are enjoyed by sadists. Likewise acts of belonephilia (needles fetish) agonophilia (pseudo rape) and other forms of extreme violence are also enjoyed by sadist [sic] and those persons with sadistic tendencies. Such tendencies would skew the mindset of the viewer of such material to believe that this is the norm. As such we feel it should not be tolerated.[13]

Although these recommendations for further inclusions were not taken up, it was clear that the government also understood viewers' mindsets were in danger of being skewed; there was little or no intention of ceding the ground relating to 'evidence of harm' despite the representations of a number of expert academics in the field.[14] In their Executive Summary, Paul Goggins and Cathy Jamieson outlined the government's position:

> As to evidence of harm, conducting research in this area is complex. We do not yet have sufficient evidence from which to draw any definite conclusions as to the likely long-term impact of this kind of material on individuals generally, or on those who may already be predisposed to violent or aberrant sexual behaviour.[15]

Not all politicians felt the same way and once the Bill reached parliament it was greeted with scepticism from sufficient numbers of MPs that research proving the claims of harm needed to be produced. A Rapid Evidence Assessment (REA) was duly brandished in parliament, claiming that:

> The REA supports the existence of some harmful effects from extreme pornography on some who access it. These included increased risk of developing pro-rape attitudes, beliefs and behaviours, and committing sexual offences. Although this was also true of some pornography which did not meet the extreme pornography threshold, it showed that the effects of extreme pornography were more serious.[16]

SHAPING RESEARCH TO FIT THE BILL

Commissioned by the Department of Health as part of its programme of research into the health and mental health effects of prostitution, pornography, and trafficking, rape and sexual assault, and sexual offending, the REA was authored by three academics known for their anti-pornography

---

13 Detective Inspector Winton, quoted in J. Petley, 'Pornography, Panopticism and the Post-Social Democratic State' (2010) 4 *Sociology Compass* (forthcoming).

14 The responses are no longer available via the Home Office website but see, for example, 'Response from Professor Martin Barker and Dr Ernest Mathijas', at: <http://www.melonfarmers.co.uk/agcmb.htm> and others available at: <http://www.backlash-uk.org.uk/responses/ >.

15 Home Office/Scottish Executive, *Consultation on the Possession of Extreme Pornographic Material* (2005), available at: <http://www.homeoffice.gov.uk/documents/cons-extreme-porn-3008051/cons-extreme-pornography?view=Binary>.

16 C. Itzin, A. Taket, and L. Kelly, *The Evidence of Harm to Adults Relating to Exposure to Extreme Pornographic Material: A Rapid Evidence Assessment (REA)* (2007) iii.

174

views – Catherine Itzin, Ann Taket, and Liz Kelly. That the authors should be partisan is a problem endemic to this kind of research exercise but that their research should have been presented as conclusive is unacceptable, given the vast body of work which has discredited and refuted the basic premises of the mass communications effects research tradition from which they drew their conclusions. The REA drew on the findings of five meta-analyses, considered 32 further studies not reviewed in those meta-analyses, and supposedly offered:

> a significant step in clarifying the position in an area subject to previous academic dispute about the findings of specific studies, and the status of the experimental – and other – research as evidence of harm.[17]

The REA made no attempt to deal with the specific criticisms of effects theorizing even though those criticisms have been widely published and debated,[18] and indeed the REA is founded on many of those criticized premises. It proceeds on the basis that:

(i)   there is something which can be counted as 'violence' – to which Itzin et al. added, 'extreme pornography' and 'sexual violence' as well as two supposedly measurable effects – 'aggressive behaviour' and 'rape myth acceptance';
(ii) effects demonstrated by research subjects in the laboratory can be directly related to 'real life' effects;
(iii) old research can be wheeled out to substantiate a supposedly new phenomenon – none of the meta-analyses deal with internet pornography, in fact, all the research 'meta-analysed' was published before the widespread availability of the Internet;
(iv) research instigated and undertaken for varying purposes and within disparate academic disciplines can be aggregated to produce similar and substantiating conclusions.

There is neither the space, nor do we have the inclination, to rehearse the many problems in effects theorizing as such; suffice to say that:

> What's wrong with effects research is that it does not acknowledge the openness of media in society, considered as a system. There is simply no way of isolating the watching of media violence among a complex of putative causes of violent behaviour among research subjects. Thus any correlation shown between the two (media and violence) may be contingent. More than this, even if one were to accept a causal link there are no means to establish the direction of causality between correlates.[19]

---

17 id., p. v.
18 See, for instance, essays in Barker and Petley, op. cit., n. 3.; D. Gauntlett, 'Ten things wrong with the "effects model"' in *Approaches to Audiences: A Reader*, eds. R. Dickinson, R. Harindranath, and O. Linne (1998).
19 J. Toynbee, 'Media Making and Social Reality' in *The Media & Social Theory*, eds. D. Hesmondhalgh and J. Toynbee (2008) 267.

In spite of these problems, the REA addressed three research questions:

(i) What effect does viewing extreme pornographic material have on those who access it?
(ii) In particular is there any evidence that it causes or contributes to sexual or violent offending?
(iii) Is there any evidence that those adults who participate in making extreme pornographic materials are harmed by their involvement?[20]

It is noteworthy that these three questions establish what will constitute their results: effects are already assumed, as are the causes and harms which ought to be found. At no point in the summary do the authors lay out an explanation of the category 'extreme pornographic material'; instead, they plunge ahead with claims that all the studies employed in their assessment focused on materials which met the REA definition of being extreme. That definition is finally given as explicit representations of sexual activities with animals, human corpses, violence in a sexual context, and serious sexual violence.[21] These were not, in fact, terms used in the majority of the research examined for the assessment, but Itzin et al. dismiss the problems this might raise for the applicability of the REA by suggesting that for ethical and accessibility reasons, early research might have avoided materials currently deemed 'extreme' and that this only presented a problem in that it 'would suggest that the REA findings are an under-estimate of the harm effects'.[22] The REA accepts as absolute that there is no dispute over what constitutes explicit representations, that there are no differences between forms of pornography, and that, indeed, pornographic imagery is so problematic that to offer any description of individual instances is likely to render their own work 'unscientific'. Hence:

> Direct quotes of ... explicit descriptions [from the studies included] have not been repeated in this report because the nature of the material was 'too extreme'. Instead it has been described in more neutral terms. This has been done to avoid the risk that these descriptions would function as extreme pornographic material for the reader, producing sexual arousal and orgasm to material that depicts or enacts serious sexual violence, explicit serious violence in a sexual context or explicit intercourse or oral sex with an animal (bestiality).[23]

Thus this material is so 'powerful' that even legislators, researchers, and other interested readers are to be protected from themselves. Yet it is precisely this unwarranted protectionism that ossifies research and debate on pornography, its forms, production and usages, as opposing positions on its appropriateness or right to existence. By this means it becomes possible to

20 Itzin et al., op. cit., n. 16, p. iii.
21 id., p. 1.
22 id., p. 4.
23 id.

produce 'evidence' from studies that are more than 30 years old and derived from discredited methodologies.

The five meta-analyses drawn on in the REA refer to a number of authors including Donnerstein, Malamuth, Linz, and Christensen, all names familiar to researchers of pornography for their continued commitment to seeking to uncover the 'effects' of pornography. Despite their interests in conducting research which pays obeisance to the idea of causal links between viewing and action, Donnerstein et al. have been unanimous in their summations of their own work that such research is inconclusive and that still further work needs to be undertaken.[24] No such caution was expressed by Itzin and her fellow authors, however. Indeed, the REA cites eighteen pieces of work co-authored by Donald Donnerstein without once mentioning his concerns about the ways in which his research has been continuously misrepresented as providing a basis for legislation. For instance, in relation to claims that their research has proved causal links between pornography and violent sexual behaviour, Linz and Donnerstein argued that:

> The Commission states there is a 'causal relationship' between exposure to sexually violent materials and aggression toward women. This is an accurate statement, as long as we are referring to laboratory studies of aggression … Whether this aggression, usually in the form of delivering [mock] electric shocks, is representative of real world aggression, such as rape, is entirely a different matter.[25]

Moreover, in their *The Question of Pornography: Research Findings and Policy Implications*, Donnerstein, Linz, and Penrod concluded:

> Should harsher penalties be leveled against persons who traffic in pornography, particularly violent pornography? We do not believe so … as we have noted, the existing research probably does not justify this approach.[26]

Even those researchers whose work is the basis of the REA suggest that the evidence does not justify legal action against the producers of pornographic materials: why then should we accept such evidence for the criminalization of possession? But in posing this question, we are naively conceptualizing the political impulses behind the legislation as rational and coherent when in fact they may owe most to emotions and morals.

---

24 See, for example, E. Donnerstein, D. Linz, and S. Penrod, *The Question of Pornography: Research Findings and Policy Implications* (1987); D. Linz, S. Penrod, and E. Donnerstein, 'The Attorney General's Commission on Pornography: The gaps between "findings" and facts' (1987) *Am. Bar Foundation Research J.* 713–36.

25 E. Donnerstein and D. Linz, 'Evidence on the causal connection between exposure to Penthouse magazine and anti-social conduct' (1990), prepared for Helen K. Wild, Auckland, New Zealand, quoted in M. Pally, *Sex and Sensibility: Reflections on Forbidden Mirrors and the Will to Censor* (1994), out of print but available at: <http://www.marciapally.com/Pages/sxsn.html>.

26 E. Donnerstein, D. Linz, and S. Penrod, *The Question of Pornography: Research Findings and Policy Implications* (1987) 172.

One of the sites named in the media coverage of the Coutts case and the legislation was *Necrobabes*, a site that deals with 'very politically incorrect fantasies' represented in a style which, as it describes, are 'fanciful, even cartoonish' and which relegates violence 'squarely into the realm of fantasy'.[27] The scenarios focus on murder, typically of women by men (there is a *Necrodudes* site which focuses on men), clearly and not especially realistically, staged in a studio setting. The disclaimer on the site, as in others of its kind, shows how producers of porn have increasingly been forced to locate themselves in relation to critiques of pornography. This assertion that what *Necrobabes* offers is the 'realm of fantasy' is given in direct challenge to those accounts of pornography which see it as a 'documentary' form: 'the content of extreme pornographic material is itself evidence of harm to those who have participated – or were used – in its making'.[28] Such 'analysis' of harms begins from identification of the 'uncomfortable, if not dreadful, sexual positions in their [porn actresses] performances of pleasure'[29] and moves on to the litany of supposed effects including 'increased callousness towards women', tolerance of rape, 'devalu[ing] ... of monogamy and lack of confidence in marriage as a lasting or viable institution'.[30]

In the media discussion following the Coutts case there was intense focus on the sites he was claimed to have visited and on the abnormality of that interest. The *Daily Mail* reported that the murder was 'unequally disturbing in that it could have happened only in this high-tech age, committed by someone whose murderous fantasies were fuelled by appalling images freely available on the Internet'.[31] The Brighton *Argus* reported that the night before he killed Jane Longhurst, 'Coutts had been downloading pictures of dead women, strangulation, rape and murder as he had done for eight years'.[32] The reporting made clear the supposed link between Coutts's visits to these websites and the murder and in so doing reproduced the popular belief in 'cases of copy-cat crimes, where men act out on women the scenarios they have seen depicted in pornography and actually use pornography during the assaults'.[33] In the use of the case to justify the legislation, proponents of the Bill broadened their attack on the 'appalling

---

27 'A word about censorship', at: <http://www.necrobabes.com/>.
28 Itzin et al., op. cit, n. 16, p. 20.
29 E. Bell, 'Performing "I do": Weddings, Pornography and Sex' in *Sexualities and Communication in Everyday Life,* eds. K.E. Lovaas and M.M. Jenkins (2006) 155.
30 'How Pornography Harms Children' at: <http://www.protectkids.com/effects/harms.htm#4>.
31 Quoted in Petley, op. cit., n. 11.
32 'Jane Longhurst: The Verdict' *The Argus*, 5 February 2004, available at: <http://archive.theargus.co.uk/2004/2/5/118369.html>.
33 C. Itzin, 'Pornography and Civil Liberties: Freedom, Harm and Human Rights' in *Pornography: Women, Violence and Civil Liberties*, ed. C. Itzin (1992) 558.

images' by claiming that no right thinking person would wish to view them. As MP Martin Salter put it:

> No-one is stopping people doing weird stuff to each other but they would be strongly advised not to put it on the internet. At the end of the day it is all too easy for this stuff to trigger an unbalanced mind. These snuff movies and other stuff are seriously disturbing. Many police officers who have to view it as part of their job have to undergo psychological counselling.[34]

A variety of languages and issues are mobilized here. Firstly the language of moral outrage – people are doing weird stuff but if they keep it to themselves the law won't intervene (just yet!) – invoking values and tastes. This bleeds into arguments of harm and the languages of safety: *seeing* this weird stuff is likely to trigger an unbalanced mind. A key indication of the danger of this material, the vulnerability of *all* viewers, is clear when even policemen, who look at the material as part of their professional duties, need counselling to help them deal with the effects. Salter invokes management as the cure: we don't have to find the evidences for harm, whether or not there are other issues at stake, the point is this stuff is weird and 'we' must take steps to get rid of it. There is an openly moral quality here. The state shouldn't just provide order and unity, it should also provide the guiding ideas around sexuality – what is appropriate sexual interest, what are appropriate responses to film forms, and so on. This is what Brown has called 'a pastoral relation of the state to its flock',[35] an approach clearly underpinning the arguments put forward by McGlynn and Rackley as they claim the Criminal Justice and Immigration Act stands as a lost opportunity to 'take much bolder, and intellectually more defensible, steps towards proscribing extreme forms of pornography'.[36]

In this and various other articles lamenting the government's retreat from the criticisms of 'arch-liberals', they claim that the 'real harm in extreme pornography' was lost from view, leading to the failure to proscribe, for example, what they term 'pro-rape websites' which 'valorise forced sex'.[37] In one article, McGlynn and Rackley claim:

> Our objection to these sites is based on their display of unlawful activity, such as rape and other forms of sexual violence, as opposed to finding the material portrayed unsavoury or distasteful or even simply too explicit. It is the harmful and violent nature of the material to which we object; that is, our perspective is one of a concern over violence against women, rather than one fuelled by a moral agenda seeking to limit expressive sexual material.[38]

34 Quoted in C. Summers, '"Extreme" porn proposals spark row' *BBC News*, 4 July 2007, available at: <http://news.bbc.co.uk/1/hi/uk/6237226.stm>.

35 W. Brown, 'American Nightmare: Neoliberalism, Neoconservativism and De-Democratization' (2006) 34 *Political Theory* 706.

36 C. McGlynn and E. Rackley, 'Criminalising Extreme Pornography: A Lost Opportunity' (2009) *Crim. Law Rev.* 245.

37 id., p. 249.

38 C. McGlynn and E. Rackley, 'The Politics of Porn' (2007) 157 (issue 7285) *New Law J.* 1142–3.

179

But their argument makes little sense. On their first premise, we should ban all representations of unlawful activity, cutting a swathe through the television schedules, cinema calendars, and bookshelves where criminal activity from burglary through to twocking is 'displayed'. Secondly, however vociferously it is argued, the claim that pornography causes harm to women as a class has yet to be established, as does the accompanying claim that pornography has a singular message which can be traced and correlated with the behaviours and attitudes of men as a class. Moreover, if concern over violence against women is what drives the impulse to legislate, that legislation should be targeting the actual practices of violence rather than representational media.

Read in combination with their other articles on this subject, it is clear that while McGlynn and her fellow authors may claim to seek a 'middle ground' which avoids excessive emotionality and moralist reactions, their arguments are underpinned by assumptions of particular kinds of usage of pornographic materials which owe much to a moralist framework. For instance, the claim that rape websites such as *brutalpassions.com* valorize rape is not argued for at any length, but simply offered as a 'fact'; a 'fact' which relies on particular assumptions about the ways in which these sites may be meaningful to those who view them. The rhetorical force of their assertion is clear, that these are *not* materials for fantasy – a point further emphasized in a footnote which states 'these rape sites are poles apart from the "rape" fantasies of women in books such as Nancy Friday's *My Secret Garden*'.[39] Here we see the division of the imaginative realm into 'harmful' and 'harmless', a strict delineation between 'reality' and what is *just* 'fantasy': to take sexual pleasure in a 'realistic' depiction of rape is presumed to be incompatible with rejection of the crime of rape. In this way we are returned to 'appropriate' and 'inappropriate' forms of sexual representation and possible interest in those representations. As McGlynn and Ward argue elsewhere, some forms of expression have no right to exist[40] and legislation will produce a proper 'responsibility'[41] in viewers where they cannot be trusted to regulate themselves.

PORN DEBATES

As Stephen Maddison has argued, debates about porn often work to degrade 'our understanding of the relationship between sexual freedom and power'.[42] Responses to the proliferation of pornographies online have worked to

---

39 C. McGlynn and E. Rackley, 'Striking a balance: arguments for the criminal regulation of extreme pornography' (2007) *Crim. Law Rev.* 690, fn. 67.
40 McGlynn and Ward, op. cit., n. 36, p. 349.
41 id., p. 350.
42 S. Maddison, 'Online Obscenity and Myths of Freedom: Dangerous Images, Child Porn and Neoliberalism' in *porn.com: Making Sense of Online Pornography,* ed. F. Attwood (2010) 17–33.

intensify views of porn as frighteningly pervasive and oppressive or wonderfully, liberatingly abundant. Both, in fact, work to mythologize porn, in the process obscuring important questions about regulatory control, civil liberties, and sexual emancipation, and diverting attention from the actual conditions of porn production and consumption.

However, it is emotional and inaccurate rhetoric about porn that has been most damaging to research into sexually explicit media. Supporters of increased regulation claim that the Internet Age has created ever more disgusting and sickening forms of pornography and make reference to what Martin Barker has termed 'scary futurology' – that if we don't do something now, the decline of public morals will be terrifying.[43] Such argumentation denies any defensible motive for a 'reasonable' person to wish to view any sexually explicit texts. Thus, appropriate research is that which ignores the voices of those who choose to engage with and take pleasure in pornographic materials in order to examine 'representation in the abstract, where theoretical assertion replaces investigation, description and analysis'.[44] Not only does this reinforce a view in which the diverse texts and uses of porn are obscured, it reproduces the characteristics of the thing that it denounces, conflating sex with violence, reducing men to brutes who hate women, and presenting women as victims. As Eithne Johnson argues, this kind of approach, evident also in the anti-porn campus roadshows of the 1980s and 1990s, draws on a rather sadistic framework in which the intention is to shock and frighten by presenting violent and highly atypical imagery as representative of all pornography. Women are positioned as incompetent readers of media texts, complicit with patriarchy – dupes of patriarchy and enemies of other women – if they do not adopt the 'correct, disciplined reading' of porn presented by anti-porn experts.[45]

Yet these emotional responses are also significant for the way they draw together a range of contemporary anxieties focused not only on pornography or even on sex, but on the new visibility of media texts and sexual activities which foreground the physicality of the body, problematize issues of control and consent, and emphasize extreme states of being. Nowhere is this more clear than in a new use of the term 'pornography' in discussions of horror films such as *Saw*,[46] *Hostel*,[47] and *Wolf Creek*,[48] which have been labelled 'torture porn' because of their graphic depiction of torture, mutilation, and

---

43 M. Barker, Plenary Speech at the IAMHIST Conference, 'Media Panics and Social Fears', Aberystwyth, 8–11 July 2009.
44 C. Smith, *One for the Girls! The Pleasures and Practices of Reading Women's Porn* (2007) 47.
45 E. Johnson, 'Appearing Live on Your Campus!: Porn-Education Roadshows' (1997) 41 *Jump Cut* 30.
46 Director, J. Wan (2004).
47 Director, E. Roth (2005).
48 Director, G. Mclean (2005).

181

murder.[49] Images of real violence have also been described as pornographic. The term 'war porn'[50] has been applied to the combat images posted by American troops in Iraq,[51] to the photographs of tortured and humiliated prisoners at Abu Ghraib prison, to footage of terrorist acts such as the beheading of Ken Bigley, and to the unofficial recording of Saddam Hussein's execution. Such uses of the term suggest a crisis over the meaning of 'porn', indicating that its users are less concerned with images of sexual pleasure than with the specularization of the body – the variety of ways of exposing the body and audiences' relationships to those exposures.[52]

The labelling of horror themes as a type of pornography is not new. It echoes the arguments of earlier anti-pornography feminists; for example, the horror film, *The Texas Chain Saw Massacre*[53] was described as pornographic in the Dworkin-McKinnon campaign to make porn actionable.[54] Nor are 'extreme' forms of porn new; *Forced Entry*, a film seen as exemplifying the new extreme pornography, is a remake of a porn film from 1973,[55] replacing the crazed Vietnam veteran of the original with real-life serial killer, Richard Ramirez, and Chuck Kleinhans has documented the existence of a 1970s porn sub-genre called 'roughies' or 'sickies', combining sex and 'overt misogynistic violence'.[56] However, violent porn films then, as now, remained relatively marginal to the genre as a whole, which is much less likely to feature images of violence than many other mainstream media genres.

Although these usages of the term 'porn' may refer to rather marginal representations, they are part of the regulatory processes of contemporary cinema which have emerged in the past two decades, profoundly influenced by media effects research, and which 'have increasingly considered the problem of film to rest with the spectator, rather than with the intrinsic obscenity or indecency of the film text'.[57] As Cronin observes when it comes to forms of 'torture porn':

---

49 'Now Playing at your Local Multiplex: Torture Porn' *New York*, 28 January 2006, available at: <http://nymag.com/movies/features/15622/>.

50 See, for example, J. Baudrillard, 'War Porn'(2005) 2 *International J. of Baudrillard Studies* 15–19, available at: <http://www.ubishops.ca/baudrillardstudies/vol2_1/taylor.htm>; and J. Harkin, 'War porn', *Guardian Comment is Free,* 12 August 2006, available at: <http://www.guardian.co.uk/commentisfree/2006/aug/12/comment.media2>.

51 For discussion, see K. Andén-Papadopoulos, 'US Soldiers Imaging the War on YouTube' (2009) 7 *Popular Communication: The International J. of Media and Culture* 17–27.

52 S. Jones and S. Mowlabocus, 'Hard Times and Rough Rides: The Legal and Ethical Impossibilities of Researching "Shock" Pornographies' (2009) 12 *Sexualities* 613–28.

53 Director, T. Hooper (1974).

54 Everywoman, *Pornography and Sexual Violence: Evidence of the Links* (1988) 19; see Jones and Mowlabocus, op. cit., n. 52 for a discussion.

55 *Forced Entry* was directed by L. Borden (2002), the original by S. Costello (1973).

56 C. Kleinhans, 'Introduction: Prior Constraints' (2007) 46 *Cinema J.* 96–101.

57 T. Cronin 'Guilty Pleasures: Media Effects and Technologies of the Self', paper to the IAMHIST Conference, 'Media Panics and Social Fears', Aberystwyth, 8–11 July 2009.

Discourses of 'media effects' are not simply the grounds on which regulatory decisions are made, but rather ... they are *technologies of power* that regulate the processes of spectatorship itself, by both problematising the 'pleasures' of viewing certain kinds of images through normative statements about the spectator's relations to these texts, and by casting doubt on the mental health of those who claim to enjoy certain kinds of 'problematic' films – like 'torture porn'.[58]

The drawing together of different types of problematic and 'extreme' texts and the mobilizing of an emotional response was particularly evident in the debate about extreme porn as the proposed legislation proceeded through its parliamentary stages; for example, in contrast to the careful, point-by-point evaluation of the Bill's clauses that Backlash contributed to in a set of papers published by Durham University in 2008,[59] the pro-legislation contributors, Jill Radford[60] and Clare Phillipson,[61] used a form of testimony relying on rhetoric and emotion, and made broad associations between porn, the filming of Bosnian war crimes, rape, forced prostitution, and death without any discussion of what the possible connections might be.

This emotive mode used by the pro-legislation contributors drew on an established anti-porn discourse in which 'pornography' has been used, not to describe a media genre, but is employed as a figure of speech for texts which enact violence against women, showing them '... tied up, stretched, hanged, fucked, gang-banged, whipped, beaten and begging for more'.[62] Here, all 'porn' is simply what is dangerous and harmful, a view expressed in the Rapid Evidence Assessment that pornography 'corrupts ... desire' by fusing arousal and orgasm with violence, objectification, and degradation.[63]

According to the Home Office, many groups who responded to the consultation document conflated concerns about extreme imagery with a view of all pornography as harmful. They referred to 'the increased availability of all types of pornography as reasons for the need for stronger legislation', 'asserted that even mainstream pornography had a detrimental effect on society', and argued that:

> the government should not only legislate in relation to extreme pornography but should also take action against the increased prevalence of pornographic

---

58 id.
59 Backlash, '"Extreme" Pornography Proposals: Ill-Conceived and Wrong' in *Positions on the Politics of Porn: A debate on government plans to criminalise the possession of extreme pornography*, eds. C. McGlynn, E. Rackley, and N. Westmarland (2007) 9–14, available at: <http://www.dur.ac.uk/resources/law/research/politicsofporn/PositionsonthePoliticsofPorn.pdf>.
60 J. Radford, 'The Politics of Pornography: A Feminist Perspective' in McGlynn et al., id., pp. 5–8.
61 C. Phillipson, 'The Reality of Pornography' in McGlynn et al., id. pp. 20–3.
62 A. Dworkin, *Pornography: Men Possessing Women* (1979/1999) 201.
63 Itzin et al., op. cit., n. 16, p. 37 (originally, C. Itzin, 'Pornography and the construction of misogyny' (2002) 8 *J. of Sexual Aggression* 4–42).

images not only on the internet, but also in top shelf magazines and in material broadcast on television and films.[64]

This view was expressed by many of the women's groups who supported the proposed legislation including Object and the Lilith Project, which responded on behalf of the Women's National Commission, the government's advisory body on women's issues. The Lilith Project argued that, 'the increasing use of pornographic images ... in advertising, magazines, music videos etc. [sic] causes psychological harm to women', said it 'would like to see the UK government acting to protect women by defining all pornography as harmful to women', and called for the restriction of 'any material which features naked women for the sole purpose of sexual gratification'. Object claimed that:

> the effects of misogynistic pornographic representations create problems regarding the welfare of women's everyday lives, for example in employment discrimination and economic exploitation,

and it called for existing laws based on the concept of 'obscenity' to be replaced by:

> specific sex-discrimination legislation against pornography (both violent and non-violent, but subordinating, material) which defines pornography concretely, specifically and objectively by the harm which it does to women.[65]

This generalizable definition is one that has been more recently taken up by those commentators who have identified the 'pornographication' or 'pornification' of culture. Although the term was first coined by academics seeking to explain the widespread fascination with porno chic,[66] 'pornographication' has now exceeded those explanations, becoming the conceptual term of choice for Christian activists, neo-con commentators, and moral lobby groups alike. It is now a part of the mix of 'terrors' assailing modern society including the supposedly debased tastes of young people evidenced both in lack of parental control and the increasingly sexualized behaviours of teenagers; claims about increasingly realistic portrayals of violence, its effects in mainstream popular cinema and television, and audiences' vulnerabilities to such materials; and the supposed ease with which everyone can access materials once kept firmly off/scene.

These concerns are condensed and made visible in debates about all kinds of popular media forms that are currently made to fit into the rubric of 'pornified' culture. Of course, as we have separately written elsewhere,[67]

---

64 Home Office, op. cit, n. 15, p. 9.
65 J. Petley, ' Matters of Decency' *Index on Censorship*, 18 January 2008, available at: <http://www.indexoncensorship.org/2008/01/britain-matters-of-decency/>.
66 B. McNair, *Striptease Culture* (2002).
67 F. Attwood, '"Other" or "one of us"?: the porn user in public and academic discourse' (2007) 4 *Participations: J. of Audience and Reception Studies*, available at: <http://www.participations.org/Volume%204/Issue%201/4_01_attwood.htm>; Smith, op. cit., n. 44.

claims about texts as overly sexually explicit, offensive, harmful, and so on are not about the texts themselves but about ways of conceptualizing those texts and their supposed 'effects' on viewers. For example, in the popular British tabloid, *The Sun*, Emma Cox claimed, in an article headlined 'Pornification of Our Kids':

> Youngsters' minds are being turned after exposure to a disturbing amount of indecent and even hardcore imagery which encourages them to copy what they have seen, says a shocking new study.[68]

And in a recent ruling, the Advertising Standards Agency declared that radio adverts for Matteson's Sausages were unsuitable for broadcast because:

> ... although it was not sexually explicit, the innuendo was sufficiently strong to present a problem if it was heard by older children. We concluded that the ads could cause harm to children ...[69]

Each of these are claims mobilizing languages of taste and values but also drawing on languages of effects, vulnerability, and *potential* harms to *possible* viewers. By making use of what Brown has called 'modalities of truth' and 'declarative statements' to present a 'truth from the gut' that derives 'from inner conviction or certainty that no amount of facticity or argument can counter', statements such as these acquire the patina of common sense and establish a problem which has to be managed.[70]

The resurgence of concern about extreme porn replays the regulatory mechanism identified by Walter Kendrick in which the identification of a victim, villain, and expert makes possible the categorization and containment of pornography and performs an 'imaginary scenario of danger and rescue'.[71] Increasingly such scenarios work to displace concerns about sex onto media. Disputes about sexual power, knowledge, and representation take the form of 'debates over pornography',[72] and 'discourse around sexuality' focuses 'more and more on visual representations',[73] in which, as Brown has argued, women are constantly presented as without agency, perpetual victims of a male sexual system predicated on violence.[74] Yet, as '"sex" has become entwined with all aspects of human desire and

---

68 'Pornification of our Kids' *Sun*, 30 March 2009, available at: <http://www.thesun.co.uk/sol/homepage/features/article2348839.ece>.
69 L. Haines, 'Watchdog bites Mattesons saucy sausage ad; Housewife boasts of her "big sausage hotpot"' *Register*, 22 July 2009, available at: <http://www.theregister.co.uk/2009/07/22/asa_sausage_ruling/>.
70 W. Brown, 'American Nightmare: Neoliberalism, Neoconservativism and De-Democratization' (2006) 34 *Political Theory* 707.
71 W. Kendrick, *The Secret Museum: Pornography in Modern Culture* (1996) xiii.
72 L. Segal, 'Introduction' in *Sex Exposed: Sexuality and the Pornography Debate*, eds. L. Segal and M. McIntosh (1992) 11.
73 C. Kleinhans,'Virtual Child Porn: The Law and the Semiotics of the Image' in *More Dirty Looks: Gender, Pornography and Power*, ed. P. Church Gibson (2004) 71.
74 W. Brown, *States of Injury* (1995).

endeavour' it has become increasingly 'difficult to isolate in an absolutely pure state of obscenity'.[75] 'Kinky' sex iconography and practice has become more visible in advertising and sex advice literature. Porn has become more accessible and porn chic texts are mainstream. Because of developments in media and communication technologies, people are able to produce their own sexual materials, to capture and circulate images of all kinds, and to take part in new forms of sexual encounter and interaction online.

The identification of all these developments as forms of 'pornographication' has been one very vocal response in the debate around 'extreme' porn in the United Kingdom. But for others, in the context of this new visibility and accessibility of sex media and the broadening out of the meanings associated with sex, the extreme porn debate has worked as a way of rearticulating the divide between obscene and on/scene. As some images and practices previously associated with porn and obscenity become recategorized as chic, cool or unremarkable, others are relegated to the realm of the taboo. And increasingly, obscenity is refigured. Whereas once it was envisaged as 'an extreme explicitness of representation',[76] it is now imagined in relation to perversity. Linda Williams has argued that, in the United States, the prosecution of sex crimes has 'moved away from the notion of explicit sex and towards the targeting of scapegoat-able "deviants"',[77] and sexual representations and villainous Others 'take their place as convenient objects of blame' for a variety of social ills.[78] A similar process is observable in the United Kingdom where child pornography has come to stand in for the material abuse of children and concerns about violence are displaced onto consensual sex practices such as BDSM, onto the figure of 'a homosexual sadomasochist stalking defenceless children',[79] and onto extreme porn.

The drama of extreme porn has, to some extent, worked to collapse together anxieties about the growing sexualization and mediatization of society, about a broader 'turn to the extreme' across a range of cultural forms, and about an appetite for graphic spectacles of the body.[80] These are apparent, not only in porn, horror or reality TV, but in scenes of 'opening up' the body in television drama and documentary, and the portrayal of torture and terror in both fictional and factual media.[81] What links these images is precisely their interest in extreme states – sexual or otherwise – and the strong reactions they evoke. In both instances, the body's unruliness or its

---

75 L. Williams, 'Second Thoughts on Hard Core: American Obscenity and the Scapegoating of Deviance' in Church-Gibson, op. cit., n. 73, p. 165.
76 L. Williams, 'Pornographies on/scene, or diff'rent strokes for diff'rent folks' in Segal and McIntosh, op. cit., n. 72, p. 233.
77 Williams, op. cit., n. 75, p. 166.
78 id., p. 170.
79 id.
80 D. Lockwood, 'All Stripped Down: The Spectacle of "Torture Porn"' (2009) 7 *Popular Communication: The International J. of Media and Culture* 40–8.
81 Jones and Mowlabocus, op. cit., n. 52, p. 622.

vulnerability is key. As Lockwood[82] notes, what the kinds of concern around extreme media highlights is the work of horror and porn as body genres, presenting and provoking sensation and affect. In the current climate, both register as extreme and unruly.

The concern with feeling is evident in the Act's concerns with the possession of images which show practices that may themselves be legal and those that feature legal certificated material if there is a suspicion that they may be used for the wrong (presumably sexual) purposes. Fears about inappropriate or 'wrong' feelings are also evident in the argument that the disturbing nature of torture porn films is dependent partly on their foregrounding of states of being, such as suffering, coupled with a moral blankness, or in the concerns with what is perceived as a general increase in graphic depictions which are 'devoid of meaning beyond the sheer delight of their (intentionally) shocking cinematic spectacle'.[83] Similarly, those fears are manifest in descriptions of mainstream media as an arena where 'cruelty ... has become a commodity' and images of catastrophe, accidents, crime, and death are about 'the inevitability of death and the excitement of observing it'; they arise too in the increased usage of the term 'porn' to denote something that turns you on.[84] Unfortunately, such usage has imported various discursive formations of panic and a generalized obfuscation of the ways in which these disparate media forms might speak to a variety of experiences, feelings, intentions, and motives that are not primarily driven by some mental sickness. This demonizing of particular groups of media users is part of the operational bridge that enables accusations or identification of possible 'harms' to translate into calls for more and more legislation against the imagination. Nowhere in the discussion of the Coutts case was there an attempt to understand his interest in *Necrobabes*; instead, commentaries simply placed the fact of his having visited these sites side by side with the details of Jane Longhurst's death. The implication was clear. Coutts was driven to murder by his arousal at the images he viewed. This is a key component of the arguments against pornography (in its myriad forms), that arousal – particularly sexual arousal – is potentially risky. In the moment of arousal, it would seem that viewers lose their abilities to be properly human, and all sense of the appropriate, the moral, and the responsible go out of the window. These are risks to be managed through legislation.

The desire to censor, to achieve a particular excising of individual parts of the sexual market place is not a unified and systematic or purposeful political drive. It is one which is messy and opportune and which seeks to *manage* what are *perceived* to be risks: hence in its individualizing of access to sexually explicit, 'obscene', and 'outrageous' materials, the internet is such a threat. Unlike the more 'social' spaces of the top-shelf magazine or lap-

---

82 Lockwood, op. cit., n. 80.
83 C. Carter and C.K. Weaver, *Violence and the Media* (2003) 65.
84 M. Presdee, *Cultural Criminology and the Carnival of Crime* (2001) 70.

dancing clubs, the internet is not limited to corporatized sexual representations where management of content is possible via withdrawal of distribution or licenses. Instead, it allows for the production and consumption of materials that operate at the furthest reaches of what some might consider respectable or desirable. All the same, the moves to regulate against extreme pornography online can be seen as part of a wider set of constraints on sexual expression, in which, on the one hand, sex in any form is depicted as dangerous, and on the other, more 'acceptable' kinds of sexual activity are normalized, while more challenging forms are demonized and criminalized.

Objections to the REA and to the legislation have been characterized as 'coalesced around two related concepts: anti-censorship generally and sexual freedom'.[85] Our objections to both are not borne out of some generalized anti-censorship impulse (though, clearly, we are anti-censorship) or, as McGlynn and Rackley dismissively characterized it in another article, 'arch-liberalism',[86] nor are we arguing for personal sexual freedoms (although those surely remain absolutely important in this discussion). Rather, we fundamentally reject the impulse to legislate based on a backwards approach to, for example, 'the prevalence of violence against women in society generally'[87] – a social phenomenon sufficiently serious to warrant proper research into the intricate mix of beliefs, motivations, and actions of those who abuse women. Rather than address the particular structural factors and material realities which contribute to women's risk of violent attack and men's propensities to violence, the current political and legal climate seeks to demonize sexually explicit media for these crimes. While opposition to legislation such as the 'Dangerous Pictures Act' may be portrayed simply as a matter of protecting personal freedoms or refusing to recognize the existence of harms, the real challenge is the interrogation of the very parameters on which the impulses to legislate in this way are based.

85 McGlynn and Rackley, op. cit., n. 39, p. 683.
86 McGlynn and Rackley, op. cit., n. 36, pp. 245–60.
87 McGlynn and Rackley, op. cit., n. 39, p. 687.

JOURNAL OF LAW AND SOCIETY
VOLUME 37, NUMBER 1, MARCH 2010
ISSN: 0263-323X, pp. 189–209

Consuming Sex: Socio-legal Shifts in the Space and Place of Sex Shops

BAPTISTE COULMONT* AND PHIL HUBBARD**

Materials defined as pornographic have always been subject to regulation because of the potential of such items to 'corrupt and deprave'. Yet the state and law has rarely sought to ban such materials, attempting instead to restrict their accessibility. The outcomes of such interventions have, however, rarely been predictable, an issue we explore with reference to the changing regulation of sex shops in Britain and France since the 1970s. Noting ambiguities in the legal definitions of spaces of sex retailing, this paper traces how diverse forms of control have combined to restrict the location of sex shops, simultaneously shaping their design, management, and marketing. Describing the emergence of gentrified and 'designer' stores, this paper demonstrates that regulation has been complicit in a process of neo-liberalization that has favoured more corporate sex shops – without this having ever been an explicit aim of those who have argued for the regulation of sex retailing.

INTRODUCTION

Objects and media designed to sexually arouse have always circulated in society, yet it was as recently as the 1970s that the sex shop emerged in the urban West as a recognizable space of sex consumption. In effect, such shops brought together various items that had previously been sold elsewhere (for example, through specialist bookshops, in pharmacies, lingerie shops or by mail order), offering them in an environment that left little ambiguity as to their sexual nature. Emerging in the wake of the 1960s 'sexual revolution',

* *Department of Sociology, University of Paris at Saint-Denis, Université Paris-8, France*
coulmont@ens.fr
** *Department of Geography, University of Loughborough, Loughborough, Leicestershire LE11 3TU, England*
P.J.Hubbard@lboro.ac.uk

189

such spaces attracted considerable press interest, much of it discussing whether the widespread consumption of sexually-explicit materials was desirable.[1] Occasionally integrated into discourses of national moral decline, for most pro-censorship groups such spaces were, however, less of a preoccupation than the increasing depiction of sex on television and in film.[2] Nevertheless, locally, the opening of such stores prompted considerable disquiet, with residents' groups, religious communities, and business leaders often opposing them on the basis they would attract incivility, decrease property prices, and lower community standards. Accordingly, the emergence of such stores prompted the introduction of new regulations concerning the sale of sexual materials. As this paper describes, these subsequently created the 'sex shop' as it is currently understood: a space forbidden to minors offering a fairly standardized repertoire of goods (videos, DVDs, magazines, vibrators, condoms, lubricants, lingerie, fetish-wear, and 'poppers').

Despite growing academic interest in pornography – and especially women's increasing use of pornography and sex toys[3] – there have been few studies of the sex shop as a social setting,[4] and even fewer considering its legality.[5] In this paper, we therefore detail how the state and law have attempted to clarify what constitutes a sex shop and impose particular conditions on its existence. Here, we focus on sex shops in Britain and France, using judicial, police, and media archives to detail the varied legal and extra-legal practices that have allowed the opening of particular types of stores in certain spaces, but repressed others. Given that the French and British legal systems are substantially different, it might be anticipated that the regulation evident in the two nations would also diverge. To the contrary, we suggest that in both jurisdictions there have been similar shifts from police repression and surveillance to more diffuse forms of commercial regulation. Making this argument, we note the legal ambiguity about what constitutes a sex shop, and suggest this lack of clarity has allowed for the emergence of shops whose legal status remains unclear but which adhere to certain shared styles of management. In demonstrating this, we argue that the

---

1 B. Coulmont, *Sex-shops: une histoire francaise* (2007); T. Kent and R.B. Brown, 'Erotic retailing in Britain 1963–2003' (2006) 12 *J. of Management History* 199–211.
2 C.E. Greek and W. Thompson, 'Anti-pornography campaigns: saving the family in America and England' (1992) 5 *International J. of Politics, Culture and Society* 601–9.
3 F. Attwood, 'Fashion and Passion: Marketing Sex to Women' (2005) 8 *Sexualities* 392–406; C. Smith, 'Designed for pleasure: style, indulgence and accessorized sex' (2007) 10 *European J. of Cultural Studies* 167–84.
4 M. Stein, *The Ethnography of an Adult Bookstore: Private Scenes and Public Places* (1997); D. Berkowitz, 'Consuming Eroticism: Gender Performances and Presentations in Pornographic Establishments' (2003) 35 *J. of Contemporary Ethnography* 583–606.
5 C. Manchester, *Sex Shops and the Law* (1986); A. Goudie, *Local Authority Licensing of Sex Shops and Sex Cinemas* (1986).

190

shape and form of the contemporary sex industry is partly the outcome of socio-legal processes which, though intended to make it less visible, have contributed to its mainstreaming.

TWO STRUCTURES OF REGULATION: SEX SHOPS IN BRITAIN AND FRANCE

Given that pornographic materials were widely-available before the 1970s, often in specialist 'gentleman's bookshops',[6] it is difficult to be precise about when shops selling a range of sex materials first emerged in either Britain or France. But it was in the 1970s that the media began to comment on the phenomenon, with the emergence of 'sex shops'[7] apparently generating considerable unease Advertised as stores where items were valued for erotic potentiality, sex shops transgressed social convention by bringing 'erotic reality' into the realms of the quotidian.[8] This given, sex shops were variously depicted as spaces of deviance, immorality, and vice. Significantly, academic discussions of sex retailing emerged within 'deviance studies', explicitly figuring patrons as a specific sub-set of the population.[9]

The underlying causes of anxiety about sex shops are open to multiple conjecture, but certainly relate to modern assumptions that sex is something that can be enjoyed in the private/personal sphere, but when encountered in the public realm disturbs as much as excites. Whatever the roots of hostility to sex shops – and it should be noted that opposition often involved 'unlikely' alliances between church groups, feminists, and local residents[10] – the initial number of stores was certainly limited, with few outside the major metropolitan centres. In both France and Britain, it was the proliferation of sex shops in the national capital that prompted most debate, with anxieties about sex shops mapped onto, and out of, specific urban spaces. In Britain, for example, it was in Soho, London, that local business groups and residents first expressed anxieties about the emergence of stores selling pornographic materials, voicing concerns that such businesses, alongside sex cinemas and 'strip shows', were displacing independent local businesses (for example, delicatessens, restaurants, craft industries).[11] However, such discourses of

6 Kent and Brown, op. cit. 1, p. 204.
7 Significantly, French shops were identified through the anglicized term, 'sex-shop', which was a way for owners to signify their modern character but also allowed opponents to characterize them as non-French, and hence a threat to the moral values of the nation-state – see Coulmont, op. cit., n. 1, p. 18.
8 Berkowitz, op. cit., n. 4, p. 584.
9 See, for example, D.A. Karp, 'Hiding in Pornographic Bookstores: A Reconsideration of the Nature of Urban Anonymity' (1973) 1 *Urban Life* 427–51.
10 Manchester, op. cit., n. 5, p. 74.
11 F. Mort, 'Striptease: the erotic female body and live sexual entertainment in mid-twentieth century London' (2007) 32 *Social History* 27–53.

opposition became mirrored in the provinces as leading operator Conegate began to target all towns with a population of over 100,000, with around 120 sex shops open by the end of the 1970s.[12]

1. *Regulating sex shops in Britain*

While the 1959 Obscene Publications Act justified police raids and seizure of British sex shops' stock, changing moral standards meant that much of the material taken was judged by the Director of Public Prosecutions as unlikely to be considered by a jury as 'corrupting', with successful prosecutions becoming scarcer through the 1970s. Likewise, when the police confiscated stock, it was often replaced within days, making police actions futile. Yet, because sex-related uses have never constituted a distinct category in the Use Classes Order in Britain, there was no possibility of using United States-style zoning powers to prevent sex shops opening in specified areas.[13] Further, if an existing retail business converted to a sex shop there was no need to apply for change of use.[14]

Given the obvious limitations of both criminal and planning law for controlling sex shops, and amidst rising concern among Soho residents in particular, Westminster City Council petitioned central government for powers to exercise control over sex businesses, initially by proposing a change to the Use Classes Order. Gradually, however, the notion that licensing might provide a more effective basis for control emerged, given premise licensing had been the main mechanism by which locally contentious land uses such as gambling and drinking spaces had been regulated in Britain as far back as the nineteenth century. It was during the second reading of the Local Government (Miscellaneous Provisions) Bill 1982 – which contained provisions dealing with the licensing of night cafes, tattooing and ear-piercing parlours – that MPs raised the possibility that such licensing be extended to sex shops. The strength of feeling was such that the government brought forward amendments at the report stage, effectively introducing a system of sex-shop licensing through the provisions of sections 2 and 3 of the Local Government (Miscellaneous Provisions) Act 1982.[15]

12 Manchester, op. cit., n. 5, p. 78.
13 M. Papayanis, 'Sex and the revanchist city: zoning out pornography in New York' (2000) 18 *Environment and Planning D: Society and Space* 341–54; D.M. Tucker, 'Preventing the secondary effects of adult entertainment establishments: Is zoning the solution?' (1997) 12 *J. of Land Use and Environmental Law* 383–431.
14 Forward planning can theoretically be used to identify areas for sex-related uses, allowing the refusal of planning permission for a sex shop outside such areas.
15 The Act was extended to Northern Ireland by the Local Government (Miscellaneous Provisions) (Northern Ireland) Order 1985 No 1208 (NI 15) with Scotland duplicating the powers of the Local Government Act in Part III of the Civic Government (Scotland) Act 1982.

This new adoptive system allowed any local authority to issue licences for:

> any premises, vehicle, vessel or stall used for a business that consists to a significant degree of selling, hiring, exchanging, lending, displaying or demonstrating sex articles or other things intended for the purpose of stimulating or encouraging sexual activity or acts of force or restraint which are associated with sexual activity.[16]

Under the Act's provisions, no person was permitted to operate a sex shop except in accordance with the terms of a licence granted by a council. With the exception of hard-core pornographic videos classified as R18 (restricted 18),[17] the grant of the licence did not affect what could be sold: however, it did affect the *quantity* of sex-related goods sold, since the license permitted the selling of sex articles 'to a significant degree'. However, the effectiveness of licensing was initially questioned, given the confusion about what this meant, with a small number of unlicenced stores continuing to trade by ensuring sex-related items did not represent a 'significant' proportion of their trade (stocking large numbers of remaindered non-pornographic novels). The legal interpretation of what constituted a 'significant proportion' was clarified in 1985 when Lambeth Borough Council unsuccessfully charged a newsagent who sold pornographic magazines with running a business with 'more than trifling sexual content', despite these constituting only 1 per cent of his stock. On appeal, the Courts ruled the 1982 Act did not 'set such a low standard' or justify intervention where sexual content was being sold by 'an otherwise inoffensive businesses'. Subsequently, it has been assumed the proportion of sexual goods should normally exceed other aspects of the business.[18]

Though the Act allowed local authorities little discretion over the nature of materials sold in sex shops (which remained subject to obscenity legislation if deemed likely to 'corrupt and deprave'), it permitted the imposition of conditions prohibiting display of products in shop windows, refusing access to under-18s, and restricting opening hours from 9am to 6pm (or rarely 7pm or 8pm). The new Act also allowed refusal of a licence on a number of grounds, such as the 'character of the applicant' or the unsuitability of the location.[19] Backed up with threats of fine and imprison-

---

16 Local Government (Miscellaneous Provisions) Act 1982, Schedule 3, Paragraph 4.

17 R18 videos/DVDs are classified by the British Board of Film Classification as 'not to be supplied to any person under 18 and only to be supplied through a licensed sex-shop' (Video Recordings Act 1984, s. 7.2.c).

18 *Lambeth London Borough Council* v. *Grewal* (1985) 84 LGR 538, 82 Cr. App. Rep. 301, 150 JP 138 (1986) *Crim. Law Rev.* 260; see, also, *Watford Borough Council* v. *Private Alternative Birth Control Information* (1985) *Crim. Law Rev.* 594 which concluded there could be no single definition of what a 'significant degree' is.

19 P. Hubbard, M. Matthews, and J. Scoular, 'Controlling sexually oriented businesses: law, licensing and the geographies of a controversial land use' (2009) 30 *Urban Geography* 185–205.

ment for running a sex shop without a license, and, latterly, the enforced closure of unlicensed premises,[20] the 1982 Act gave considerable powers to local authorities. Controversially, it also allowed local authorities to generate considerable revenue through variable fees for sex shop licenses (for example, an annual license costs £1,500 in Peterborough, £4,500 in Salford, £5,000 in Liverpool, £12,500 in Glasgow, and £20,000 in Westminster), suggesting that sex shops can be lucrative for both owners and local authorities.[21]

2. *Regulating sex shops in France*

Rather than having a system of licensing, France has been characterized by a steady accumulation of local and national legislation designed to contain and control sex shops. During the post-war years, the principal weapon against pornography was the police's use of the Penal Code provisions concerning *l'outrage aux bonnes moeurs* ('outrages against morality'), with the exchange of objects outside the boundaries of 'common' morality potentially leading to a fine and imprisonment. But from the 1960s, judges were less inclined to condemn: more than 350 people were fined or jailed in 1962, but only around 50 in 1978.[22] '*Les moeurs*' (morals) were deemed to be evolving rather too rapidly, with the common morality of French citizenry increasingly described by the courts as a problematic basis for legal action ('*outrage aux bonnes moeurs*' hence disappeared from the French penal code in 1994).

As the '*outrages aux bonnes moeurs*' got weaker, stores opened which did little to disguise the sexual content of their stock. The first recognized French 'sex shops' opened in 1969 and 1970 at the centre of touristic, civic, and intellectual Paris (for example, the Quartier Latin, the Champs Elysées). They sold objects that were legal (small vibrators, condoms, various novelties) as well as posters, small artistic statues, and books deemed to be unfit for minors. But even if, separately, such objects were legal, their gathering in a single outlet created tensions. From the beginning, protests were voiced by journalists, politicians, and 'concerned citizens' in both newspapers and town halls. For example, in 1969, the conservative daily *Le Figaro* proclaimed 'Eroticism is threatening Paris!'[23] when a store opened under the name '*Sexologie, insolite*'. Press reports at the time identified this

---

20 Under the provisions of the City of Westminster Act 1996.
21 This fee is supposed to represent the costs of operating the licensing system: however, one local authority – York – deliberately sets fees to reflect the perceived profitability of the stores concerned, with fees highest for a shop specializing in R18 DVDs.
22 *Compte général de l'administration de la justice criminelle et de la justice civile et commerciale* (Statistical Yearbook of Justice).
23 *Le Figaro*, 26 November 1969. A copy of the article was found in the proceedings of a trial: Archives de Paris, 1886W 11.

194

shop as undermining French moral values, describing the owner as 'a Chinese' and the shop more suited to 'Copenhagen'. Elected Parisian officials angrily voiced their opposition, asking the Prefect for 'extremely drastic, forceful measures' against sex shops.[24]

The consequence of such opposition was a two-pronged legal and administrative action. In September 1970, an order (*ordonnance*) of the Paris Prefect created a regulation for bookstores that openly advertised their sexual goods.[25] This '*ordonnance*' created a new class of stores on which the police could act. To counter the weakening of the '*OBM*', the Prefect based this decree on another set of laws: namely, the 1949 regulation that identified certain books as unsuitable for children and required that the titles of such books be regularly published in the *Journal Officiel* (the public gazette of the French Republic). Such books could not be advertised, nor made directly available (being stored in closed cabinets). The Prefect accordingly adopted the principle that if certain stores specialized in the sale of books forbidden to minors, then such stores should also be off-limits for minors, with the police deemed responsible for ensuring this.[26] Further, because sex shop windows became increasingly 'graphic' with the progressive liberalization of magazine content, the Prefect ordered a blackening or opacification of the windows in 1973.[27] The rationale was based on an extension of the previous '*ordonnance*', arguing that minors should not be able to see what was for sale in the stores. But while the aim was to hide the stores' paraphernalia and restrict it to the private realm, it conversely lent the stores themselves heightened visibility as they were the only ones without real windows. In so doing it created something of a mystique around sex shops, rendering them taboo and somewhat transgressive. It is hence possible to trace the production of a specific cultural form defined by the law: after all, law is not only repressive – even when its stated aim is to repress – it is also *expressive* (affirming a common good) and *productive* (enacting material constraints). The law effectively brought the 'pornographic bookstore' into being as a distinctive legal, physical, and even moral category – one so 'solid' that it persisted even when adult 'bookstores' stopped selling books in favour of videos and then DVDs.

---

24 *Bulletin municipal officiel de la ville de Paris,* 6 March 1970, 401.

25 *Bulletin municipal officiel de la ville de Paris*, 16 September 1970, 1505.

26 This was a local municipal law erroneously thought to be enforceable throughout France. In fact, the Minister of Interior declared in 1971 that no new national law was required as the police had sufficient powers. The Minister of Justice concurred: the sex-shop owners, he declared 'are probably aware of their precarious situation' and 'discipline themselves' – see *Journal officiel de la République française, Débats parlementaires, Assemblée nationale*, 21 August 1971, 3956, Réponse du Ministre de la Justice à la question n19210 du député Brocard.

27 *Bulletin municipal officiel de la ville de Paris*, 16 September 1973, 1782.

195

In societies where the consumption of sex was regarded as most appropriate in the context of *private* sexual intimacy, the emergence of sex shops clearly posed significant questions about the place of pornographic materials. However, the impossibility of defining some objects as unambiguously obscene (and hence likely to corrupt) instead encouraged legislation designed to prevent them being seen by 'those whose minds are open to immoral influences'.[28] The forms of regulation introduced to identify – and repress – shops selling sexual materials were thus introduced on the pretext of protecting those considered vulnerable to the 'corrosive' effects of pornography. Explicit in the will to control was the will to protect, with the state and law adopting the liberal principle that power should only be exercised over individuals against their will if it is in the interests of preventing harm to others.[29] Within the European Union, Article 10 of the 1998 Human Rights Act has become significant in this respect, implying that the right to freedom of expression can be extended to those who distribute, buy or look at pornography. Yet the same Act argues this can be subject to appropriate restriction – a caveat that suggests that a consumer's right to access pornography should not be allowed to impinge on the lives of those who do not wish to be confronted by it. This argument was indeed made by those feminist movements which sought to condemn sex shops in the late 1970s, with 'Take back the night' demonstrations ('*La nuit est à nous*' in France) implicating sex shops in wider process of sexual objectification that limited that women's rights to public space.[30] These protests highlighted the tensions within women's movements at the time, with pornography identified both as a legitimate source of women's pleasure as well as a source of gendered exploitation.[31]

Perhaps informed by such arguments, the state and law has accordingly sought to prevent sex shops from intruding on the lives of those who do not want to be confronted by sexual commerce.[32] In Britain, the most obvious manifestation has been the licensing conditions that demand 'the displays of articles sold at the premises shall not be visible at any time to persons outside the building'. This desire for strong separation of the public realm and the publicly accessible space of the sex shop is underlined by guidance stipulat-

---

28 id, p. 35.
29 J.S. Mill, *On Liberty* (1869).
30 See J.R. Walkowitz, *City of Dreadful Delight. Narrative of Sexual Danger in Late-Victorian London* (1992) 235–6. For French feminist actions against sex shops, see Folder 396 FEM (1978) in the Bibliothèque Marguerite Durand, Paris.
31 This schism of course still evident in feminist writing: see S. Jeffreys, *The Industrial Vagina: The Global Political Economy of the Sex Trade* (2008).
32 See D. Cornell, *The Imaginary Domain: Abortion, Pornography and Sexual Harassment* (1997) for a politicized discussion of the importance of zoning pornography rather than outlawing it outright.

196

ing that 'the external doors shall be fitted with automatic closing devices'.[33] In France, judicial decisions in 1972 and 1978 likewise established the 'sex shop' as a black box, arguing that if it is impossible to see the store's content from the street, and if people are sufficiently aware of the character of the store before entering, the sex shop cannot constitute an '*outrage aux bonnes moeurs.*'[34] Such organizational devices ensure those who do not wish to be consumers of sexual materials are not confronted with such objects, while the widespread adoption of names such as the 'Private Shop' in Britain further protects the prudish.[35]

In a wider sense, allowing sex shops to persist under certain conditions rather than banning them outright reflected wider shifts in the regulation of sexuality: Michel Foucault, in a 1978 debate, spoke of a transition from a prohibition of certain acts to the protection of society from 'dangerous individuals'. He termed this 'a new regime for the supervision of sexuality' whose function 'is not so much to punish offences against these general laws concerning decency, as to protect populations and parts of populations regarded as particularly vulnerable':

> In the past, laws prohibited a number of acts … Now what we are defining and, therefore, what will be found by the intervention of the law, the judge, and the doctor, are dangerous individuals. We're going to have a society of dangers, with, on the one side, those who are in danger, and on the other, those who are dangerous. And sexuality will no longer be a kind of behavior hedged-in by precise prohibitions, but a kind of roaming danger, a sort of omnipresent phantom … It is on this shadow, this phantom, this fear that the authorities would try to get a grip through an apparently generous and, at least general, legislation.[36]

Accordingly, the core of French regulation was protection of the child, first, because pornographic books had been defined as 'children-adverse', and secondly, because children were increasingly depicted as 'endangered'.[37] This was explicit in political debates, with one MP arguing that while the law 'forbids the implantation of bars and cafés too close to schools, the implantation of "sex shops" is certainly more dangerous (*redoutable*) than that of cafés for the moral security of children'.[38] From the late 1970s, French politicians increasingly argued for tighter regulation of sex shops to

33 Standard conditions for sex-shop licence, as issued by all local authorities who have adopted a sex-shop licensing scheme under the powers of Local Government (Miscellaneous Provisions) Act 1982, Schedule 3.
34 *Cour d'Appel de Besançon*, 9 May 1972, *Gaz. Pal.* 1972.2.558 note Lambert, and *Chambre Correctionnelle de Reims*, 7 October 1978, *Gaz. Pal.* 1978.2.somm.122.
35 Kent and Brown, op. cit., n. 1, p. 193.
36 M. Foucault 'Sexuality Morality and the Law' in *Michel Foucault. Politics, Philosophy, Culture: Interviews and Other Writings*, ed. L.D. Kritzman (1988).
37 On obscenity law and the protection of children, see M. Heims, *Not in Front of the Children* (2001).
38 *Journal officiel de la République française* 10 February 1986, 508, question n77934 du député Édouard Frédéric-Dupont.

prevent them opening near schools, arguing that, like bars, sex shops should be considered very dangerous for some people, and especially the young.

Here, there was an implicit understanding that 'too early an exposure' to sexual content might inhibit normal sexual development or convey a 'distorted view of sexuality' in which recreational notions of sex would overwhelm ideas of commitment and emotional reciprocity.[39] The incompatibility of sex commerce and childhood was emphasized time and again by French judges in lawsuits: in a suburb of Paris, Houilles, the judge remarked that 'a bus stop serving the schools is located precisely in front of this store'.[40] In Avignon, the location of a sex shop was considered 'incompatible' with 'an orthodontics practice welcoming a clientele of young children'.[41] In Rouen, a judge decreed that children passing in front of a store twice a day, risked 'moral and psychological damage ... [from exposure at] a young age to images or messages from the pornography'.[42] The judge noted that the images were not pornographic in themselves, but that the shop's visibility might normalize '*la pornographie*'.

In Britain too, a major aim of licensing has been the protection of children. However, this is not explicit in the 1982 Act, and the justification for excluding under-18s from sex shops is not clear, given the Sexual Offences Act 2003 seeks to protect only under-16s.[43] However, the fact that many stock R18 DVDs suggests that the legislation surrounding sex shops took its lead from the existing BBFC regulations that stipulate only over-18s can be exposed to 'real' as opposed to simulated sex. To these ends, standard conditions on sex shops in Britain suggest:

> At each entrance there shall be prominently displayed ... a notice prohibiting entry to all persons under 18 years of age. Such a Notice shall be in letters at least 50mm high and 6.25mm thick and shall be in dark letters on a light background. The Licensee of every premises licensed as a sex shop shall ensure that all persons employed on the premises are aware of the age restriction on clients and ... exclude or remove from the premises any person attempting to evade the restriction.[44]

Despite such efforts to ensure these spaces are off-limits to minors, the vulnerable child remains a potent figure in debates around sex shops, with opposition to their opening often couched in terms of potential impact on

---

39 Manchester, op. cit., n. 5, p. 118.
40 *Cour administrative d'appel de Versailles* (2008) 13 March [N06VE01662].
41 *Cour d'appel de Nimes* (1998) 28 September [N97/5355].
42 *Cour d'appel de Rouen* (2003) 29 April [N02/03110]; see, also, *Tribunal de Grande Instance de Lyon*, Ordonnance de référé (2002) 7 June [N02/01541].
43 The 2003 Sexual Offences Act makes it an offence to intentionally show another person an image of sexual activity where a person is under 13 or where the person is under 16 and there is no reason to believe they are over 16.
44 Standard conditions for sex-shop licences, as issued by all local authorities who have adopted a sex-shop licensing scheme under the powers of Local Government (Miscellaneous Provisions) Act 1982, Schedule 3.

children. For example, Trafford Council's refusal of a licence for a sex shop in 2005 was portrayed in the local media as a victory for a local schoolgirl, who had written (alongside other objectors) that: 'this shop will attract paedophiles, perverts and rapists ... As well as the fact that the crime rate may well rise, we will be letting children in the community get contaminated'.[45] Invoking exclusionary metaphors, the case for repression was clear and, in this instance, a local councillor claimed 'the large concentration of schools in the area, several residential streets, and a popular nursery' all made the refusal 'common sense'.[46] Similarly, a successful campaign against a Kendal sex shop was led by two 'divorced women who have eight sons between them', who claimed 'the job of being single parents would only be made harder if the shop opened' as 'youngsters would be tempted to go inside and the shop would prompt them to think about sex'.[47]

Such license refusals, and related appeal cases, suggest that while councils cannot refuse licences on moral grounds as such, they can do so if:

> the sort of people likely to be in the locality or vicinity are more liable than most to find a sex establishment in that location intrinsically objectionable, morally offensive [or] intrusive upon their sensibilities.[48]

Indeed, when adjudicating an appeal case against Newham Council, Justice Brown went on to state that:

> the only reason I can envisage why sex establishments should ever be regarded as inappropriate in a given locality, assuming always that they satisfy the requirements of planning legislation, is because they may be thought to constitute a temptation to those in the area, perhaps particularly children, to sample their wares.[49]

Although the argument that customers of sex shops might be a danger to young people has not been legally supported, given the lack of reliable evidence that sexual attacks are higher around such premises,[50] this has clearly not prevented opponents of sex shops from making allegations that they render children susceptible to physical harm.

The discourse of youth vulnerability is similar in the French case, with children regularly depicted as potential victims of sex-shop customers, ('animals, would-be paedophiles and perverts').[51] This argument is the correlate of a shift in focus: at the beginning of the 1970s, journalists and

---

45 *Manchester Evening News*, 30 September 2005, 19.
46 id.
47 *Westmorland Gazette*, 7 October 2005, 2.
48 J. Brown, cited in *R* v. *London Borough of Newham ex parte Sheptonhurst Ltd* Q.B.D. (Crown Office List) (1987) CO/980/85.
49 id.
50 D. Linz, B. Paul, and M. Yao, 'Peep show establishments, police activity, public place and time' (2006) 43 *J. of Sex Research* 182–95.
51 30 October 1997 session of the French Senate, available at: <http://www.senat.fr/ seances/s199710/s19971030/sc19971030013.html>.

199

elected officials stigmatized the sex-shop owners as professional perverts, or *'libertines'*, but those owners could easily be depicted as isolated individuals. Later, the focus shifted to customers, who were depicted as more numerous yet not readily identifiable (being indistinct from any other 'man on the street').[52] For such reasons, debates around the legal protection of children in France regularly invoked discussion of sex shops. The drafting of child protection laws (1996–1998, 2007) effectively crystallized this, conflating the protection of children with the protection of neighbourhood spaces: residents and children alike spoke in the same sentence of protecting their children and 'their' streets.[53]

LOCATION, LOCATION, LOCATION

Given the stated aim of regulating sex shops has been protecting particular 'vulnerable' and 'worthy' populations whilst respecting the rights of consenting adults to consume sexual materials, limiting them to specific locales has been a key regulatory tactic. In Britain, such spatial control is facilitated by the licensing system, which encourages local authorities to consider the character of the relevant locality and the uses to which any premises in the vicinity are put. Refusal of a sex-shop licence is thus possible if 'the number of sex establishments in the relevant locality at the time the application is made is equal to or exceeds the number which the authority consider is appropriate for the locality', with the local authority able to decide that none may be appropriate.[54]

Despite this, in practice, it remains difficult for local authorities to state there is no suitable location for a sex shop within the entire borough, albeit this was the line adopted by many local authorities in the 1980s. For example, Cheltenham Borough Council rejected numerous applications for sex shops, arguing that those in the town who wished to visit such premises could do so by travelling to a neighbouring area.[55] By 1983, Swansea, Chester, Preston, Trafford, Watford, and Havant had all refused licenses on these grounds. But subsequent to the passing of the EU 1998 Human Rights Act, and particularly Article 10, most local authorities have not sought to enforce a total ban on sex shops, given this might be seen to reduce freedom of expression. In some cases, local authorities that previously stated they

---

52 Compare, for example, an article published in *Adam et Ève*, May 1970, focused on the young entrepreneurs, with *Paris-Demain*, March 1979, 9 (describing the patrons as 'fauna').

53 A. Dassonville, 'Un projet de loi prévoit le renforcement de la répression des abus sexuels sur les enfants' *Le Monde*, 21 November 1996, 13. See, also, the private archives of a Parisian apartment buildings studied in Coulmont, op. cit., n. 1, pp. 122–9.

54 Local Government (Miscellaneous Provisions) Act 1982, Schedule 3, s. 12, para. 5(a).

55 *Quietlynn Limited* v. *Cheltenham Borough Council* C.A. (Civil Division) LJJ [1986] 85 LGR 249.

would not grant licenses have been seen to recant (for example, Richmond Council granted a licence to a sex shop on Kew Road in December 2004 despite having earlier stated that such establishments would not be suitable anywhere in the borough).[56] However, how far freedom of expression extends to the right to sell pornography is debatable, given all freedoms are deemed to carry responsibilities – including the 'prevention of disorder and crime' and the 'protection of health and morals'.[57] Rejecting an appeal against license refusal made under article 10(b) and 1(c) of the First Protocol to the European Convention for the Protection of Human Rights and Fundamental Freedoms 1950 (as set out in Schedule One to the Human Rights Act 1998), Lord Hoffmann indeed stressed that:

> the right to vend pornography is not the most important right of free expression in a democratic society and the licensing system does not prohibit anyone from exercising it – it only prevents him [sic] from using unlicensed premises for that purpose.[58]

Given this, a licensing authority must always give grounds for licence refusal, explaining why a shop would be inappropriate in a given locality.[59] Here, reasonable grounds for refusal appear to include the presence in the locality of schools or nurseries, places of public worship, 'family housing', and even 'the presence of a number of shops which would be of particular attraction to families and children'.[60] Nevertheless, questions remain as to what 'the relevant locality' means: although this is straightforwardly defined as the 'locality where [premises] are situated', judicial rulings suggest this is 'to be decided on the particular circumstances of a particular application'.[61] Localities have hence been defined variously as approximately 'one-quarter of a mile'[62] and 'one-third of a mile'[63] around a sex shop, whilst some local authorities stipulate in their general licensing policies that objections to the opening of a licensed premise will be ignored if they originate from residents who live more than 100 metres from a premise (the implication being that beyond this distance, they could not be directly affected).[64] Again, the courts

---

56 'Sex-shop is inappropriate in our community say residents' *Richmond and Twickenham Times*, 10 December 2005, 7.
57 Article 10 (2) Human Rights Act (1998).
58 *Miss Behavin' Ltd* v. *Belfast City Council* (2007) UKHL.
59 *R* v. *Birmingham City Council and others, ex parte Quietlynn Ltd* (1985) 83 LGR 461.
60 *Miss Behavin' Ltd* v. *Belfast City Council* (2007) 3 All E.R. 1007.
61 *Quietlynn Limited* v. *Peterborough City Council*; *Quietlynn Limited* v. *Northampton Borough Council*; *Quietlynn Limited* v. *City of Worcester*; *Quietlynn Limited* v. *City of Birmingham*; *Quietlynn Limited* v. *Tunbridge Wells Borough Council*; *Quietlynn Limited* v. *Cheltenham Borough Council* CA (Civil Division) [1986] 85 LGR 249.
62 *R* v. *Leeds City Council, ex parte Quietlynn Ltd* CA (Civil Division) [1986] 85 LGR 249.
63 *R* v. *Peterborough City Council, ex parte Quietlynn Ltd* CA (Civil Division) [1986] 85 LGR 249.
64 Manchester, op. cit., n. 5, pp. 224–5.

have left such questions a matter for discretion, suggesting a locality cannot be defined with any precision, being 'highly dependent on local knowledge'.[65] This exercise of discretion contrasts with the rigid zoning powers employed in the United States, where sex shops are typically forbidden within 1,000 feet of one another, schools, and religious facilities according to previously established guidelines which may appear inflexible in some instances.

In contrast, French regulation appears more influenced by United States zoning laws than British licensing legislation. Indeed, continuing outrage during the 1980s led some French MPs to ask for a national law restricting where sex shops could open and, from 1987, new stores were forbidden within 100 metres of any school – a law that imposes considerable restrictions given the sheer density of schools in many French towns.[66] This represents what could be called 'inverse zoning' – 'inverse' because, contrary to United States-style zoning, the zones are not precisely drawn on a map, and identifying the forbidden zone is left to the would-be storeowner (who has to make sure no school is located near the prospective location). There is no published information on where new sex shops can be opened, with no municipal department charged with gathering the relevant information. Even a list of addresses of teaching institutions (*établissements d'enseignement*) is difficult to find, meaning that city-wide mappings of possible sex shop locations cannot be attempted. The result, as Robert Badinter, a senior French senator, has observed, is a de facto prohibition of sex shops in city centres.[67]

The new law thus represented a shift from local '*arrangements*' (including chronic police surveillance and veiled threats of administrative closure) to a national law predicated on more universal notions of spatial order.[68] Yet, as had been the case for the Prefect of Paris in 1970 and 1973, MPs seemed to feel a need to base their regulation on the protection of something 'fixed' (that is, a school building in which pupils from the age of 3 to 18 years are taught) rather than children themselves. This law hence changed the space being regulated from the sex shop to the school and neighbourhood around the school. As part of this neighbourhood-based surveillance, the local '*associations de parents d'élèves*' (associations of pupils' parents, present in each and every school in France) were given the possibility of suing if a sex shop tried to open nearby. Yet, existing sex shops were not targeted, and

65 *4 Wins Leisure Ltd* v. *Blackpool Council* (2007) EWHC 2213, para. 8.
66 Article 99, loi n87-588 du 30 juillet 1987 portant diverses mesures d'ordre social, *Journal officiel de la République française* (1987) 31 July, 8583. This article was modified by Article 6, loi n 2007-293 du 5 mars 2007 réformant la protection de l'enfance, *Journal Officiel de la République française* (2007) 6 March, 4215.
67 French Senate, 30 October 1997 session, available at: <http://www.senat.fr/seances/ s199710/s19971030/sc19971030014.html>.
68 *Journal officiel de la République française* (1978) 18 February, 584, question n44323 of M.P. Valleix to the Minister of Interior.

sometimes benefited from the elimination of would-be competitors, although profits were checked by other initiatives. For instance, from 1987 the Ministry of Finance enforced an over-taxation of 'every commercial operation realised in stores forbidden to minors', targeting *boutiques du sexe*.[69] This meant that books, magazines or condoms were liable to 5 per cent Value Added Tax (VAT) in most stores but 33 per cent VAT in a sex shop.[70] Simultaneously, rising rents made some businesses less viable. For a few years, sex shops resisted the gentrification of the centre of Paris, though the purchase of a few stores on Rue Saint-Denis around 2003 by a public-private joint venture signalled the beginning of the end for many sex shops in the capital.

COMMERCIAL REGULATION AND SELF-REGULATION

Attempts to regulate sex shops – whether through censorship, licensing or planning controls – are essentially about *boundary drawing*, making clear where and when pornography can be bought and sold. However, in making such distinctions, Valverde argues that the state draws not on a repository of evidence about the harm that is caused by buying pornography, but rather a series of prior legal judgments in which the *potential* risks of opening a sex shop are deliberated. In such ways, Valverde shows that the knowledges on which decisions about the appropriateness of a sex shop in a particular locality are made may be sufficient for legal purposes, but lack the objectivity that one might associate, for example, with social science research that seeks to establish causality. This stresses that the knowledge that informs the regulation of sex shops is a curious hybrid, based on claims to knowledge in which the opinions of elected governors and 'interested parties' are privileged over factual evidence. Furthermore, given 'sex shops' have never constituted a pressing social problem on which there has been social consensus, these hybrid knowledges are the result of 'piecemeal' pronouncements that lack co-ordination.

This hybridity, and the entwining of the moral and legal, means it is never entirely clear where and how pornography may be sold. One obvious example of this is the definition of a sex shop itself, with Valverde arguing that while 'as a matter of urban experience it is not difficult to distinguish a convenience store that sells porn from a porn bookstore', the law cannot offer such a clear distinction.[71] This is because while pornography is defined

---

69 *Bulletin officiel des impôts*, n25 (1987) 16 February and *Journal officiel de la République française*, Article 42.I, Loi n86-1317 du 30 décembre 1986 de finance pour 1987 (1986) 31 December, 15826.
70 The income raised was intended to help fund local museums.
71 M. Valverde, 'Authorising the production of urban moral order: appellate courts and their knowledge games' (2005*)* 39 *Law and Society Rev.* 450.

in Britain as any object intended for the purpose of stimulating sexual activity, and in France as a publication unsuitable for children, it is not pornography in itself that is the regulatory object; rather, the presence of pornography is 'merely a clue to the character of the business in question'.[72] And, as Valverde continues, 'great imprecision is found at the key switch-point linking the publications to the business',[73] given a sex shop is defined as one having a 'significant proportion' of its stock in adult publications.

Such legal indistinction appears particularly important in the French context, given that magazines and DVDs forbidden to minors are sold in most press stands and tobacconists (most often high up in an 'adult' section). Similarly, 'sex toys' are sold without restriction when they are deemed 'unrealistic' (in terms of colour or shape). This is not a legal definition but a 'common-sense' understanding of what is considered 'obscene', meaning the sale of sex toys can be stopped suddenly if a patron expresses concern that they are pornographic.[74] In Britain too, there remains significant discretion for local authorities to employ 'common-sense' understandings of which shops actually require a sex-shop licence. For example, it is notable that in some towns (for example Bristol) Ann Summers shops selling sex toys, lingerie, and soft-core DVDs but no R18 videos are still required to possess a sex-shop licence on the basis that a significant proportion of their stock is sex-related. In others, licensing officials are aware there are sex superstores or lingerie stores which are publicly perceived to be sex shops, but have not required them to seek a licence because there are no R18 videos being sold.[75] Conversely, in some instances where an application for a sex-shop license has been refused, a 'sex shop' has opened anyway – albeit not offering R18 videos. For example, in the process of making an unsuccessful licence application, one owner stated 'the licence laws with regard to sex establish-ments are very mish-mash. Rather than retreat on refusal we will still open the shop. We'd just adjust the stocks. It's an exercise in stock control, it's not difficult to do'.[76] Although local residents might still argue the store is a sex shop, and the manager may market the business as if it were a sex shop, it is not subject to licensing conditions and, as such, may be able to display lingerie and even sex toys in the window, leaving passers-by in no doubt as to what the business is.[77]

72 id, p. 451.
73 id.
74 Ph. R. [Philippe Rivière], 'Cachez ce sex toy que je ne saurais voir' *La Nouvelle République du Centre*, 13 February 2008, 2.
75 For example, Bexhill Council's licensing officer stated a sex shop 'would be able to operate without a licence so long as it sells no more than 50 per cent sex stimulators', cited in 'Secret desires in Bexhill' *Sussex Courier*, 29 October 2005. The basis of this figure is unclear.
76 *This is Trafford*, 26 September 2005, 7.
77 When Shop Tonight Ltd was refused a sex-shop license in Worthing, they opened an unlicensed shop selling lingerie and sex toys, with a view into the shop. See 'Bid to halt sex-shop receives police backing' *Worthing Herald*, 12 January 2006.

204

In the context of the retail restructuring of the 1990s that effectively gentrified Britain's high streets, the emergence of this more 'open' type of sex shop is worthy of note. Partly reflecting the changing acceptance and visibility of sexual imagery in British society[78] – as well as emerging synergies between the physical spaces of sex retailing and an ever-expanding Internet pornography industry – these more visible and accessible stores have been taken as a symptom of the democratization of desire.[79] Elaborating, Clarissa Smith argues that British sex shops licensed in the 1970s and 1980s remained 'oases of ugliness' whose blacked-out windows created a fear of what lurked within for many female consumers.[80] In her view, this encouraged a furtive and anonymous consumption of pornography, and reproduced these spaces as male preserves. In contrast, the more open and often unlicensed sex shop challenges the traditional notion of pornography as a male domain (some welcoming men only if they are accompanied by a 'female friend').[81] Commenting on unlicensed 'concept' sex stores aimed at women (including *Sh!, Coco de Mer, Bliss, Nua* and *Ann Summers*), Kent and Brown argue 'the new female focus on sex shops has altered both the design of shops and the products they sell'.[82] Described as women's erotic emporia, 'new-style' sex stores sell sex toys and accessories in a 'relaxed and unpretentious environment, where staff are happy to offer advice over a cup of tea', with the interior imagined as a 'female playspace'.[83] Many also stress that women can take their children into these shops, albeit there is a company policy that areas where sex toys are sold are off-limits to under-18s.

What is notable is that many 'traditional' sex shops have mimicked some of these strategies in an attempt to make their stores more 'couple-friendly'. Several *Harmony* stores, for example, have separate doorways leading to licensed and unlicensed sections respectively, one leading to what is described a more 'girlie' ground floor, the other a more 'hard-core' basement.[84] Arguing that a visit should be as everyday 'as going to any other chain-store in your lunch hour',[85] *Nice'n'Naughty* stress their stores have both male and female staff and offer 'comfortable shopping'. Increasingly, such licensed shops have also sought permission to vary from standard licensing conditions that insist on blanked-out or frosted windows, with many local authorities acceding to requests where the objects to be displayed

78 Attwood, op. cit., n. 3.
79 B. McNair, *Striptease Culture: Sex, Media and the Democatisation of Desire* (2002).
80 Smith, op. cit., n. 3, p. 170.
81 See <www.sh-womenstore.com>.
82 Kent and Brown, op. cit., n. 1, p. 204.
83 D. Molina and R. Schmidt, 'It's a business doing pleasure with you: Sh! A women's sex shop case' (1997) 15 *Marketing, Intelligence and Planning* 356.
84 A number of Adult World shops in Britain are licensed on a similar basis.
85 Company spokesperson, cited in 'Sex-shops are making their way to the high street' *Los Angeles Times*, 11 October 2004.

are 'not outside what is considered decent',[86] and where banners are used to prevent the interior being fully-visible from the street. From the perspective of the owners, such window displays, if 'tasteful', make the 'store far more appealing', potentially breaking down the boundary between licensed and unlicensed space.

Making the stores 'couple-friendly' or 'women-friendly' is all the more important when the goal is to escape the French over-taxation of licentious stores and open in lucrative city-centre locations. Many ploys may help the store owner to escape the dreaded 'sex shop' category: for example, the use of the anglicized 'love shop' instead of 'sex shop', the refusal to forbid entry to minors, facades designed to appeal to upper-class tastes, the recruitment of professional interior designers, the use of music to induce particular ambiences, and so on. Some owners insist on making a distinction between 'sex shops' and their own stores at every occasion. For instance, one registered the trademark *developpement durable du couple* ('sustainable development of the couple') to emphasize the (hetero)normality of their business. Another insisted his store should not be in a phone directory under the 'sex shop' category.[87]

Given such attempts to evade regulation, a 2007 modification of the 1987 French 'inverse zoning' law redefined sex shops as stores selling 'objects of a pornographic character' or 'sex toys' without any lower limitation specified, effectively extending accepted definitions of pornography.[88] Significantly, this new law also extended the forbidden zone to 200 metres around a school, granting more suing possibilities to various associations. A recent shifting jurisprudence is further routinizing such legal uncertainty, with the administrative Court of Appeal of Versailles and the supreme administrative court (*Conseil d'Etat*) suggesting definitions of 'public tranquillity' which would allow a mayor to forbid the opening of a sex shop in residential areas.[89] According to the jurists who studied the decision, this widens notions of 'public tranquillity' and abandons reliance on explicit references to public morality. Yet, because the law does not offer a clear definition, owners are faced with further insecurity. The main threat comes from the possibility of lawsuits initiated by residents, and consequently owners have begun to open sex shops near malls or industrial zones: these benefit from low rentals, parking spaces, and from the kind of anonymity that such zones

86 Sandwell Borough Council, Licensing (Miscellaneous) Committee Minutes, 17 June 2008, 2.
87 Coulmont, op. cit., n. 1, p. 207.
88 André Lardeux, *Rapport (n205), au nom de la commission des Affaires sociales, sur le projet de loi, modifié par l'Assemblée nationale, réformant la protection de l'enfance*, Sénat, 1 February 2007.
89 Conseil d'Etat, juge des référés, *Commune de Houilles c. Société Cassandre* (2005) 8 June. [N281084] and *Cour administrative d'appel de Versailles*, 13 March 2008 [N06VE01662].

offer. In recent times, the opening of such stores has paralleled the closure of sex shops in French city centres.[90]

Such examples underline the putative shift from police regulation to a more permanent regulating gaze exercised by the citizenry, effectively institutionalizing a 'regulation by uncertainty' (that is, uncertainty about what might be considered pornographic). Likewise in Britain, this lack of clarity means that those who run stores where sexual items are on sale manage their store *as if it were* a sex shop, being uncertain as to whether they risk prosecution. An example of this is that many unlicensed stores have policies that under-18s should not be admitted alone, despite the fact they have no items it would illegal to sell to 16- or 17-year-olds, and many that can legally be sold to all. Window displays of unlicensed stores and sex superstores may also be obscured, allowing no view into the interior, or contain innocuous displays of lingerie even though many sex toys and vibrators could be publicly displayed without contravening Indecent Advertisements Acts.

What is interesting here is that despite the lack of formal guidelines or rules about how sex shops should be laid out and managed, sex shops and love shops throughout Britain and France have come to share many characteristics. The sales desk is normally immediately visible upon entry, subjecting the customer to the gaze of the proprietor, who may ask for proof of age. In front of the sales desk or counter, one typically finds racks of DVDs and magazines, organized by category – usually those featuring heterosexual couples and 'glamour girls' first, then more 'specialist' and 'gonzo' titles featuring BDSM or fetish scenarios, lesbian and girl-on-girl sex or public sex. In many stores DVDs featuring gay male sex are less visible, the assumption seeming to be that these will be of marginal appeal to the majority of (presumed heterosexual) customers. At the front of the store, lingerie and adult-themed 'fancy dress' may be on display: normally sex toys, vibrators, stimulants, and lubricants are nearer the back, but in clear view of the sales desk: fetishwear and BDSM accessories, as well as 'gay' clothing/paraphernalia may be in a separate room, or in the basement.

The layout of the sex shop thus manifests particular assumptions about sexual morality, with 'harder' items only becoming visible once one has negotiated the 'softer'. Even in Ann Summers, now ubiquitously offering 'cheap and cheerful sexual paraphernalia' on British high streets,[91] 'clothing is displayed in standardised units, which become more specialised until false fur and leather finally give way to sex toys which are discretely, almost apologetically, hidden in a rear alcove'.[92] Touristic guidebooks emphasize

---

90 The *libertine* tourist guidebooks *France Coquine* (published since 1998) and *Guide du kokin* (since 2005) provide evidence of this shift. See D. Menduni (ed.), *France Coquine* (1998–2009) and S. Beninca, *Guide du Kokin* (2005–2009).
91 F. Attwood, *Mainstreaming Sex* (2009) xv.
92 Kent and Brown, op. cit., n. 1, p. 209.

207

this: the *Guide Musardine du Paris Sexy* describes with appreciation a 'quasi-ideal store, with lingerie at the window and a progression from banal objects at the entry to the pornographic inferno at the back of the store'.[93] Concerns about visibility and morality thus appear to entwine with marketing considerations, creating a standardized layout. Thus, even where there are no rules, shop owners act *as if there are rules* – the rules coming from the regulated as much as the regulators.

CONCLUSIONS

This paper has considered how shops selling pornography and sexual materials have been regulated in Britain and France over the last four decades. In both cases, there has been an important shift from the use of criminal law (enforced through punitive policing and stock seizure) to more diffuse forms of control in which the management of risk is devolved to the owners and managers of shops. In Britain, this has been through licensing – a technique of governance that instrumentalizes social actors' capacity for self-governance rather than relying on panoptic surveillance.[94] In France this has been through the progressive outsourcing of the regulating gaze from the police to the '*riverains*' (local residents) and a tentative legal exclusion of sex shops from city centres. In both cases, however, the invention of a distinct legal category – the 'sex shop' – has proved fraught, with attempts to contain and repress its transgressive potential reliant not so much on understandings of what is pornographic but who needs protection from its corrupting influence. In this sense, the law invokes both spaces and subjectivities (the vulnerable child, the family, the predatory male), bequeathing a moral geography that separates these populations through acts of boundary drawing, distancing, and 'inverse zoning'.

In both cases, the forms of regulation enacted by the state allow it to claim that it is uninterested in questions of private sexual morality whilst allowing it to address issues of public order, principally by locating sex shops away from those areas where their presence is deemed problematic. Yet, beyond this form of spatial control, and the maintenance of a clear boundary between the public and private realm, the state and the law generally leave decisions about the running of the business to the operator, who takes on responsibility for ensuring that the shop is well-run and has no detrimental impacts on its locality.[95] In general terms, this has favoured the more corporate, 'well-managed' sex shops, and encouraged the development of more 'open', women- or couple-friendly stores. While it is tempting to describe this as a

---

93 M. Dannam, *Guide musardine du Paris sexy* (2006) 60.
94 P. Hadfield, *Bar Wars* (2006).
95 C. Manchester, S. Poppleston, and J. Allen, *Alcohol and Entertainment Licensing Law* (2007) 6.

planned regulatory outcome, the gentrification of sex shops is perhaps better viewed as the cumulative outcome of a series of situated decisions that had no a priori predicted outcomes but which effectively encouraged similar market-oriented forms of management. As such, we conclude by suggesting that the up-scaling of sex shops needs to be interpreted as part and parcel of wider shifts in the sex industry, which in the last forty years has changed from being a 'small, privately-owned, illegitimate and almost feudal set of businesses dependent on local sheriffs looking the other way' to being a 'multi-billion dollar business dominated by corporations'.[96]

96 K. Hausbeck and B. Brents, 'McDonaldization of the sex industry?' in *McDonaldization: The Reader*, ed. G. Ritzer (2002) 91–107.

209

JOURNAL OF LAW AND SOCIETY
VOLUME 37, NUMBER 1, MARCH 2010
ISSN: 0263-323X, pp. 210–32

Cultural Criminology and Sex Work: Resisting Regulation through Radical Democracy and Participatory Action Research (PAR)

Maggie O'Neill*

Taking a feminist cultural criminological analysis to the regulation of sex work in the United Kingdom, this paper argues against the dominant deviancy and the increasingly abolitionist criminal justice model for regulating sex work. The paper begins by offering a critique of the dominant regulatory regimes which have operated since the Victorian era, amended in part in the 1950s with Wolfenden, and currently being reinscribed with the Home Office strategy on prostitution and various pieces of legislation. The focus is specifically upon research with female sex workers and the usefulness of using Participatory Action research methodologies (PAR) with sex workers, agencies, and policy makers in order to foreground the diverse voices and experiences of sex workers, challenge the current focus on abolitionist criminal justice regimes and outcomes, and offer an alternative framework for a cultural materialist analysis of sex work, drawing upon the work of Nancy Fraser.

INTRODUCTION

This paper takes a feminist cultural criminological analysis to the regulation of sex work in the United Kingdom. It argues against the dominant deviancy and criminal justice model for regulating sex work and suggests that Participatory Action Research methodologies (PAR) and Participatory Arts (PA) have a vital role in the process of developing a radical democratic imaginary. PAR and PA offer interventions in the governance of sex work by

* School of Applied Social Sciences, University of Durham, 32 Old Elvet, Durham DH1 3HN, England
maggie.o'neill@durham.ac.uk

Thanks to Jane Scoular for sound editorial advice and to Kate Green for permission to use the artworks.

creating spaces for dialogue and fostering more integrated horizontal and vertical processes of inclusion around the principles of social justice and cultural citizenship[1] that include rights, recognition, respect, and redistribution for sex workers.[2] Moreover, our task as researchers is to take responsibility for catalysing what Bauman describes as the need for 'dialogic understanding in the general public, to opening up and keeping open spaces for what has been called "critical discourse".'[3]

The paper proceeds by: highlighting key themes, discourses, and interventions in the regulation of sex work; outlining the trajectory of cultural criminology as the basis for a cultural materialist analysis of sex work; and moves the debate on prostitution beyond binaries (that lead to divisions and paralysis and ultimately help to reinforce the Othering of women and men who sell sex), arguing for a politics of inclusion. A politics of inclusion makes use of participatory, biographical, and visual methods in order to create spaces for the voices of sex workers, leading to dialogue, knowledge transfer, and transformative interventions in the governance of sex work.

REGULATING SEX WORK: DISCOURSES, INTERVENTIONS, AND IDEOLOGY

Prostitution and the broader sex industry is a deeply embedded global institution that is tied to social, cultural, economic, and political structures, processes, and practices. Prostitution and sex tourism are global phenomena and they help to constitute the political economy of prostitution. Structured currently by capitalism, commodification, sexuality, and sexual relations,[4] it is a major task to generate knowledge and understanding of this complex issue; and concomitantly to develop feminist responses that take us beyond the fixity of a deviance model towards a cultural materialist analysis that may lead to a more realistic model for the governance of sex work in the twenty-first century. The selling of sex is associated in the public imagination and embedded in law as (moral) deviance. The regulation of the sale and purchase of sex takes place predominantly through the enforcement of laws which focus mainly on women who sell sex. In the process, a particular ideology of prostitution is reproduced.[5] By ideology, I mean

1 J. Pakulski, 'Cultural Citizenship' (1997) 1 *Citizenship Studies* 73–86.
2 N. Fraser, 'Recognition as Justice? A Proposal for avoiding Philosophical Schizophrenia' in *Law, Justice and Power Between Reason and Will*, ed. S. Cheng (2004).
3 Z. Bauman, *Life in Fragments: Essays in Postmodern Morality* (1995) 242.
4 C. Pateman, 'Defending Prostitution: Charges against Ericsson' (1983) 19 *Ethics* 561–5.
5 M. McIntosh, 'Who needs prostitutes? The ideology of male sexual needs' in *Women, Sexuality and Social Control*, eds. C. Smart and B. Smart (1978).

211

(following Marx in *The German Ideology*)[6] that which serves to conceal unequal and oppressive sexual and social relations and practices; the ways that sectional interests are presented as universal; the denial of contradictions and the naturalization of that which has been socially constructed. Ideology is also linked very closely to 'identity thinking',[7] a concept from critical theory which describes a process by which unlike things appear as like or equivalent, such as the perceived equivalence between the label 'prostitute' and dirt or disease or a victim identity/role.[8]

1. *Regulatory regimes: the making of an outcast group*

Historical analysis evidences relationships between women selling sex, the state, working-class/underclass communities, and the regulation of public space and moral order. The development of a deviancy model is tied to the identification of women selling sex with symbols of immorality and disease and the enactment of laws that prevent women's access to public spaces where they might sell or exchange sex for money.

Historians working in this area have identified the Victorian era, in particular, as a time in which we find evidence of identity thinking in relation to the targeting of women who sell sex and what Walkowtiz calls 'the making of an outcast group'.[9] For example, the 1824 Vagrancy Act introduced into statutory law the term 'common prostitute'.[10] The 1839 Metropolitan Police Act made loitering an offence in London, and was extended to towns/cities outside of London in the 1847 Town Police Clauses Act. The Contagious Diseases Acts of 1846, 1866, and 1869[11] introduced the compulsory medical examination of prostitute women in eleven naval ports and garrison towns (1846); extended police powers and introduced (following the French

---

6 K. Marx, *The German Ideology* (1845/1936):
> The ideas of the ruling class are in every epoch the ruling ideas, i.e. the class which is the ruling material force of society, is at the same time its ruling intellectual force. The ruling ideas are nothing more than the ideal expression of the dominant material relationships, the dominant material relationships grasped as ideas; hence of the relationships which make the one class the ruling one, therefore, the ideas of its dominance …

available at: <http://www.marxists.org/archive/marx/works/1845/german-ideology/ch01b.htm>.

7 See T.W. Adorno, *Aesthetic Theory*, tr. R. Hullot-Kentor (1984).

8 See, also, M. O'Neill, *Prostitution and Feminism: Towards a Politics of Feeling* (2001); J. Scoular and M. O'Neill, 'Regulating Prostitution: Social Inclusion, Responsibilization and the Politics of Prostitution Reform' (2007) 47 *Brit. J. of Criminology* 764–78.

9 J. Walkowitz, *Prostitution and Victorian Society* (1980). See, also, T. Sanders, M. O'Neill, and J. Pitcher, *Prostitution: Sex Work, Politics and Policy* (2009).

10 H. Self, *Prostitution, Women and Misuse of the Law: The Fallen Daughters of Eve* (2003).

11 In 1872 Parliament suspended the Acts and repealed them three years later. For more information, see Self, id.; Sanders et al., op. cit., n. 9, ch. 7.

212

system) registration and fortnightly inspection (1866); and, in 1869, extended the number of towns where the Act was in force. This legislature enshrined in law the category 'prostitute' – what she does (sells sex) becomes who she is. Her identity is fixed as 'prostitute' through registration, cautioning, imprisonment in pseudo-prisons – lock hospitals. She is also made an 'outcast' from the working-class communities she lived and worked in, set apart as 'Other', labelled a 'common prostitute'.

Such identity thinking also serves to reinforce and reproduce the ideology of prostitution, that is to say, that which conceals unequal and oppressive sexual and social relations, presents sectional interests as universal, denies contradictions, and naturalizes what has been socially constructed. For example, poor women sold sex in Victorian England to survive, and many sold sex in addition to their 'day' jobs, for which they earned a pittance.[12] The economic basis for entry into sex work is thus based upon social inequalities as well as the organization of sexual and labour relations.

There were alternative voices at the time that offered some resistance to the identitarian logic of the moral deviancy model. Parent-Duchatalet described prostitution for poor women in 1836 as a transitional occupation not a lifetime identity.[13] Bracebrydge Hemynge similarly describes selling sex as a temporal phenomenon and rooted in economic need: 'the greatest, and one equally difficult to combat, is the low rate of wages that the female industrial classes of this great city receive, in return for the most arduous and wearisome labour'.[14] He talks of a particular example:

> A French woman ... said that she came to town four or five times in the week for the purposes of obtaining money by the prostitution of her body. She loved her husband, but he was unable to find any respectable employment, and was she not to supply him with the necessary funds for their household expenditure they would sink into a state of destitution, and anything she added, with simplicity, was better than that.[15]

Walkowtiz writes in 'The making of an outcast group':

> For most 'public' women prostitution represented only a temporary stage in their life that they would pass through. The age concentration of registered women in their early twenties strongly supports the likelihood that they had prior work experience outside the home as well as having engaged in non-commercial sexual activity. In addition registered women appear to have stayed in prostitution for two or three years, leaving in their mid twenties at a critical point in their lives – when most working class women were settling

---

12 J. Rendell, 'Industrious Females and Professional Beauties, or, Fine Articles for Sale in the Burlington Arcade' in *Strangely Familiar: Narratives of Architecture in the City*, eds. I. Borden, J. Kerr, A. Pivaro, and J. Rendell (1995).
13 Walkowitz, op. cit., n. 9, pp. 336–7.
14 B. Hemynge, 'Prostitution in London' in *London Labour and the London Poor*, ed. H. Mayhew (1967) 213–14. Also reprinted in R. Matthews and M.ONeill (eds.), *Prostitution: A Reader* (2003).
15 id.

into some domestic situation with a man, whether it be formal law or common-law marriage. The timing here is very important. For as long as prostitution represented a temporary stage in a woman's career, and as long as she could leave it at her discretion, she was not irrevocably scarred or limited in her future choices.[16]

Moreover, for Walkowitz the registration of women as common prostitutes facilitated 'official intervention into their lives' and offered the police:

> An easy opportunity for general surveillance of the poor neighbourhoods in which they resided ... Their temporary move into prostitution reflected the fluid social identity among the casual labouring poor who so violated Victorian society's sense of order and place.[17]

Hence, sectional interests, such as fear for the nation's – that is, men's – health, and a strong focus on morality and immorality, were presented as universal, denying contradictions such as sexual and social inequalities and the absolute poverty that many of the labouring poor endured. The identity of the prostitute was naturalized and reified around the notion of the deviant individual woman contravening moral order, patriarchal order, and the law.

The problem of prostitution was dealt with by regulating the women involved through a combination of legal and medical discourses that regulate and control women's sexuality, women's bodies, with particular regard to the sexual health of their bodies, *and* women's access to public spaces.[18] The dominant mode of regulation from the Victorian period onwards is thus rooted for Corbin in discourses of containment and surveillance as well as a degree of tolerance that emerge from the interrelated discourses of municipal authorities, hygienists, the police and judiciary who combined to protect the nation's health, morality, as well as male prosperity. He writes:

> The first task of regulation is to bring the prostitute out of the foul darkness and remove her from the clandestine swarming of vice, in order to drive her back into an enclosed space, under the purifying light of power.[19]

The effects of Victorian morality and the social purity movement together with the social organization of gender relations (hegemonic heterosexuality) have in Britain created a legacy enshrined in law that was further extended by Wolfenden and the Street Offences Act of 1959. In this second period of legislative activity, we witness the reinforcement of identity thinking through the labelling of prostitutes as 'morally deviant'; at the same time,

---

16 J. Walkowitz, 'The Making of an Outcast Group: Prostitutes and Working Women in Nineteenth-century Plymouth and Southampton' in *A Widening Sphere: Changing Roles of Victorian Women*, ed. M. Vicinus (1977) 77. Also reprinted in Matthews and ONeill, op. cit., n. 14.
17 Walkowitz, id., p. 72.
18 A. Corbin, *Women For Hire: Prostitution and Sexuality in France after 1850* (1990); O'Neill, op. cit., n. 8, pp. 129–31.
19 Corbin, id., p. 215.

this focus serves to conceal the sexual and social inequalities experienced by women who sold sex.

The Wolfenden committee, chaired by John Wolfenden, was set up by the post-war government to examine homosexuality and prostitution, at the request of the Secretary of State for the Home Office, Sir David Maxwell Fyfe. Fyfe was 'concerned that London streets gave a deplorable impression of British immorality to foreign visitors'.[20] Wolfenden stated that the law was concerned only with 'the manner in which the activities of prostitutes and those associated with them offend against public order and decency, expose the ordinary citizen to what is offensive and injurious, or involve the exploitation of others'.[21] Here we see a shift in the governance of sex work that reflects the classic liberalism of these times. And, as Matthews writes, it:

> applied a more rigid distinction between law and morality ... claiming that however 'immoral' prostitution was it was not the law's business; it also rationalised resources directed towards the control of prostitution while increasing the certainty of convictions; and ... it encouraged a more system-atic policing of the public sphere in order to remove visible manifestations ... in London and other urban centres.[22]

Women were identified as 'common prostitute', their guilt assumed in advance, and they could be convicted on police evidence alone, serving to reinforce the ideology of prostitution as moral deviance and preserve the sectional interests of the liberal government and patriarchal society as universal. The travesty here is that, due to sexual inequalities and the label of stigmatized 'Other' and 'common prostitute', women were powerless to challenge the double moral standards upon which the legislation was based. This, in turn, 'reinforced the liberal claim that the law was not concerned with private morality'.[23]

The next major period for legislative activity is, as Brooks-Gordon writes, 'set against a contemporary climate in which most sexual activity has been commodified'[24] and is marked by increasing criminalization, not only of sex workers but also their clients. There is a clear shift from enforcement to welfarism in the policing and regulation of sex workers within the broader context of neo-liberalism and a shift from 'coordination through hierarchy or competition towards network-based forms of coordination'.[25] Multi-agency welfarist responses to street sex work appeared in the 1980s in response to

---

20 Self, op. cit., n. 10, p. 3.
21 *Report of the Committee on Homosexual Offences and Prostitution* (Cmnd. 247; 1957; Chair, Lord Wolfenden) 80.
22 R. Matthews, 'Beyond Wolfenden: Prostitution, Politics and the Law' in *Prostitution*, eds. R. Matthews and M. O'Neill (2002) 492.
23 id.; see Scoular's chapter in this volume, pp. 12–39.
24 B. Brooks-Gordon, *The Price of Sex: Prostitution, Policy and Society* (2006) 19.
25 J. Newman, 'New Labour, Governance and the Politics of Diversity' in *Gender and the Public Sector: Professionals and Managerial Change*, eds. J. Barry, M. Dent, and M. O'Neill (2003) 16.

conflicting interests and tensions around the needs of communities in the first instance (with more welfare-based forms of policing to address community concerns), as well as perceived sexual health needs of sex workers in relation to fears and risks about AIDS and HIV.[26]

Hence a key feature of contemporary regulation is the emergence of a welfarist model and as Scoular and I argue in a recent article:

> the move from enforcement towards multi-agency interventions can be explained by reference not only to shifting police imperatives and the opening up of welfarist responses, but also, crucially, to changes in governance ... which upon closer examination, reveal more expansive forms of control, which are often masked by the emphasis in government rhetoric upon 'inclusion', 'participation' and 'active citizenship'.[27]

The Home Office Strategy on Prostitution,[28] alongside various pieces of legislation such as Sexual Offences Act 2003, Criminal Justice and Immigration Act 2007, and the Police and Crime Bill 2008 serve increasingly to regulate the women selling and the men buying sex using abolitionist discourses, yet also claim concern for women's welfare. However, what is contained in this legislation includes compulsory rehabilitation schemes for sex workers on arrest,[29] and criminalizing the clients of sex workers.[30] A number of researchers and experts have argued that this will serve further to criminalize and stigmatize sex workers, reinforce the abject status of the women concerned, and ultimately have a detrimental effect on their safety.[31]

We can say that the historical context of prostitution policy reform in the United Kingdom includes regulationism, suppression, and welfarism.[32] And, as Phoenix argues, 'research has indicated that regulating prostitution through criminal justice has a profoundly negative impact on many women's lives (especially those working on the street)'.[33] The piecemeal legislation developed from the Victorian period, Wolfenden, and the flurry of

---

26 For more information on the growth of support services to sex workers, see the United Kingdom National Network of Sex Worker Projects (UKNSWP) website at: <http://www.uknswp.org/>.

27 Scoular and O'Neill, op. cit., n. 8, p. 764. See Scoular in this volume, pp. 12–39, for a more detailed analysis of the operation of the law in the regulation of sex work.

28 Home Office, *A Coordinated Prostitution Strategy and Summary of Responses to Paying the Price* (2006). A series of articles that offer a rigorous critique of the Strategy can be found in issue (2007) 6 *Community Safety J.*

29 Home Office, *Policing and Crime Bill 2009* Part Two, s. 16, available at: <http://services.parliament.uk/bills/2008-09/policingandcrime.html>.

30 id., ss. 18 and 19.

31 For more information, see the range of evidence submitted by various academics and researchers in response to the Police and Crime Bill, including evidence submitted by the author, at: <http://www.publications.parliament.uk/pa/cm200809/cmpublic/cmpbpol.htm>.

32 Matthews and O'Neill, op. cit., n. 22, p. xvii.

33 J. Phoenix, 'Be helped or Else! Economic Exploitation, Male Violence and Prostitution Policy in the UK' in *Demanding Sex: Critical Reflections on the Regulation of Prostitution*, eds. V. Munro and M. Della Giusta (2008) 37.

legislation in the wake of the review of sexual offences legislation in the 1990s has reinforced the regulation of women in the 'realm of criminal justice'[34] as well as their victim status as Other and Othered.

Contemporary social interventions, both welfare- and law-based, have served to raise awareness about women's lives but crucially, tied to the deviancy model, the focus has become skewed towards helping women out of sex work, through processes of rescue, desistance, self-governance, and rehabilitation for which the individual women must take responsibility.[35]

The regulation of sex work built up through these three major periods of regulatory reform – the Victorian era, the 1950s with Wolfenden and the Street Offences Act, and the legislative activity and policy guidance of the current period – instantiates in law, discourses, and representations the abject status of the sex worker, who is defined as a morally deviant Other who may also be a victim, of her own making or of another: a man, brothel owner, or trafficker. What consistently remains hidden in all of these periods of regulatory reform is the poverty experienced by women and their families, the growing market and availability for sex work at a local and global level, and the fact that social justice for sex workers is hence circumscribed.

Thus, any attempt to understand prostitution in current times must be very clear about the various ways that selling sex is constructed and maintained as a social problem and regulated via discourses of deviance, control, and social order, out of which emerges ideological interventions in law, welfare, policies, and guidance, especially given that, 'deviant identities become the basis of law reform rather than the social factors that construct those identities in the first place'.[36]

Phoenix neatly summarizes the key discourses and ideologies in the contemporary policy and politics of sex work as, first, the battle over meanings, that is, how might we:

> critique or engage with policy in a field where the key signifier (i.e. prostitution) is one which is both highly contested and . . . capable of signifying almost any type of social anxiety about sex, danger, violence and community destruction.[37]

Hence, the abject status of the 'prostitute', the fact that she/he is Other, the end stop in discourses on normative concepts of womanhood/manhood, and current responses to prostitution by the Home Office are inevitably linked to a much broader shift to intolerance and greater punitiveness in Western

---

34 id.
35 Home Office, op. cit., n. 28; Scoular and O'Neill, op. cit., n. 8; M. O'Neill and R. Campbell, 'Desistence from sex work: feminist cultural criminology and intersectionality – the complexities of moving in and out of sex work!' in *Theorizing Intersectionality and Sexuality*, eds. Y. Taylor, S. Hines, and M. Casey (2010).
36 J. Phoenix, 'Frameworks of Understanding' in *Regulating Sex for Sale: Prostitution, Policy Reform and the UK*, ed. J. Phoenix (2009) 160.
37 id.

217

societies. This has been defined by Phoenix and Oerton as 'the new moral authoritarianism',[38] evidenced in the United Kingdom by the 'the increased levels of regulation and criminalisation that specific populations of sex workers are now facing'.[39]

Second, Phoenix asks what counts as evidence in prostitution policy reform. She summarizes critiques from a significant number of academics about the selective practices employed by the Home Office in generating evidence-based research on prostitution and the way this 'evidence' is then used in consultation documents to 'decontextualize' the issue and problem of prostitution. For much of the work by scholars, feminists, and academics that present evidence to counter the ideological position taken by the Home Office does not figure in policy making.[40] Of course, the dynamics of prostitution reform at government level are framed and informed by the cumulative impact of the various social, historical, and legal discourses and practices, such as the operation and interpretation of the law and discourses emerging from various state (and non-state led) research and practice that are negotiated and filtered through the ideological stance to sex work taken by ministers and civil servants.

Third, she highlights that the 'process of reforming the UK's prostitution policy at the beginning of the Twenty First century has amounted to little more than the ideological legitimation of an abolitionist stance on selling sex'.[41] In the Home Office strategy, prostitution is defined as commercial exploitation with no reference to the agency of the women and men concerned, nor the social context within which they make choices nor the intersections and multiple subject positions they occupy as mothers, daughters or partners that are inscribed also through race, class, and sexuality.

Susan Edwards argued more than a decade ago that different ideological constructions of prostitution will have an effect on shaping law and policy; this describes very aptly the current governance of sex work. For Edwards, the schism between prostitution as sex and a matter of privacy (Wolfenden) and prostitution as exploitation (a strong discourse in the current regulation of sex work) shapes the climate in which the reconstruction of legal prostitution in Europe takes place.[42] What is clear from the available research is that abolitionist discourses are gaining ground in Europe today around clear 'anti-trafficking and anti-immigration agendas'[43] and key

---

38 J. Phoenix and S. Oerton, *Illicit and Illegal: Sex, Regulation and Social Control* (2005).
39 Phoenix, op. cit., n. 36, p. 165
40 id., p. 164.
41 id.
42 S. Edwards, 'Abused and Exploited – Young Girls in Prostitution' in *Whose Daughter Next? Children abused through prostitution*, Barnardo's (1998) 67.
43 G. Allwood, 'The Constructions of Prostitutes and Clients in French Policy Debates' in Munro and Della Giusta, op. cit., n. 33; N. Mai, *Migrants in the UK Sex Industry: First Findings* (2009), available at: <http://www.londonmet.ac.uk/research-units/iset/projects/esrc-migrant-workers.cfm>.

discourses have bifurcated around prostitution as exploitation and prostitution as work/labour.

Responses by feminists and other commentators and theorists have supported this bifurcation along pro or anti sex work lines. On the one hand, feminist discourses seek to re-frame prostitution as work/labour within the context of capitalism and market principles and on the other, prostitution is framed as exploitation, as violence, and the women involved are deemed to be victims – of patriarchy, power relations, traffickers, and sometimes of themselves. Building upon previous work,[44] I argue that we desperately need to move beyond the binaries and overcome the three major barriers inherent in current discourses (identified by Phoenix above as the abject status of the sex worker; what counts as research in supporting the development of government policy; and the broader shifts to intolerance and punitiveness in Western societies) that prevent both imagining and actioning an inclusive, holistic strategy for prostitution reform in the United Kingdom.

I also propose that we might better understand the complexities involved using cultural materialist analysis informed by feminist work on inter-sectionality,[45] in order to move debate forward beyond the confines of criminal justice and the deviancy/regulatory model and the entrenched feminist positions that argue either for (or against) selling sex as a form of labour or survival strategy. Methodologically, I propose to employ a cultural criminological analysis that contextualizes debates within historical, cultural, and material analysis, that explores the cultural, structural, and emotional experiences of the people involved, and also determines that the knowledge produced looks towards policy making to facilitate social justice and a politics of inclusion with, and for, sex workers, rather than the semblance of inclusion witnessed in the recent government 'consultations'. In this way, we move debates forward, away from identity thinking, the partial justice contained in the criminal justice response, and the paralysis that constrains

---

44 M. O'Neill, 'Community Safety, Rights and Recognition: Towards a Coordinated Prostitution Strategy?' (2007) 6 *Community Safety J.* 45–52; M. O'Neill, 'Sex, violence and work services to sex workers and public policy reform' in *Sex and Crime*, eds. G. Letherby, P. Birch, M. Cain, and K. Williams (2008); M. O'Neill, 'Community Safety, Rights, Redistribution and Recognition: Towards a Coordinated Prostitution Strategy?' in Phoenix, op. cit., n. 36.

45 Feminist work on inter-sectionality is described as the variety of 'social and structural cultures and practices at work in the maintenance of the current gendered and heterosexual social order': S. Jackson, 'Sexuality, Heterosexuality and Gender Hierarchy: Getting Our Priorities Straight' in *Thinking Straight. The Power, the Promise, and the Paradox of Heterosexuality*, ed. C. Ingraham (2005) 15–38, at 16. Davis further articulates this as 'the interaction of multiple identities and experiences of exclusion and subordination': K. Davis, 'Intersectionality as buzzword. A sociology of science perspective on what makes a feminist theory successful' (2008) 9 *Feminist Theory* 67–85. See, also, Y. Taylor, 'Complexities and Complications: Intersections of Class and Sexuality' (2009) 13 *J. of Lesbian Studies* 189–203.

feminist thinking in this area. To do this we could work with the women and men who sell sex and develop knowledge about both the phenomenological and the structural, material conditions and constraints they experience, using cultural criminological analysis and participatory methods.

BEYOND BINARIES: RECOGNITION, REDISTRIBUTION, AND SOCIAL JUSTICE

I propose that cultural criminological analysis using participatory methods could move us beyond binaries and help us to access a richer understanding of the complexities of sex work, developing inter-sectional knowledge and analysis that might foster a more radically democratic governance of sex work. Such knowledge would include recognition claims as well as redistribution claims – addressing both the materiality of women and men's lives and the need for recognition as full, not partial, subjects.[46] Participatory action research could demonstrate a politics of inclusion and representation by facilitating recognition. For example, in collaborative research, Pitcher, Campbell, Hubbard, Scoular, and myself addressed the concept of community conferencing in the Home Office strategy[47] and suggested that through participatory and cultural methodologies we might bring together 'all stakeholders who can make a difference to problems identified by communities, including communities themselves'[48] and that it is vital that we engage in processes of *recognition* through the inclusion of sex workers in research, debates, and dialogue.

However, in our search for social justice, do we not also need to address the issue of *redistribution*, the materiality of sex work that includes poverty and economic routes in, as identified through the narratives presented in this chapter? Yet, in current discourses, the issue of redistribution is largely hidden or silenced by claims for recognition.[49]

A recent article by Nancy Fraser throws some light (and hope) on this issue. Fraser argues that currently we are faced with new dynamics centered on the discourse of social justice. On the one hand, social justice concerns focus upon redistribution (class politics and materialism) and on the other, the focus is squarely upon recognition (identity politics); and often, 'the two discourses are dissociated from one another. The cultural politics of difference is

---

46 See J. Scoular, 'The "Subject" of Prostitution: Interpreting the Discursive, Symbolic and Material Position of Sex/Work in Feminist Theory' (2004) 5 *Feminist Theory* 343–55.
47 Home Office, op. cit., n. 28, p. 16.
48 M. O'Neill, R. Campbell, P. Hubbard, J. Pitcher, and J. Scoular, 'Living with the Other: Street sex work, contingent communities' (2008) 4 *Crime, Media, Culture* 73–93.
49 O'Neill, op. cit. (2007), n. 44.

decoupled from the social politics of equality'.[50] Fraser argues that the emancipatory aspects of the two paradigms need to be integrated into a single comprehensive framework by devising an expanded concept of social justice.

In previous work I suggested that the polarization amounted to, on the one hand, too great a focus upon claims to recognition at the expense of claims for redistribution and that redistribution (the economic basis for sex work) is displaced by identity politics (recognition claims).[51] I further argued that feminists need to work across this divide and challenge sexual and social inequalities with respect to both redistribution/materiality and recognition/ideology (identity politics). We need to acknowledge that structural inequalities form the entry point for many women's routes in to sex work and sustain involvement. Poverty, the need for money, or more lucrative earning potential is evident in the available research. Struggles for recognition that transgress cultural value patterns (sex worker as deviant/diseased/victim/Other) need to be integrated with struggles for redistribution that also 'examine the structure of capitalism'[52] and critically explore the marketization of sex.

Put simply, Fraser argues that we need to integrate 'recognition' and 'materiality' and replace the identity politics model of recognition with what she calls 'status misrecognition'. Hence, identity politics misrecognition involves the deprecation by the dominant culture and damage to group members' sense of self – the sex worker labelled as abject Other. Redressing this means demanding recognition through, for example, collective identity as identity politics, unionization, solidarity, and sex-worker organization. Fraser also argues that identity politics misrecognition reifies group identity and has the tendency to pressure individuals to:

> conform to group culture while masking the power of dominant factions and reinforcing intra-group domination. In general then, the identity model lends itself all too easily to separatism and political correctness.[53]

Fraser goes on to suggest that instead of treating (mis)recognition through group identity we should treat recognition as an issue of *social status* not group-specific identify. Misrecognition in this sense means social subordination – being prevented from participating as a peer in social life, and much research with sex workers evidences this point. When asked 'do you feel part of the community?' in research led by Jane Pitcher for the Joseph Rowntree Foundation, one sex worker answered as follows. 'I didn't feel part of anything, I was just there'.[54]

---

50 Fraser, op. cit., n. 2, p. 139.
51 See O'Neill, op. cit. (2007), n. 44, pp. 45–52; O'Neill, op. cit. (2009), n. 44; J. Scoular and M. O'Neill, 'Legal Incursions into Supply/Demand, Criminalising and Responsibilising the Buyers and Sellers of Sex' in Munro and Della Giusta, op. cit., n. 33.
52 O'Neill id. (2009), p. 145.
53 Fraser, op. cit., n. 2, p. 142.
54 O'Neill et al., op. cit., n. 48, p. 81.

Overcoming status recognitions (as opposed to identity politics) means establishing the group member – sex worker – as a full member of society capable of participating on a par with other members.[55] So the focus of analysis is on the institutionalized patterns of cultural value for their effects on the relative standing of social actors and moving beyond status misrecognition by establishing the misrecognized party as a full member of society through reciprocal recognition and status equality.

An example of status misrecognition is the institutionalized structuring of sex workers as absent presence, an Other, in the Home Office strategy, and the way that women who sell sex/sex workers are represented as partial citizens. Supported by the mainstream media and agencies of social control, the 'cultural value' assigned to sex workers is non-normative, deficient, inferior: therefore, claims to recognition are needed. Fraser cautions against recognition 'based on valorizing group identity, but rather at overcoming subordination', for the aim is 'to deinstitutionalize patterns of cultural value that impede parity of participation and to replace them with *patterns that foster it*'.[56] Moreover, for Fraser, treating recognition as a matter of justice and 'construing recognition on the model of status permits us to treat it as a matter of justice'[57] – that is to say, social justice, not criminal justice.

Yet, for Fraser, a theory of justice must 'reach beyond cultural value patterns' to also 'examine the structure of capitalism'.[58] For this, she develops an expanded concept of justice to include both recognition and redistribution. Justice requires parity of participation and for this to happen, material resources must be such as to enable 'participants' independence and a voice' through both 'objective' and 'inter-subjective' conditions.[59] The objective condition relates to distributive justice, the economic structure, and class differentials and the inter-subjective relates to recognition linked to status order, associations, and culturally defined hierarchies, 'thus an expanded conception of justice oriented to the norm of participatory parity encompasses both redistribution and recognition, without reducing either one to the other'.[60]

Fraser concludes her paper by arguing that if we cling to false antithesis and misleading dichotomies we will:

> miss the chance to envision social arrangements that can redress both economic and cultural injustices. Only by looking to integrative approaches that unite redistribution and recognition can we meet the requirements of justice for all.[61]

---

55 Fraser, op. cit., n. 2, p. 142.
56 id., pp. 142–3.
57 id., p. 145.
58 id.
59 id.
60 id.
61 id., p. 155.

222

In supporting Fraser's approach we can draw upon Lister's body of work on citizenship. Lister argues that whilst 'the redistribution paradigm is concerned with economic injustice; the recognition paradigm addresses cultural or symbolic injustice'.[62] Hence, rights, recognition, and redistribution are inter-connected.

What is clear is that any strategic response should focus upon the complexity of sex work in the United Kingdom in the twenty-first century and that understanding complexity in order to improve the situation of women and men involved in selling sex should be based upon an integrated approach to recognition and redistribution that involves developing patterns of participation to support processes and practices of parity.

To progress this vision, it is important to make use of cultural analysis and inclusive research methodologies such as participatory action research that might overcome subordination and progress parity of participation, by creating safe spaces for dialogue with sex workers, as well as organizations supporting sex workers, criminal justice agencies, and residents and businesses in communities affected by on- and off-street sex work. I suggest that we might move forward on this, using cultural criminology.

CULTURAL CRIMINOLOGICAL ANALYSIS OF SEX WORK

Cultural criminology explores the many ways in which cultural dynamics intertwine with the practices of crime and crime control in contemporary society.[63]

Cultural criminology can be described as an inter-disciplinary field, emerging from synthesis of sociology, criminology, anthropology, and cultural studies. There is a focus on the everyday meanings of crime and crime control and phenomenological analysis – a focus on city/urban spaces and upon psycho-social analysis and methodologies that are predominantly ethnographic, textual, and visual.[64] In my own work there is also a focus upon materiality and the political constructions of deviance, crime, and crime control in the lives of marginalized groups and communities; and how praxis (purposeful knowledge) can be developed that includes interventions in policy and practice. The cultural turn in criminology (and sociology) can be charted by looking at the development of cultural studies since the 1950s,

---

62 R. Lister, 'Social justice: meanings and politics' (2007) 15(2) *J. of Poverty and Social Justice* 4, based on a public lecture, 'The Scales of Social Justice', given, as Donald Dewar Visiting Professor of Social Justice, at Glasgow University. The lecture is published by the Scottish Centre for Research on Social Justice, available at: <www.scrsj.ac.uk>.

63 J. Ferrell, K. Hayward, and J. Young, *Cultural Criminology: An Invitation* (2008) 4.

64 See: M. Presdee, *Cultural Criminology and the Carnival of Crime* (2000); J. Ferrell and C.R. Sanders, (eds.), *Cultural Criminology* (1995); Ferrell et al., id.

223

the importance of Marxism, the influence of critical theory and critical criminology, and the ways that ethnography emerged as an effective and popular approach to researching cultural processes.[65]

For myself, the emergence of postmodernism and the cultural turn through the work of the Birmingham School was pivotal and best expresses my own engagement with issues of culture, gender, and crime empirically/ methodologically and theoretically. My engagement with western Marxism inspired me to engage with participatory methodologies such as participatory action research (PAR) in the work of Maria Mies,[66] the community research of Hanmer and Saunders,[67] Orlando Fals Borda,[68] Paulo Friere,[69] and William Foote Whyte.[70] I explored the possibilities for more democratic and radical ways of doing social research with marginalized groups using ethnographic, narrative, and arts-based methods. Through my engagement with western Marxism, the Frankfurt School, and feminisms, I was committed to producing knowledge as praxis. Fals Borda's work had huge resonances as a way of seeing and knowing through participatory democratic ways of doing research that included asking questions such as 'whose knowledge counts?', 'knowledge for what?' 'knowledge for whom?'[71]

A cultural criminological analysis of sex work can be described using the category of inter-sectionality, the entwining of ethnographic (cultural) and structural analysis as an interdisciplinary field of study and as a form of radical politics and praxis using participatory action research methodologies.

1. *Participatory action research (PAR)*

Fals Borda describes PAR as a transformative methodology linked to social justice especially for those who are most marginalized. Thus, for Fals Borda,

---

65 S. Hall, 'Cultural Studies: two paradigms' in *Culture, Ideology and Social Process*, eds. T. Bennett et al. (1982). Framed by these specific theoretical and methodological orientations, cultural criminological research and analysis has developed for Ferrell around crime as a sub-cultural phenomenon, in that it is organized around shared aesthetics, symbolic communication, and an embodied, collective activity. See J. Ferrell, 'Style Matters' in *Cultural Criminology Unleashed*, eds. J. Ferrell et al. (2004) 61–3. See, also, J. Ferrell, 'Cultural Criminology' in *The Sage Dictionary of Criminology*, eds. E. McLaughlin and J. Muncie (2005).

66 M. Mies, 'Towards a Methodology for Feminist Research' in *Theories of Women's Studies*, eds. G. Bowles and D. Klein (1983).

67 J. Hanmer and S. Saunders, *Well Founded Fear: A Community Study of Violence to Women* (1984).

68 O. Fals Borda, *Knowledge and People's Power: Lessons with Peasants in Nicaragua, Mexico and Colombia* (1988).

69 P. Friere, *Pedagogy of the Oppressed* (1996).

70 W. Foot Whyte, 'Advancing scientific knowledge through participatory action research' (1989) 4 *Sociological Forum* 367–85.

71 Fals Borda, op. cit, n. 68, p. 78. I was introduced to Fals Borda's work by Professor Richard Harvey Brown of the University of Maryland. Ferrell et al., op. cit., n. 63, p. 184, have described my participatory approach as an example of liquid ethnography.

224

vivencia[72] or *erfahrung* (life experience gained through immersion in fieldwork with local communities, identifying with them without giving oneself over or projecting oneself into the other) and *commitment* with change processes and their actors are the two core orientations of PAR. William Foot Whyte suggests that PAR can advance sociological knowledge in ways that would be unlikely to emerge from more orthodox sociological research. For Whyte, the element of creative surprise (which comes with working *with* – not on or for – participants whose experiences and knowledges are different from our own) is a central aspect in conducting participatory action research and advancing social-scientific knowledge.[73]

This approach gives rise to a subject-subject approach to generating understanding and knowledge which, as Fals Borda states, takes us beyond the classical 'participant observer role' (subject-object) in fieldwork and enables recognition. This methodological approach can also give rise to the 'critical recovery of history',[74] fostering mutual recognition, trust, and responsibility. It also enriches the life experiences and skills of the researcher. So, with regard to sex work and sex working, alternative histories can be written reflecting materiality, lived experience, diversity, and difference, as well as engaging in the creative process of looking at regulatory practices and experiences and exploring what might work better. Moreover, respect for communicating such knowledge is written into the processes and practices of PAR, so that meanings are understood by all involved and shared with a wider population: with sex workers, as well as projects, communities and government, responsible authorities and policy makers.

Fals Borda talks of four key aspects or skills that are part of PAR's contribution to social research methodology that I argue offers a way of doing a cultural-materialist analysis of sex work. First, there is an emphasis on collectivities. This is helpful in documenting processes and practices of solidarity and diversity, as well as methodologically ensuring cross-referencing of data and triangulation in sex-work research. The focus is on collective memories, building up knowledge and analysis over time and

---

72 PAR is therefore a combination of experience and commitment. Certainly, a combination of experience and commitment allows us to see and shape the relationship between knowledge and social change. For Fals Borda, the sum of knowledge from both the participants and academics/researchers allows us to acquire a much more accurate picture of the reality we want to transform. For him, academic knowledge combined with popular knowledge and wisdom may give us a new paradigm. Certainly, renewed methodologies which aim to get at the reflexive nature of human thought and action, and the meanings given, both conscious and semi-conscious, could enable us to better understand people's everyday experiences and, at the same time, enable us to better understand broader social institutions and work towards social change.

73 Foot Whyte, op. cit., n. 70.

74 Fals Borda, op. cit., n. 68, p. 81.

225

focusing upon specific locations and locales. For example, the work conducted by Jane Pitcher et al.,[75] funded by the Joseph Rowntree Foundation, provides a good example of this, even though the research was informed by participatory approaches rather than defined as PAR. The UKNSWP databases, archives, and research are another example of this work on and with collectivities.[76]

Second is the critical recovery of history based upon use of personal, folk, and archival materials, the oral tradition, which is supportive of community dignity and facilitates cultural inclusion and involvement (a vital aspect of working *with* sex workers, as well as communities) on and off street and links back to the notion of knowledge for what and knowledge for whom. Nick Mai and Laura Agustín have both conducted ethnographic and participatory work with migrant sex workers which offers good examples of an approach to knowledge production that develops a more complex and critical recovery of history, and which challenges dominant ideologies of 'trafficking' in relation to migrant sex work and sex working.[77]

The third is devolving knowledge in understandable and meaningful ways that reinforces the need for dialogue and interpretation, and can lead to concientization. For example, in the PAR research conducted by Rosie Campbell and myself with community co-researchers, who were residents of the street sex market area in Walsall, huge shifts in understanding were made, including addressing residents' concerns and fears. The community co-researchers learnt more about sex work and sex working and collaborated in the development of recommendations. As a result, shifts in attitude and tolerance emerged. These residents who were also co-researchers wrote a leaflet to summarize the research and posted this to every house in the local area (three wards). They also created a website, with the help of Walsall Community Arts, where our report, the leaflet they created, and the participatory arts work with residents, sex workers, and young people can be found.[78]

Fourth, praxis as purposeful knowledge (action) emerged, that involved drawing upon the knowledge and experience of participants in report form, in the leaflet, but also visually, in an exhibition at the Walsall new art gallery, as well as on-line. Attention to rigour, validity and ethical imperatives are, of course, central to PAR research. Crucially, PAR involves a commitment to research that develops partnership responses: it includes all those involved, where possible, thus facilitating shared ownership of the development and outcomes of the research, and it uses innovative ways of

---

75 J. Pitcher, J.R. Campbell, P. Hubbard, M. O'Neill, and J. Scoular, *Living and Working in Areas of Street Sex Work: From Conflict to Coexistence* (2006).
76 Available at: <http://www.uknswp.org/>.
77 L.M. Agustín, *Sex at the Margins: Migration, Labour Markets and the Rescue Industry* (2007); Mai, op. cit., n. 43.
78 Safety Soap Box, at: <www.safetysoapbox.co.uk>.

consulting and working with local people, facilitating change with communities and groups. Methodologically, PAR involves working with participants as co-researchers (sex workers/community members as experts) through democratic processes and decision making.[79] This involves mutual recognition, using what Freire calls dialogic techniques,[80] for example, through community and participatory arts workshops, forum theatre and ethno-drama methods, alongside stakeholder events. But perhaps most importantly, PAR is a process directed towards social change *with* the participants.

O'Neill and Campbell suggest that PAR develops social knowledge that is interventionist in partnership with sex workers and communities and, because it seeks to promote social change, it provides 'a testimony to the possibilities for participation in local governance that can shed light on broader structures, practises and processes' and might lead to better governance of sex work.[81]

Methodologically, PAR seeks to foster social justice and can provide resistance and challenges to the fixed identity of the 'prostitute' as victim and abject Other by documenting the multiple subjecthoods of female and male sex workers, in direct opposition to the identity thinking marked by inequalities, ideological effects, and social divisions which identify 'prostitutes' as 'Other', as the end stop in discourses on good or honest women. Women who sell sex are indexical.[82] PAR is a social research methodology which includes the stereotypical subjects of research as co-creators of the research. It creates a space for the voices of the marginalized to become involved actively in change or transformation. Participatory action research seeks to understand the world from the perspective of the participants. Outcomes of participatory research can inform, educate, remind, challenge, empower, and lead to action/interventions.[83]

Participatory research can provide important counter-voices that document subjecthood, amidst narratives of routes in, making out, material lives, managing sexual and social inequalities, and managing multiple identities as well as, for some, desistence. Immersion in the life worlds of women selling sex through participatory research enables the foregrounding of feelings, meanings, emotions, and experiences from multiple standpoints

---

79 O'Neill, op. cit., n. 8 ; M. O'Neill and R. Campbell, *Working Together to Create Change* (2004), available at: <www.safetysoapbox.co.uk/>.
80 Freire, op. cit., n. 69.
81 O'Neill and Campbell, op. cit., n. 79; M. O'Neill and R. Campbell, 'Prostitution and Communities' in *Sex Work Now*, eds. R. Campbell and M. O'Neill (2006) 59.
82 O'Neill, op. cit., n. 8.
83 Yet, participatory action research is little used in the United Kingdom. Rarely will it get a mention in research methods texts, other than in the literature on development, and it is most prevalent in countries of the South, North and South America, and India. In contrast to this, see the work of Rachel Pain, Kye Askins, and colleagues at Durham University, England, at: <http://www.dur.ac.uk/beacon/socialjustice/>.

that facilitates the development of 'thick' descriptions of lived cultures and resists identity thinking.

For example, the following narratives from three women involved in participatory research conducted by Rosie Campbell and myself illustrate this point.[84] They speak of the ways that money – materiality – is a central organizing feature of involvement in sex work, *not* deviant identities, and also the stigma and deviancy associated with sex work and the way this can serve as a 'trapping' factor[85] that impacts on their lives and personal development:

> The hours and the money suit my needs and I couldn't earn this money in a 'proper' job.[86]

> That's where a lot of us girls are stuck. We've got children of our own and often we go on the streets when times are hard but there are certain jobs we can't do because we are sex offenders ... We can't work in banks ... we can't work with children.[87]

> I've been looking to do some courses ... but, you see, what stopped me ... what's stopping me really looking too hard is the fact that I'm working here and people ask what I'm doing. It's always a barrier. That's what I'm worried about now, that's what's stopping me doing it, because I want to do it, but I don't know what to say to them when they ask me what have you been doing ... If they asked me the wrong question I won't know what to say ... you ain't given a fair chance really. I don't want that stuck to me for the rest of my life anyway ...[88]

The image reproduced as Figure 1 was produced in participatory action research and participatory arts workshops that were an intrinsic part of research Rosie Campbell and I led on, commissioned and funded by Walsall South Health Action Zone.[89] The image visually represents the themes expressed in the narratives above and challenges the limited and limiting identity thinking used to represent and define sex workers in the current regulatory regime that feeds into the public imagination. The woman who created this image worked with community artist Kate Green to produce in visual form her own experience of sex work as work.

The combination of narrative, text, and image resists the binary of work/victimhood and can be described as an example of non-identitarian thinking. The image/text also highlights struggles for cultural citizenship, participation, and inclusion that include the right to presence and visibility versus marginalization; the right to dignifying representation versus

---

84 O'Neill and Campbell, op. cit., n. 35.
85 T. Sanders, 'Becoming An Ex-Sex Worker: Making Transitions out of a Deviant Career' (2007) 2 *Feminist Criminology* 1–22.
86 O'Neill and Campbell, op. cit., n. 35.
87 id.
88 id.
89 See the full report, O'Neill and Campbell, op. cit., n. 79. To see more images produced in the participatory arts workshops, see <www.safetysoapbox.co.uk>.

Figure 1. Curriculum Vitae

EMPLOYMENT HISTORY
(Please list in order the organisations for which you have worked).

Name and address of <u>current</u> employer:		Please summarise the main duties of the post
self		*customer satisfaction* *negotiating prices* *communication skills* *advertising*
Post held: *sex worker*		Date started: *1995* Until: *2002/3*

Salary:	Period of notice:	OR Reason for leaving (if applicable)
£500 - 1000/wk	*?*	

PREVIOUS POSTS

From Month/ Year	To Month/ Year	Name and Address of Employer	Post Held	Salary	Reason for leaving
93	*94*	*Posh Hotel*	*2nd chef*	*£110/wk*	*career change*
94	*95*	*Local council*	*admin officer*	*£100/wk*	*seeking more money*

FURTHER INFORMATION:
Please use this section to provide evidence that you possess the skills and experience required for this post.

(Please use additional sheets if necessary)

Despite what you may think about my current employment I feel that you need to value me as a whole person with a range of positive skills gained often working in difficult circumstances. Your prejudices should not hinder me from progressing with my life and with my future plans to move forward.

stigmatization; and the right to identity and maintenance of lifestyle versus assimilation. One can read the image as prioritizing the human dignity of the woman concerned – she asks directly for the reader to see her as a whole person, not just in relation to the category prostitute. Using participatory arts and visual methodologies can help to foster reflective/safe spaces for

229

dialogue, thinking through issues, and representing the voices of sex workers as well as project workers, residents, and other related individuals and groups. Such work can speak of the multiple subject positions of women, what they have to negotiate, and how they do or do not manage this, whilst seeking dignity, recognition, and making a life in total contrast to the way the current governance of sex work focuses upon the exclusion of women through a victim/abject identity. Sharing the images, in exhibitions (as in the Walsall gallery) and on-line, as well as in newspaper coverage (the Walsall exhibition was covered by the Big Issue) can raise awareness about women's lives and the importance of public sharing and participation for democratization in supporting the human dignity of sex workers, thus allowing women the space to speak and be heard, to articulate their own needs and not simply have needs imposed upon them through discourses of responsibilization and rehabilitation.[90]

These struggles for human dignity, cultural citizenship, and social justice are currently being fought regionally, nationally, and internationally from bottom-up or grassroots positions by organizations and agencies and by prostitutes' rights' movements, for example, the UKNSWP, the English Collective of Prostitutes, and ScotPep in the United Kingdom, and EUROPAP in Europe. Yet, claims for social justice revolve for sex-worker feminists around calling for decriminalization and for sex workers to be recognized as workers. For radical feminists, social justice claims involve calling for abolition, and the recognition of sex work as exploitation. For both groups these claims are based upon recognition as identity politics. My argument here (following Nancy Fraser) is that we can use participatory, cultural, and visual methodologies to show the intersection of recognition and redistribution; to ask for status recognition as well as addressing material sexual and social inequalities.

RESISTING REGULATION: TOWARDS A POLITICS OF INCLUSION

The political potential of cultural criminological analysis of sex work is an important theme in this paper. Developing cultural/phenomenological analysis of sex work may help us to access richer understanding of the

90 Evelin Lindner founded a global transdisciplinary network and fellowship of concerned academics and practitioners that focuses upon the relationship between humiliation and human dignity:
> The field of dignity/humiliation research is novel and a larger body of research has still to be built. Our aim is to avoid single interest scholarship, work transdisciplinary, and probe how even local micro-changes may be embedded within larger global changes. In our meetings we aim at creating a humiliation-free, collaborative learning environment characterized by mutual respect, mutual empathy, and openness to difference'. Available at: <http://www.humiliation studies.org/research/research.php>.

complexities of sex work and impact upon the governance of sex work. Moreover, knowledge produced through participatory analysis may help us to avoid identitarian thinking and feeling and help us to engage in rethinking and reimagining relationships between the lived experiences of the people who sell sex, social regulation, the culture of control, and policies for real social inclusion – towards a more holistic concept of social justice than is present in the deviancy model. Phenomenological and participatory modes of exploring and analysing sex work may produce knowledge as praxis, raise awareness, and develop critical reflexive texts that may help to mobilize social change with the very people who are currently both abject and Othered in the governance of sex work. Methodologically, participatory methodologies can support a radical democratic imaginary. Given the closing down of spaces for public resistance under the auspices of the Thatcher, Major, Blair, and Brown governments, PAR provides a potentially powerful tool for resistance and a platform for civic participation – a critical theory in practice.

Thus, 'a politics of inclusion'[91] could brush against the grain of the abolitionist approach and the dominant deviancy/criminal justice model for regulating sex work by providing spaces for the voices and meanings of sex workers, highlighting the need to address the cultural citizenship of sex workers, and promoting social justice as an integration of recognition and redistribution.

I will conclude with some suggestions for further discussion and debate that may point us in the direction of an effective strategy that bears reference to the wealth of research on sex work, *with* sex workers, within the context of governance. Fraser's politics of recognition and redistribution and cultural criminological analysis evidences the complex lived relations and structural/ social inequalities experienced by women selling sex. A way forward based upon cultural criminological and participatory research would be to:

(i) continue to engage with the theories and practices of governance despite the barriers and difficulties of who is invited to the table and which research is taken to evidence or develop policy;
(ii) think beyond the labels and binaries by working in participatory ways using participatory action research and performance and participatory arts;
(iii) establish chains of equivalence[92] and seek transformative change through dialogue, participation, inclusion, and reciprocal recognition;

---

91 Following the usage of this term by Janet Newman: J. Newman, 'New Labour, Governance and the Politics of Diversity' in Barry et al. (eds.), op. cit., n. 25.
92 This is akin to Smith's thesis (drawing upon Laclau and Mouffe) that: 'radical democracy is the best route towards social change for the Left Today' and fosters 'a democratic politics that aims at the articulation of the various different struggles against oppression. What emerges is the possibility of a project of radical and plural democracy': A.M. Smith, *Laclau and Mouffe, The Radical Democratic Imaginary* (1998) 328. See, also, Scoular and O'Neill, op. cit, n. 8.

231

(iv) imagine a radical democratic politics of prostitution reform *with* the very women and men who are the currently the subject-objects of the governance and reform of sex-work legislation, policy, and guidance.

In a recent seminar Ruth Lister,[93] drawing on Naila Kabeer, identified certain values of inclusive citizenship that I suggest we need to consider when focusing upon imagining a radical democratic politics of sex work that moves us beyond abolitionist discourses and binaries, and towards a politics of inclusion. These include the need to strengthen belonging and participation in the civic (the right to work and the right to dignity), political (rights to participate and to a political voice), and social (legal and social rights) spheres. This stands in contrast to the current policy and practice rooted in abolitionist discourse. Together these points coalesce into an account and understanding of the importance of cultural citizenship – as the right to recognition, dignity, and respect.

This paper has sought to challenge the exclusionary discourses of disease, victimhood, rehabilitation, and control rooted in the deviancy and criminal justice model of regulating sex work. It invites readers to imagine what a sea-change a radical democratic approach to the governance of sex work would mean, rooted in dignity, recognition, and respect for the women and men who sell sex, as well as an active engagement with redistribution: for their identities, subjecthood, and rights; for shifting the socio-cultural structures that set limits to our imaginings; but also for our analysis and policy making.

93 Professor Lister's talk is summarized in M. O'Neill and L. Cohen, *Women and Migration: Art, Politics and Policy* (2008), available at: <http://www.lboro.ac.uk/departments/ss/global_refugees/reports.html>.

232